"When first published, Teilhard de Chardin's seminal work attracted worldwide attention and immediately became a bestseller, but few realized then how many mistakes the first translation contained. Sarah Appleton-Weber has done us a great service by providing a much more exact, more coherent and more poetic text based on many years of meticulous research. This fresh translation invites readers to enter and share Teilhard's powerful vision of science and religion, of the direction and meaning of life in a world so large and complex. It is a vision of great spiritual significance and strength. It provides a perspective of hope, energy, love and meaningful coherence which can inspire and uplift people's lives."

Professor Ursula King, University of Bristol, author
of Spirit of Fire: The Life and Vision of Teilhard de Chardin

"This book reads so splendidly—with precision, fidelity, beauty of presentation, comprehensiveness, forcefulness . . . it has a magic quality you don't find in writing in the science world. This new translation of the *The Human Phenomenon* gives us a new Teilhard. No one so far has caught the lyric style of Teilhard so well as the author of this translation. A precise understanding of Teilhard's style of writing is especially important, for the nuances of his thought are so subtle that any translation that fails in this regard will necessarily fail in transmitting the full meaning of his thought. We have now, for the first time, this most comprehensive work of Teilhard in a translation worthy of its importance. This translation will in the future be the basic text for any serious study of Teilhard in the English language."

Thomas Berry, co-author of The Universe Story,
and author of The Great Work

"This is an entirely new and authoritative translation by Sarah Appleton-Weber of the original French text of *The Human Phenomenon* by Teilhard de Chardin. It will provide scholars, and the general reader, with a manuscript that is faithful in every detail not only to the epic quality and vibrant energy of Teilhard's thought but also to nuances of expression so important to an in-depth understanding of the theological, philosophical and scientific implications which he intended."

James W. Skehan, SJ, Professor and Director Emeritus,
Weston Observatory, Boston College

"Teilhardians have long been aware of limitations in the standard English version of *Le phénomène humain*. Now they have access to a new and felicitous translation by Sarah Weber. But Weber offers more than a new translation, for she has spent years visiting archives and restoring passages that were lost as Teilhard and others revised the original text. Now we have access to a stunning new version of a twentieth-century classic."

Thomas M. King, SJ, Georgetown University,
author of Teilhard's Mysticism of Knowing
and Teilhard de Chardin; *co-editor of*
Teilhard and the Unity of Knowledge
and Letters of Teilhard de Chardin
and Lucile Swan

"The Teilhard de Chardin Foundation (Paris) endorses Ms Weber's new translation, which will undoubtedly contribute to spreading the thought of Teilhard in English-speaking countries."

Maurice Ernst, Administrator Delegate,
Fondation Teilhard de Chardin, Paris

"One of the most significant debates in evolutionary history has been postponed into the twenty-first century. That is, the intellectual clash between the schools of purpose and direction within evolution with the modernist schools of randomness and non-teleology. Sarah Weber's new translation of Telhard's major work, *The Human Phenomenon*, comes just as these schools seek to clarify their positions. Teilhard's work occupies a central role in these discussions not only because of his prescient understandings of complexity and convergence in the emergence of life, but also because of his concerns regarding the deeper spiritual meanings in contemplating evolution.

Teilhard's insights find prominent expression in the increasingly intense discussions on religion and science. In addition to her painstaking translation, Sarah Weber provides in her introduction helpful keys for an initial understanding of the novel literary genre which Teilhard used in his work, namely, his description of the unfolding of cosmological powers in the history of the Earth."

John A. Grim, Department of Religion,
Bucknell University

THE HUMAN PHENOMENON

Pierre Teilhard de Chardin

The best of my thought and time
goes into writing the book on the human,
which I have told you about, where I am trying
to transmit the essential part of my vision of the world:
thought rooted in matter, and by the very fact of its awakening,
calling for the reality of some sort of superlife. Just what you have
created in your "Man Emerging out of the Elemental Forces"—the
best possible illustration for the frontispiece of my book . . .
If my pages could be ready when the war has ended—
when human beings will truly feel the need of
building and hoping—my time
will not have been wasted.

Teilhard to Malvina Hoffman
Peking, January 14, 1940

The quotation is courtesy of the Getty Research
Institute, Research Library, 850042

THE HUMAN PHENOMENON

Pierre Teilhard de Chardin

A New Edition and Translation
of *Le phénomène humain* by

Sarah Appleton-Weber

With a Foreword by
Brian Swimme

sussex
ACADEMIC
PRESS

BRIGHTON • PORTLAND

Originally published as *Le phénomène humain,* copyright © Editions du Seuil, 1955 and
1970; published in the USA by arrangement with HarperCollins Publishers, Inc.;
published in this English edition as *The Human Phenomenon,* translation
and editorial copyright © 1999 Sarah Appleton-Weber; "Teilhard's
Transforming Thought: Editor-Translator's Introduction" and
"Editor-Translator's Appendix" copyright © 1999 Sarah
Appleton-Weber; typeset text, jacket design, index,
copyright © 1999 Sussex Academic Press.

The right of Sarah Appleton-Weber to be
identified as editor and translator of this work has been
asserted in accordance with the Copyright, Designs and Patents Act 1988.

2 4 6 8 10 9 7 5 3 1

Published 1999 in Great Britain by
SUSSEX ACADEMIC PRESS
Box 2950
Brighton BN2 5SP

and in the United States of America by
SUSSEX ACADEMIC PRESS
5804 N.E. Hassalo St.
Portland, Oregon 97213-3644

British Library Cataloguing in Publication Data
Teilhard de Chardin, Pierre
The human phenomenon
1. Cosmology   2. Evolution   3. Philosophical anthropology
I. Title
113
ISBN 1–902210–29–8 (hardcover)

Library of Congress Cataloging-in-Publication Data
Teilhard de Chardin, Pierre.
[Phénomène humain. English]
The human phenomenon / Pierre Teilhard de Chardin ; a new edition
and translation of Le phénomène humain by Sarah Appleton-Weber.
p. cm.
Includes bibliographical references and index.
ISBN 1–902210–29–8 (alk. paper)
1. Cosmology   2. Evolution.   3. Philosophical anthropology.
I. Title.
B2430.T373P5613   1999
113—dc21   99–32883
CIP

Typeset and designed by G&G Editorial, Brighton
Printed in the UK by Biddles Ltd, Guildford and King's Lynn
This book is printed on acid-free paper

CONTENTS

THE HUMAN PHENOMENON

Part I   Prelife

Part II   Life

Part III Thought

ILLUSTRATIONS

Jacket picture: Photograph by Steven Santori (Syracuse University Photo Center) of Malvina Hoffman's bronze statue of "Elemental Man," or, as Teilhard described it, "Man emerging out of elemental forces," which stands on the campus grounds of Syracuse University.

Frontispiece: A photo-portrait of Teilhard taken by Malvina Hoffman in preparation for making her final bust of Teilhard prior to preparing her sculpture. The photo is reproduced courtesy of the Getty Research Institute, Research Library, 850042.

Endpapers: Facsimile of the Delamarre medal, struck by the French Mint, Paris, 1951. The reverse is based on a design by Teilhard to illustrate his idea of convergence.

ACKNOWLEDGMENTS

Without the cooperation, encouragement, and support of both the French and American Teilhard Associations, this new English edition and translation of *Le phénomène humain* could never have been completed. Through the late Jeanne Mortier, I received permission to work with the earlier texts of *Le phénomène humain*, and through her successor as General Secretary of the Fondation Teilhard de Chardin in Paris, Simone Clair-Michot, I was given access to material in the archives of the Fondation. I also received the warm support of Maurice Ernst, Administrator Delegate of the Fondation and head of the Association des Amis de Pierre Teilhard de Chardin; and the art and friendship of Anne-Marie Caffort-Ernst have been an inspiration to me. Under the leadership of Maurice Ernst, the French, American, and Canadian Associations have signed a charter of cooperation with the British Teilhard Association, and with other European Associations. My particular thanks go to Siôn Cowell, Chairman of the British Teilhard Association, for reading the text and for essential suggestions about important terms. I extend a warm thank you to the British Committee, and Association members, for organizing the formal launch of this edition at the Reform Club in London. It is much appreciated.

I would also like to thank Catherine Rousslin of Editions du Seuil, Paris, for her assistance and support in liaising with Sussex Academic Press in bringing this publication to fruition.

Furthermore, I am deeply indebted to the late Pierre Leroy, SJ, for making his copy of the 1949 text of *Le phénomène humain* available for my research. Pierre Leroy, a biologist, became a close friend of Teilhard while they were exiled together in China during World War II and remained so until Teilhard's death. Pierre Leroy read the most technical section of my translation, advised me on scientific terms, spoke to me at length about his memories of Teilhard, and gave me encouragement at different stages of my work. He subsequently gave his copy of the 1949 text of *Le phénomène humain*, along with other personal papers, to the important special collection of Teilhard material at the Lauinger Library of Georgetown University. This warm bond has been continued by Solange Soulié, who assisted Pierre Leroy in the editing and publication of his last works, and who provided me with the new location of Teilhard's journals and retreat notes.

Claude Cuénot, Teilhard's first and most comprehensive biographer, who helped Jeanne Mortier prepare the text of *Le phénomène humain* for Les Editions du Seuil, and who was a strong promoter of French-American cooperation, also gave me invaluable information. In return, I was able to find for him certain Teilhard material located in the United States, which included the correspondence between Teilhard and Malvina Hoffman now at the Getty Institute. It was in reading Hoffman's correspondence with Teilhard that I discovered Teilhard's wish to use the figure of "Man emerging out of the elemental forces" as his frontispiece for *Le phénomène humain*, a photo by Hoffman on the jacket cover of her book *Sculpture Inside and Out*, which she had sent to Teilhard in China in 1939. By coincidence (or serendipity) the statue of Elemental Man itself stood on the campus of Syracuse University, where I had walked by it for many years. With its extraordinary manifestation of the upward thrust of human energy, the statue of Elemental Man has been used as the jacket photo for *The Human Phenomenon*.

During their years of friendship Malvina Hoffman sculpted several busts of Teilhard. As she worked, they had long conversations during which Teilhard came to grasp the high function of art for humanity and to discern the parallels between Hoffman's thought and his own work (see "Teilhard's Transforming Thought," VII, par. 3 and note 20, pp. 261–2). The frontispiece of *The Human Phenomenon* is a photo-portrait of Teilhard taken by Malvina Hoffman as they talked, one of several photos she made in preparation for her final bust of Teilhard.

I am also equally indebted to Pierre Noir, SJ, for his study groups, lectures, and retreats on Teilhard. Pierre Noir originally provided me with access to Teilhard's retreat notes and journals, and initiated me into Teilhard's use of symbols and abbreviations. Through him I received warm hospitality at the Centre St. François Xavier in Colmar, and in Strasbourg was introduced to Mère Marie-Augustine and the Sisters of the Convent of Marie Réparatrice, where I was given a quiet parlor in which to work.

In May 1985 my husband and I traveled with Pierre Noir and a group of about twenty-five of Les Amis de Pierre Teilhard de Chardin to follow the itinerary of Teilhard's research in China. Reading aloud Teilhard's descriptions of the areas as we journeyed through them, we traveled from Beijing to Zhoukoudian and the site of Peking Man; to Inner Mongolia; then followed the curve of the Yellow River around the Ordos Desert;

traveled westward toward Tibet to Xining; and finally turned back to Xi'an, Luoyang, and Zhengzhou, visiting the great park built on the high banks of loess washed up by the Yellow River. It was an extraordinary and adventure-filled encounter with the Teilhardian spirit among the French, Americans, and Chinese!

Of vital importance throughout these years of research and translation have been the support, encouragement, and friendship of the late Winifred McCulloch, and of the officers and members of the American Teilhard Association, in particular Thomas Berry, John Grim, and Mary Evelyn Tucker. I especially thank Thomas King, SJ, through whom I was given access to the major collections of Teilhard material at Georgetown University in both the Lauinger and Woodstock libraries. The American Teilhard Association provides a community infused with that spirit of unanimity described by Teilhard and it has provided a stimulating forum to present phases of my work. "Teilhard's Transforming Thought" first appeared in the Association's publication, *Teilhard Perspective* (vol. 24, no. 2, Dec. 1991). Not only has the Association furthered my understanding of Teilhard, but it embodies the many ways in which the dynamism of Teilhard's thought is being carried into the future. The American Teilhard Association has also provided me with a generous grant for the typing and proofreading of the electronic text of *The Human Phenomenon*, for which I am deeply grateful.

I would like to thank the Corporation of Yaddo in Saratoga Springs, New York for offering me the space and the uninterrupted time for concentration on my work. Yaddo was where the inspiration for this project began in 1974, and where parts of the translation have been written. I would like to thank the director of the community of Blue Mountain Lake for a month of hospitality, as well as the Sisters of St. Joseph at the Convent of St. Vincent de Paul Church in Syracuse, New York for a quiet winter's working place.

The office space, support, and community provided by The Bunting Institute of Radcliffe College in July 1997 made it possible for me to complete my final revisions of the English text.

I would like to express my profound gratitude to Ursula King for her support and guidance, for her reading of my completed manuscript of *The Human Phenomenon* and the invaluable suggestions she has made. Her biography of Teilhard, *Spirit of Fire: The Life and Vision of Teilhard de Chardin*, her more recent *Pierre Teilhard de Chardin: Writings* (Orbis Books Modern Spiritual Masters Series), and her other books and essays, are indispensable for a full understanding of Teilhard.

It was through Ursula King that my manuscript came to the attention of Anthony Grahame, my editor, who with his incredible and patient skill opened the way forward for the publication of this new edition and translation of *The Human Phenomenon* throughout the English-speaking world. I am especially grateful for his time, care, and creative presentation and editing of the text and illustrations of *The Human Phenomenon* to make it possible for the work of Teilhard to come together in all its depth, its beauty, balance and structure.

The beauty and depth of Teilhard's work is brought forth in Brian Swimme's remarkable foreword, which leads us, through his own personal journey, into Teilhard's transforming thought and to a vision of where we stand at this moment in a transforming universe.

I would also like to express my thanks to many others who have given their time and effort to the making of the text of *The Human Phenomenon*. To Elizabeth Bartelme, for her invaluable editorial work and years of friendship and encouragement. To Kristin Fogdall, for her great skill in typing the electronic text, for her editorial acumen, and her personal commitment to the project. My gratitude to Sally Treadwell, who edited the project of translation as I first presented it. To Julia Ketcham for her thoughtful reading of the whole, her textual comments and suggestions, as well as to others who have read or worked with parts of the text: Elizabeth Sewell, Jean Valentine, Jane Cooper, Padma Hejmadi, Leslie Ann Donovan, and Danny Marcus.

And finally, I am most deeply indebted to my husband Joseph G. Weber, scholar and healer, who over the years has advised and accompanied me through each and every step of the way and given invaluable suggestions about the phraseology and accuracy of my translation from the French.

*　　*　　*

This translation is dedicated to the memory of Ida Treat Bergeret, paleontologist, journalist, and writer, who was my teacher at Vassar College and in whose home in 1952 I first saw a photo portrait of Teilhard and first heard his name.

FOREWORD

There are days in New York City where you never see the sun but only feel its presence in the blasts of hot air that sweep through the concrete canyons and in the heat waves that radiate up from the asphalt. When my clothes finally became heavy with my own sweat and I was lost for the third time I was tempted to hide out in some air-conditioned hotel but all I had to remember was my own misery and that was enough to keep me going. I had recently resigned as a professor of mathematics and physics and was now on a search for wisdom, and a number of people had pointed me toward New York, most notably the founder of the Club of Rome, that seminal gathering of planetary thinkers and visionaries. On his death bed, when asked who of all the brilliant minds he had worked with he would most recommend, Aurelio Peccei had said simply, "Our best hope is Thomas Berry."

By the time I made it to Berry's Riverdale Research Center and was invited into his library, I could not have had higher expectations. He listened carefully as I tried to explain my misery and confusion over the destruction of the planet and what to do about it. After a long pause, and without saying a word, Thomas Berry pulled a book from the thousands on his shelves. With stern visage he tossed across the table Teilhard de Chardin's great work, the one you now hold in your hands.

My disappointment was instantaneous. This was old stuff. I had come all the way across the continent to receive a book I had read back in my Jesuit high school? Even worse, some famous scientists had objected to Teilhard's ideas, and I brought that up. Thomas Berry just smiled, and broke into easy laughter.

"Teilhard was the first to see the universe in a new way, so I suppose it's inevitable that he would be criticized. If you're bothered by what a few scientists have to say you should read some of the theologians! Fundamentally the difficulty is one of scale. Any attempt to understand Teilhard that does not begin with the entire complex of civilizations as well as the vast panorama of the evolutionary universe is doomed to failure for it is simply too small to grasp what he is about. Surely, similar situations have occurred in the history of science?"

My mind raced with thoughts of Albert Einstein and Niels Bohr and the revolutions they initiated and how these could not be contained in the world of classical physics, but he had only asked the question in a rhetorical way. He was soon to bring our brief meeting to a close but not before he uttered a most unforgettable statement. "To see as Teilhard saw is a challenge, but increasingly his vision is becoming available to us. I fully expect that in the next millennium Teilhard will be generally regarded as the fourth major thinker of the western Christian tradition. These would be St. Paul, Augustine, Thomas Aquinas, and Teilhard."

He smiled again, aware of so much that needed to be said by way of explanation, but also aware that I would be incapable at this time of taking it in. He pointed to the book he had put in my hands. "Begin with Teilhard. There's no substitute for a close reading of his work."

I would read on my own and once a week discuss the ideas with Thomas Berry; I would be regularly amazed by how much of the world's intellectual history it seemed necessary to refer to. He drew constantly not just from physics and biology but also from philosophy, poetry, linguistics, music and above all world history and cosmology. As the months went by I began to suspect that the fundamental categories of my mind were undergoing some sort of change. The unexamined assumptions that had been organizing my experiences in the world were now writhing under the pressure from Teilhard's massive and penetrating cosmology. But all the confusion was worthwhile for it led to a singular experience, the moment when I had what I understood to be my fullest understanding of Teilhard's ideas.

This epiphany came not in my discussions nor in my reading but rather in a quiet moment while I watched my four year old son climb on top of a large boulder in a deciduous forest just north of New York City. The rock, staying just what it was, suddenly became molten, and my son, staying just as he was, also became molten as did the cool forest shade and the multicolored leaves—some damp, some rotting—and the dark burbling stream. All of it blazed now with the same fire that had flared forth in the beginning and was now in the form of this forest. I floated in the moment, buoyed up with these feelings. I knew most likely I would soon crash back into normality, but I was also aware of delightful mystery: it had taken me years to get to this profoundly moving moment, and yet nothing could have been closer to me or even more obvious during all that time.

I sprinted to my next meeting with Thomas Berry. I could hardly contain myself as the words tumbled out of me. I was so excited to be able to demonstrate to him that I had finally understood what Teilhard was saying, and I was sure he would be thrilled to hear it. But halfway through my description I stopped altogether for his eyes had drifted off. When he spoke it was not with the delight I had expected but with a depth of sadness I had not heard before.

"So much of western civilization has been dedicated to erecting a discontinuity between the human and the rest of the universe. You see it in our law, in our jurisprudence. You see it in our narrow focus on human rights. It's there in our religions and in the very structure and rationale of our corporations. It is this illusory discontinuity that enables us to carry out so much destruction of the natural world. The tragedy could not be more complete. We destroy the greatest beauty in the known universe, and we do so convinced we are making things better.

"Teilhard was one of the first scientists to realize that the human and the universe are inseparable. The only universe we know about is a universe that brought forth the human. Teilhard understood this, he understood that the human story and the universe story identify with each other.

"The spiritual formation of humans in the third millennium will undoubtedly include something similar to what you experienced. An immersion into the deep creative powers of the universe is the most direct contact a human can have of the divine. Such is the spirituality that Teilhard makes available to us, a spirituality that is rooted not in the spatial cosmos of Ptolemy but in the time-developmental universe that the scientists have detected.

"You've waded into the shallows of this, but Teilhard offers a multitude of such experiences. He points to an ocean of energy suffusing the universe. One of his principal aims is to teach us the art of drawing this energy into our lives."

I am attempting, in this short foreword to Sarah Appleton-Weber's beautiful, lucid, and authoritative new translation of *The Human Phenomenon*, to give a sense of how to approach a first reading of Teilhard. I have suggested that one might begin with a sense of gratitude for his planetary wisdom, with a sense of humility before the challenge of fully appropriating his comprehensive vision, and with a sense of expectancy for those contemplative illuminations a study of Teilhard evokes. It is time to bring this to a close with my final suggestion.

A number of years ago I was asked to give the annual lecture of the American Teilhard Association in New York City, and I arrived several days early to finish my work on the address. A bitter cold spell gripped the city and as I wandered the frozen slabs of concrete I thought of Teilhard as he hurried along these same sidewalks during the last lonely years of his life in New York. It was perfect weather to reflect on his end. He had been forced into isolation, had been denied any opportunity to teach, been refused permission to publish his works. As I walked and reflected, wondering if I were actually walking along the same path as he, I eventually decided to wander all the way out of the city up north to the old Jesuit novitiate where he is buried.

His tombstone is ramrod straight, one of hundreds in the Jesuit cemetery organized with military discipline. I stood there reflecting on the bones a few feet below me in his grave, and suddenly found myself thinking of the expansion of the universe and of how much Teilhard would have loved learning what we now know about this fiery birth. Had the expansion been even slightly different the universe would not have blossomed forth with such beauty: a slower expansion would have ended in a massive black hole; a faster expansion would have quickly become cold hard dust. Even after many discussions at scientific conferences organized around this amazing discovery and others like it, we do not yet know what to make of all this so-called "fine tuning" in the universe. Some physicists are even weary of discussing the matter. Teilhard, on the other hand, would be thrilled.

The universe is about something. Thirteen billion years ago it was about giving birth to an expanding elegance that could stabilize the baryons and knit together hydrogen and helium. Twelve billion years ago it was about giving birth to galactic structures capable of fashioning the complexities of matter necessary for organic life and intelligence. In each moment the universe is about something new, something that had been but a dream until this moment now when the necessary conditions have been created for a new and stunning transformation. You hold *The Human Phenomenon* in your hands and one way to understand this is to point to your human agency in grabbing the book. But it is just as true to say that you hold this book because the universe has labored for billions of years to reach a point in its complexification where it can now bring forth something new through you. It comes to you with its own ideas for your future, for what is needed now for the universe's unfolding story is not a new galaxy or a new star. What is needed now is a new form of human being.

Begin your study of Teilhard with the confidence that it is the creative intelligence of the universe that has seized upon you. Teilhard spoke of this power as Omega, as God, as the future of the universe that is always present in subtle ways. There is work to be done, and the universe through Teilhard's words has now swooped into your life with the aim of transforming you into a power that can participate in our great work of building a vibrant Earth Community.

Brian Swimme
California Institute of Integral Studies
San Francisco

TEILHARD'S TRANSFORMING THOUGHT

EDITOR-TRANSLATOR'S INTRODUCTION

I THE NEED FOR A NEW EDITION AND TRANSLATION

I first read *Le phénomène humain* in the Seuil edition of 1955.[1] Later I
reread it as *The Phenomenon of Man* in Bernard Wall's translation of
1959.[2] But it was while writing a series of poems on poetry and plantlife
in 1974 that I read *Le phénomène humain* as a formal source of poetry.
From the energy and joy I experienced in discovering through Teilhard
the coherence of creation, I wrote a long sequence of poems, *Ladder of
the World's Joy*.[3] Since 1974, to discover the secret of the energy of the
book and to transform my own sense of life and form, I have been reading
and rereading *Le phénomène humain* in the light of Teilhard's essays,
letters, notebooks and retreat notes, his autobiography, and key biographical and interpretive studies.

To enter *Le phénomène humain* more meditatively, exactly, from 1979
to 1981 I made a preliminary word-for-word translation of the work into
English, pacing myself and my understanding with the rhythms of the
work. It was this close reading and translating of the French text which
revealed to me the many serious inaccuracies of the 1959 translation and
led me to see the urgent need to make a new translation for English-
speaking readers.

The very nature of Teilhard's book is "to develop a *homogeneous* and
coherent perspective of our general experience extended to the human
being" for increased vision and thus increase of consciousness (HP, p. 6,
par. 5). Therefore, it calls for a translation that represents Teilhard's
thought accurately and consistently in all its coherence. In Teilhard's
words: "Truth is the total coherence of the universe in relation to each

point of itself. . . . The truth of the human being is the truth of the universe for the human being, that is to say, quite simply, truth." ("Esquisse d'un univers personnel," *Oeuvres*, VI, 71).

The most far-reaching error of the 1959 translation is the failure to differentiate between Teilhard's two terms "homme" and "humain." The title itself of the 1959 translation is incorrect. Teilhard's subject is not the "phenomenon of man" as one among other species, but the ever-evolving human phenomenon as it is developing in and around us at this very moment. The human phenomenon is a unique biological, collective, and global phenomenon, whose past, present, and future is intimately bound up with the formation, life, and ultimate transformation of the Earth. Human speciation remains virtual. Its unique and unifying mode of phylogenesis, which is at once physical and spiritual, has given it the extraordinary power of expansion over the planet in a single unbroken membrane.

The term "homme" in *Le phénomène humain* develops between the two extremes of meaning that Teilhard presents in the Prologue. As seen from a certain limited perspective of science, the human being appears to be an object of study only in the body—a trivial thing in nature, and nature itself appears to be fragmented. The human is seen as analogous to "bee" or "rose." But once the whole of the human is integrated—the "inside" as well as the "outside"—into a coherent representation of the world, the human comes to be seen as the very axis and arrow pointing the direction of evolution itself. If we are to see ourselves completely and survive, it must be as part of humanity, with humanity as part of life, and life as part of the universe (HP, p. 5, par. 9).

The subject of the human phenomenon was developed by Teilhard in three earlier essays of 1925, 1928 and 1930, and it became the pivotal point for all his thought (*Oeuvres*, XIII, 38 ff.). It is through the human phenomenon that the imponderable universal current of spirit is manifested. The magnitude of the human phenomenon is on the level of matter's first forming of the planet Earth, imprisoning the human future within its globe and motion; it is on the level of the first condensation of life on Earth. The human phenomenon represents a new zone in the universe, independent yet somehow born of the entire maturation of the Earth. "Humanity is the Earth (we can even say 'nature') 'hominized'" (*Oeuvres*, IX, 125). It gives us the vision to see the human being as continuous and yet unique among other animals, and it is a zone necessary for the equilibrium of the universe. As such it warrants the foundation of a supreme branch of science, even at the cost of an overall reshaping of our perspectives.

This confusion of the title and focus of Teilhard's work by the first translator has been compounded for English-speaking readers for forty years by being carried into translations of Teilhard's other essays, into translations of *Le phénomène humain* based on the English, and into most discussions and evaluations of Teilhard's work. The work must be called by its proper title: *The Human Phenomenon*.

But there are also other dimensions and qualities of Teilhard's thought, just as fundamental for our understanding, which the 1959 translation has obscured. I have already pointed out the biological reality of the human phenomenon within the evolution of space–time. The 1959 translation also seems blind to the biological reality of "collective unity" in *The Human Phenomenon*, which is one of the three types of the unity of matter introduced in the opening chapter. A collective reality is more than the sum-total of its parts. It has a mysterious unity and active power in itself— a birth, unfolding, and a passing. Humanity belongs to this category.[4]

The 1959 translation misrepresents the relationship of the part, or "element," within the whole. For Teilhard "there are no isolated 'things' in the world. There are only elements of a whole in process" (*Oeuvres*, X, 122 ff.). Those who see are those who have the sense of the world as a unified whole. Those who do not see, do not see beyond the multiple. They perceive the world as fragmented and ultimately absurd. The relationship of the part to the whole is the ultimate problem to be solved by science (HP, p. 177), and for theology it is the foundation of its critique of pantheism.

This relationship of the part to the whole is also used by Teilhard to create a fundamental proportion in the development of the narrative of *The Human Phenomenon*. In each of the four parts, first the element is presented, then the whole of which it is a part, and then the whole is set within its context of the global evolution of the Earth. This proportion is clearly embodied in the structure of Teilhard's table of contents. The 1959 translation, however, may substitute various terms for "element" or shift the reader's focus from the part to the whole, or the whole to the part, or it may represent the part as absorbed by the whole.

Furthermore, the 1959 translation breaks down the essay's coherence of development in space–time as well as the movement of synthesis of Teilhard's thought: by reversing the direction of movement in space–time, or by interchanging terms appropriate to different degrees or phases of synthesis, or by ignoring axial or functional differences between different parts of the tree of life. By omitting or substituting terms inappropriately, it also blurs the continuity of Teilhard's development of individual terms.

For Teilhard's terms "grow" in space–time, becoming more inclusive in their application as the work progresses. A term may embrace more than one domain, and the terms from one domain may be applied to another, expressing, sometimes in a startling way, a fundamental difference yet continuity of development.

For example, Teilhard extends the term "molecule" ahead in time, from its use in the physical analysis of matter before life, to reflect a reality of physics within the human phenomenon; so that "molecule" becomes "mega-molecule" and then "human molecule." In Part II, in a similar extension, "aggregate," the loosest form of grouping at the level of the cell or isolated groups of cells, is applied to the collective reality of humanity, a "super-aggregation" of souls (HP, p. 175), the biological "grain" of life is used to refer to the atom as well as to a "single vast grain of thought on the sidereal scale" (HP, p. 178). Or, extending back in time from the human being, in a descending direction, Teilhard integrates the human's inner dimension within the parameters of physics and biology; "consciousness" and "spontaneity" are found within the primordial dust and within the prelife particles of the juvenile Earth (HP, pp. 24–5).

Teilhard does not use metaphor, but analogy founded in nature. For the reader, Teilhard's use of a term, seen out of its proper context within the whole, may appear to be metaphorical, as, for example, in Teilhard's representations of life's actions of combat and its power of imagination (Part II, Ch. II, 1 and Corollary). But in reality, these apparently metaphorical comparisons are the expression of physical and biological structural realities. Human research and invention are life's groping and ingenuity, transformed: i.e., hominized. For Teilhard, research and invention are indispensable for explaining the movements of life and the ramifications of the living mass. Because of the biological quality and properties of thought that make the human both center of perspective and center of construction of the universe, metaphor is virtually eliminated from Teilhard's text, which develops by structural analogy, analogy that holds from a deep natural bond (HP, p. 71). This bond is revealed in *The Human Phenomenon* with humanity's discovery of evolution, when the summit point of perspective, or "illumination," has been reached— the node in space–time spoken of in the Prologue (HP, pp. 154–8)—and human vision unfolds from its genetic place in the evolutionary landscape. Here we realize that it is in being reflected in the consciousness of each of us that evolution sees itself.

On the one hand the 1959 translation suppresses what appear to be human qualities applied to life, while, on the other, it introduces extraneous metaphors and inappropriate English clichés, which serve no structural or scientific purpose and which confuse the universal "note" of the affinity of beings reverberating within the heart of *The Human Phenomenon* (see "L'amour-energie," HP, pp. 188 ff. and below).

If Teilhard's terms are not translated consistently within their space–time dimensions, the reader can catch only glimmers of the presence of the human dimension. The coherence, which is the source of the work's transforming power and truth, is lost.

In fact, a major lack in the 1959 translation is that it does not retain the very human tone and quality that pervades the whole of *The Human Phenomenon*.

In *The Human Phenomenon* Teilhard is in living dialogue with his readers. He writes at a time of world war, from a sense of organic crisis in evolution, to free humanity from fear and despair so as to give new hope and heart for life. The issue is critical: "See or perish." *The Human Phenomenon* is a long approach to the naming of humanity's deepest fear and unique grandeur, with heightened points of dialogue along the way. Where in the French the dialogue bursts forth, the 1959 translation may eliminate quotation marks or add them inappropriately, and at times blur the dramatic and human urgency by rephrasing Teilhard's questions in indirect discourse.

One of the most dramatic moments is Teilhard's address to Demeter, which opens "Life," Chapter III: "Demeter! Mother Earth! A fruit? What kind of fruit? Is it trying to be born on the tree of life?" (HP, p. 91). The 1959 translation simply omits the address—an address which serves not only a dramatic function, but as a transition from Part II to the content and questions of Part III, and also sets Part II in the context of the Earth. It omits the role of the feminine in creation and the implicit role of "Mary, Queen and Mother of all things, the true Demeter" (*Oeuvres*, XII, 68). Finally, by not translating the words "Terre-Mère" in the text of Part II, Ch. III and Teilhard's reference to it in the table of contents as well, all direct reference to "Mother Earth" has been eliminated from the 1959 translation.

Teilhard's method of phrasing and paragraphing embodies the movement and argument of his thought (see below). By changing Teilhard's system of subheadings and by breaking down the structure and movement of Teilhard's phrasing, the 1959 translation has introduced causal and metaphysical relationships into *The Human Phenomenon* that are alien to Teilhard's phenomenological approach and the scientific method of his work. Yet we must not forget that the 1959 translation was made in other circumstances from ours, in a climate of controversy, without the full context and benefit of Teilhard's essays, other scientific writings, correspondence, biographical material and commentary available to us now. Our global perspective was not as clear and generally recognized.

My purpose in this somewhat extended discussion has not been so much to stress inaccuracies of the 1959 translation as to establish for the reader a basis for understanding the power of Teilhard's transforming thought and, also, what I have come to realize in reading *The Human Phenomenon*: the startling fact that Teilhard's essay is itself a biological step forward in space–time. It has the power to initiate the reader, in the act of reading, into the epic and drama of space–time.

II   Three Earlier Versions of *Le phénomène humain*

The fundamental work of my new translation has been to restore the dimension of biological space–time to the reading of *Le phénomène humain*, and in doing so to restore the dimension of the human, which creates the unity of science and poetry in Teilhard's work. This has entailed a study of texts.

During the years of 1981–83, while living in Strasbourg France. I frequently consulted three earlier versions of *Le phénomène humain* and Teilhard's unpublished correspondence in the archives of the Fondation Teilhard de Chardin in Paris. I was able to establish that MS B Non-corrigé[5] is one of the first three copies Teilhard had typed for him in Peking in 1940 and to compare its text with the later revisions that Teilhard made in response to his Jesuit censors, as well as with his final stencilled version made in 1948–49.

My research also revealed certain important errors and omissions in the Seuil texts of 1955 and 1970 (which have been carried over into other translations). A major contribution of this new translation is to correct these elements and to prepare an authentic new English text for the general reader that will allow the clarity, the dynamics, and the coherence of Teilhard's thought to reveal itself.

The core of *Le phénomène humain* was written down between June 1938 and June 1940. The first typed version, MS B Non-corrigé, consisted of a prologue, four parts, and an epilogue. This core, as Teilhard himself said in his correspondence with Jeanne Mortier, was never fundamentally changed, but in the periods of revision following his return to France from China in May 1946, the work was pruned, elaborated and clarified. In 1947, preparing to submit *Le phénomène humain* to Jesuit censors in Lyons, Teilhard added a foreword (see "Author's Note"), he substantially simplified his description of tangential and radial energy, and omitted the two diagrams that illustrated his earlier description.[6] He also eliminated his diagram of the development of the phylum.[7] In October of 1948, he travelled to Rome to affirm in person his fidelity to the Jesuit order and to try to obtain permission for publication of *Le phénomène humain*. While he was there, in response to his Roman censors, Teilhard added a "Summary or Postface" as well as certain corrections and footnotes,[8] and the appendix "Some Comments on the Place and the Role of Evil in a World in Evolution." In 1949, after receiving the ultimate refusal from Rome, Teilhard revised some twenty or more pages for a final version, which was then stencilled and distributed among scientific colleagues and friends. Upon Teilhard's death, Jeanne Mortier, to whom Teilhard had entrusted and later willed his writings, prepared one of these copies, MS

Corrigé,[9] for publication. I have verified that this text is the basis of the first French edition by Seuil in 1955.

Thus what we have in the Seuil edition represents the essence of Teilhard's thought on the human phenomenon as it was refined and elaborated over a period of eleven years. The final text embodies Teilhard's thought in process.

The three texts of *Le phénomène humain* that are in the archives of the Fondation Teilhard de Chardin in Paris represent the stages of Teilhard's thought and revision over this eleven-year period. MS B Non-corrigé, which I will refer to here as "MS B 1940," contains the typed "core" of *Le phénomène humain*. Later revisions by Teilhard appear in ink between the lines and on the verso of a number of pages. Four diagrams corresponding to the diagrams in MS 1949 have been cut out of the text, perhaps to be used for the preparation of MS 1949. The second version, MS Avant Carmaux,[10] is apparently a rough copy of a version resembling MS B 1940, and it was one of the texts used for the session of revision at Carmaux with Msgr. Bruno de Solages and Henri de Lubac, SJ, in January 1947. Its special interest is that it contains all seven diagrams in Teilhard's own hand, the four represented in Seuil as well as three diagrams similar to numbers A1, A2, and B1 of MS B 1940. The diagrams of MS Avant Carmaux, taken together, provide a graphic embodiment of the astonishingly dynamic and integrated structure of *Le phénomène humain* as I show in the Editor-Translator's Appendix A and B below. The third version, MS Corrigé, is, as I said, the stencilled copy used to prepare the Seuil text of 1955. A fourth copy, one of the 1949 stencilled texts, a copy given by Teilhard to his close friend, the late Pierre Leroy, SJ, was loaned to me by Father Leroy for my work and presented by him to the special collection of Teilhard material at Georgetown University's Lauinger Library.

The four diagrams used in the text of my translation are based on the diagrams made for the stencilled text of 1949 from the tracings of four diagrams which now are lost. Teilhard's letters to Jeanne Mortier and the four final textual revisions made in MS Corrigé in Teilhard's hand show that Teilhard had direct familiarity with this text.

The identification and use of the three versions have been essential for discerning omissions, changes, or errors made in the text of the Seuil editions of 1955 and 1970. I have corrected these as they occur. They have been helpful for establishing Teilhard's principle of organization of subheadings and the table of contents, for correction of the diagrams, and for providing a key to the context, choice, and development of Teilhard's terms, as well as for clarifying Teilhard's use of capitalization and italics.

MS B 1940 has been especially valuable for my work of translation. The typed core is clearly visible beneath an overlay of later ink revisions in Teilhard's hand. The dramatic movement and human dialogue of *Le phénomène humain* stand luminously expressed in the simpler rhythms of phrasing and paragraphing. In more than one letter, and in his journal, Teilhard said that the purpose of his work was perhaps not to create something new, but, as he stated in a letter to Jeanne Mortier two months before he finished: "to create a quality, a tone—to help a new soul to be born within what already exists."[11] MS B 1940 is a source of inspiration for the translator who seeks to convey the urgent human sense, the human resonances, and the dramatic quality and tone of Teilhard's work.

III   TEILHARD'S TRANSFORMING THOUGHT

While pursuing my research at the Fondation, I also reread Teilhard's essays chronologically, coordinating the essays with his published and unpublished correspondence. For Teilhard, thought is a prolongation of life, but life "hominized." The very end of thought is to have no end. This fact lies behind the tremendous exuberance and quantity of his writings. Teilhard's correspondence became central to the very life of his thought as he suffered repeated restrictions and discouragement from his superiors. His correspondence shows that in writing *Le phénomène humain* Teilhard was bringing to bear his many essays, distilling from them the best of his thought, into a work of peace which would be ready for the time after the fighting of World War II had ended. In 1939, when Teilhard returned to China from a trip to the United States, England, and France, and remained there, prevented from returning to Europe by the German invasion of France, his letters tell us that he gave himself to the writing of *Le phénomène humain* as his part in the combat—war being sublimated into a work to form new eyes, to enable the world to see and to become more.

During this same period of my research I spent many days in Colmar, where Pierre Noir, SJ, was preparing an edition of Teilhard's later journal of 1944–55.[12] Guided by Father Noir in the understanding of Teilhard's system of abbreviations and symbols, I studied both the retreat notes and the journal written during Teilhard's period of composing and revising *Le phénomène humain*.

Reading Teilhard's work chronologically while studying Teilhard's journal, I came to see how Teilhard's thought constantly transforms. His thought on a theme is never finished, but it develops with a forward movement, while centering and deepening. Each thought is the seed of a new thought. Throughout the pages of his journal, one can see how Teilhard's thought grows and branches, how he gathers it into larger central themes, and how these themes develop. This movement of Teilhard's thought in space–time is embodied in his style.

IV   Teilhard's Method of Phrasing and Paragraphing, and Arrangement in Space–time

For Teilhard, evolution itself is so fully reducible and identifiable with the advance toward thought that the movement of our soul expresses and measures the very progression of evolution (HP, p. 154). The coherence of *Le phénomène humain* demands faithfulness on the part of the translator to Teilhard's method and terminology, as well as to every degree of complexity of phrasing: for the phrasing in Teilhard's work reflects the coherence of arrangement in space–time and thus the degree of light and energy of his synthesis.

By comparing the earlier versions of *Le phénomène humain* to the Seuil edition, I have been able in my translation to verify Teilhard's method of phrasing, paragraphing, and punctuation as well as to clarify Teilhard's textual format, which itself embodies his principle of organization for subheadings.

Phrase. The smallest element of structure is the phrase in relation to the larger unit of the paragraph. Paragraphing and punctuation are relative, varying with the dramatic movement and rhythm of thought. Just as to perceive the collective unity of the phylum (the natural unit of life's movement as a whole) one has to stand back somewhat (HP, p. 70 ff.), so, to see Teilhard's sentence as a whole, one has to look at it from a certain distance. As in the case of the phylum, Teilhard's sentence varies in size and movement.

Phrase and sentence. For emphasis, or to connect a subsection, section, or chapter to the larger movement, the phrase may stand alone, as a paragraph. Or sometimes a paragraph will appear to be composed of phrases, each set off from the other by a full stop; yet if one stands back, one sees that, in fact, when the phrases are taken together, the whole paragraph they comprise forms grammatically a single sentence. Or a paragraph itself may serve as part of a sentence, which was begun in the paragraph before it, or which will be completed by the paragraph that follows it. A single sentence may stretch over several paragraphs.

The rhythmic use of a full pause and of paragraphing provides space, allowing the resonances among the parts to be perceived. The rhythm may gather and continue from section to section.

Teilhard uses suspension points (. . .) to mark rhythmic pauses and points of suspense, which in leading the reader forward also create a structural relationship among the phrases and paragraphs to follow.[13]

Paragraph, subsection, section, chapter, and part. Thought is measured in paragraphs, which are the units of the larger movement within a subsection. Each subsection develops and unifies at a deeper level what has led up to it, while it leads forward, itself, to what follows. The single *phrase-* or *sentence-paragraph* may be used both within a subsection and as one of a series of subsection headings.

Table of Contents. The variation in organization of subheadings in the text is reflected in Teilhard's table of contents, which is not simply an index of the parts of the text, but a visual embodiment of the development and proportions in space–time of *Le phénomène humain*. The table itself is a unique synthesis, which for the reader adds a dimension of meaning to the text.

Translation of *Le phénomène humain* is not a matter of translating Teilhard's thought into what is already familiar to us, or of translating French into the conventional idioms of English for readability (as the 1959 translation so vividly does). It is, rather, at the most fundamental level, a matter of translating ourselves, the readers, through the vision of the book, so that in passing through the sequence of cosmogenesis, biogenesis, noogenesis, our vision may be transformed into what it must be today in order for us to see, not simply to survive, but to be fully alive (HP, p. 4).

V SCIENCE AND POETRY

The Human Phenomenon is a synthesis of science and poetry: for the reader, to read is to enter on an epic journey (of seeing) and a drama (of becoming).

> Because the individual human being represents a *corpuscular magnitude* we *must* be subject to the same development as every other species of corpuscles in the world: that means that we *must* coalesce into physical relationships and groupings that belong to a higher order than ours. It is, of course, quite impossible for us to apprehend these groupings directly *as such* . . . but there are many indications that enable us to recognize perfectly well their existence and the influences they exercise.[14]

To overcome the illusions of smallness, plurality, and immobility—to be able to see—over the ages the human being has struggled to acquire a whole series of qualities of sight: a sense of space, followed by a sense of time, a sense of number (of the multitude of material and living elements), a sense of differences in physical scale (between the infinitesimal and the immense), a sense of what is new and also certain absolute stages of growth, a sense of movement hidden beneath seemingly monotonous repose, and a sense of the organic (of underlying physical relationships and structural unity) (HP, p. 5).

In an immense combat, or effort of vision, as Dante was guided by Virgil, Teilhard takes the reader down into the deeper zones of matter and life in a quest of the human. Teilhard guides the reader through fears and false perspectives in order to form new eyes (HP, p. 200, par. 3). He names these specific sources of incomplete or faulty vision: instinct, habit, impression, and illusion.

Part I opens where the fibers of the human composite are seen to merge in our sight with the stuff of the universe. The reader enters into three major events of evolution in order to come in Part III, "Thought," to the node of perspective in space–time where humanity stands today, and we see how the option for the evolving future of the Earth and her thinking layer (ourselves) lies in our own hands. It is in "Thought," ch. I, sec. 2 B, that along each of the threads distinguished by anthropology and sociology, a hereditary and collective current of reflection is established and propagated as the human branch emerges through human phylogenesis. The fire of thought spreads from place to place until its incandescence covers the whole Earth. Psychogenesis, relayed to the higher function of "noogenesis" (HP, p. 123), forms the "thinking-layer" of the Earth. With its discovery of evolution, humankind enters a new age and a new spirit of the Earth is born. Part IV concludes with the end of the Earth and Teilhard's projection ahead of a single possible biological point of emersion for humanity at the Omega Point.

Just as the fibers of the human are extended back to where they merge in our sight with the stuff of the universe, so the boundaries of science, which have been too narrow to include the totality of the human, are widened ahead to embrace thought and Omega, on the planetary scale, in a "mega-synthesis" and a "hyperphysics." Toward the final ramification of the human phenomenon at the Omega Point, science and religion conjoin, in a single act of consciousness.

This backward and forward extension of the human with the apparent incongruities it creates is expressive of the actual antinomies in the human condition felt by the modern human. In *The Human Phenomenon* they are used by Teilhard to create dramatic irony and increasing dramatic tension.

For example, in Part II, at the deep level of the cell and clusters of cells, after having described the elementary movements of life and before continuing on to consider how these movements extend to life as a whole, in a corollary called "The Ways of Life," Teilhard pauses with the reader to point out the general characteristics marking every development and occurrence of life: the characteristics of profusion, ingenuity, and indifference (HP, pp. 65–8).

The Corollary is a mysterious passage. It resonates with our human lives, with the revelation of invention and imagination within the constructive power of life, as well as with that blind indifference life appears to have toward the individual.

Here, through the Corollary, the reader enters and suffers the movements of life at the level of cells, lost in number, caught up in the collective, and drawn ahead into the future.

The human and the personal call from within ourselves, caught in the midst of the stark drama of life's early stages. The resonance strikes that tone of pathos fundamental to poetry and drama, coming not from metaphor, but from the structural reality of our human condition in space–time and unlocked here so that we feel it through Teilhard's text.

It is the conflict, Teilhard says, which is still cruelly recognizable in the present time and will remain so, even to the end: that of the "dramatic and perpetual opposition in the course of evolution between the element born of the multiple and the multiple constantly being born of the element" (HP, p. 67 (c) *Indifference*, par. 4). This phrase expresses both dramatic action and the fundamental issue of thought to be solved by science. The conflict will be resolved in Part IV, within the sphere of the person, where humanity comes to accept "the possibility and the reality that there is some magnetic love, and that it is lovable, at the summit of the world" so that the universe takes on ahead of us "a face and a heart," becomes "personified for us, so to speak" (HP, p. 190, par. 4 and footnote*).

VI THE COSMIC RHYTHMS OF BECOMING

Having reached the summit or node of space–time (HP, 154–8), human vision unfolds from its genetic place in the evolutionary landscape. In reading, the reader enters into the cosmic rhythms of becoming, and we recognize them as our own. The same instructions Teilhard gives on how to see the phylum in its collective reality can be applied to seeing cosmic motion: for cosmic movements to become visible, we need to look at them from high enough and far enough away. We need to know how to make them out at any dimension and to see them over a deep enough duration so their movement becomes apparent. Immobilized in time, the features are lost, as well as the life (HP, p. 121 ff.).

Some cosmic events are immense. Some happened in the far distant past. Some are infinitesimally small and take place right under our eyes. Some are so fast or so slow that for our ordinary senses they remain invisible. Yet the material world shown by Teilhard is not the static world of common sense. The mountains are rising and sinking under our feet, while we are being swept along in a cyclone of stars.

To make us see these cosmic motions, Teilhard uses a method he identifies as "kinematic." This kinematic technique of Teilhard's, as the biologist and zoologist Lucien Cuénot pointed out, is fundamentally the method used by paleontologists to represent the development of vertebrate and human forms based on fossil evidence over very long periods of evolution.[15]

In *The Human Phenomenon*, distant or slow movements of evolution, their beginnings erased by the passage of time and at this moment imperceptible directly to ordinary experience, are represented through a visual sequence of forms speeded up by something akin to time-lapse photography. But there is a radical difference between the paleontological representation of the tree of life and time-lapse photography. In the case of the branching of forms on the tree of life, the moment captured is not, as for the camera, a single day's sunrise, the formation of clouds, or the unfolding of a flower, but each evolutionary verticil or "fan" (and in Part II, ch. II, sec. 3 each paragraph of text) represents a different form, a different being—mammal, reptile, amphibian, fish—at a different stage of evolution. And these are seen, from our perspective of the present, across immense gaps left by the fragility of all beginnings now erased by the corrosive effect of time, and with adjustments made in our vision to compensate for the continually expanding dimensions of space–time in the past and the future. This is how we must learn to see, now, if we are to survive and prolong life over the millions of years that lie ahead of us.

In *The Human Phenomenon*, because of our axial position on the tree of life, these movements on the cosmic scale are, at the deepest level, in harmony with our own. And the fact of this cosmic-human harmony has the force of argument, through beauty and through experience, and the power to transform the reader, who is being created (HP pp. 88–90).

Two passages from *The Human Phenomenon* illustrate this power dramatically. In Part II, ch. II, the reader descends with Teilhard back down into the past of the tree of life through a descending series of ever more inclusive animal forms, the expansional zoological "fans" folding back up and disappearing at the level of their peduncles, as if into a "tunnel"; from the layer of trituberculate mammals, to the layer of layers of the tetrapods, to the main branch of the vertebrates, until, as the three main branches of the tree of life rejoin the trunk, everything sinks out of sight in the realm of the soft. Then suddenly, in a single paragraph, the descent is recapitulated in one rapid sequence, from the smallest most faintly outlined microfans to the entire living, rising reality of life as a whole:

No one would think of doubting the giratory origin of the spiral nebulas; or the successive aggregation of particles in a crystal or stalagmite; or the concrescence of woody bundles around the axis of a stem. Certain geometrical dispositions, which to our eyes are perfectly stable, are the trace and irrefutable sign of a kinematics. How is it possible, even for an instant, to doubt the evolutionary origins of the Earth's living layer?

Through our efforts of analysis, life peels apart. It disarticulates indefinitely into an anatomically and physiologically coherent system of overlapping fans. Of faintly sketched microfans of subspecies and races. Of already broader fans of species and genuses. Of more and more enormous fans of biotas, and then of layers, and then of main branches—until we have, at last, the whole assemblage of animals and plants, forming by association just one single gigantic biota, perhaps rooted as a simple ray, in some verticil drowned at the bottom of the mega-molecular world. With life as a simple main branch upon something else . . .

From top to bottom, from smallest to largest, the same structure is visible, whose pattern, reenforced by the very distribution of its shadows and gaps, is accentuated and prolonged (*beyond all hypothesis!*) by the quasi-spontaneous ordering of the unforeseen elements each day brings. Each newly discovered form finds its natural place within the framework already traced—in reality, not one of them is absolutely "new". What more do we need to be convinced that all this *was born*—that is *has grown?*" (HP, p. 89)

The kinematic method is used by Teilhard in Part III to draw the whole of matter and life into the birth of thought, as the whole body of factors established in Parts I and II simultaneously come together in a marvelous conjunction, making the single movement of what Teilhard names the "externalized" act of reflection. This act represents for the reader the only way we will ever see the imperceptible first step of reflection:

Ultimately it is true that from the organic point of view the entire hominizing metamorphosis comes down to the question of a better brain. But how did this cerebral perfectioning take place—how could it have functioned—unless a whole series of other conditions had not been realized together at exactly the same time? If the being the human was born of had not been a biped, its hands would not have been free in time enough to relieve the jaws of their prehensile function, and as a result the thick band of maxillary muscles that imprisoned the skull would not have been relaxed. Thanks to bipedalism freeing the hands the brain could enlarge; and thanks to it at the same time the eyes, drawing near to each other on the diminished face, could begin to converge, and fix their gaze on what the hands took hold of, brought near, and, in every sense of the word, presented: the very act of reflection, exteriorized! In itself there is nothing surprising in this marvelous conjunction. Is not the smallest thing formed in the world in this way always the fruit of an incredible coincidence—a knot of fibers running together forever from the four corners of space? Life works not by following an isolated thread or by starting over. It pushes its whole net ahead at the same time. This is how the embryo is formed in the womb that bears it. We should have known. And, this is precisely why we feel some satisfaction in recognizing that the human being was born under the same maternal law. We are glad to admit that the birth of intelligence corresponds to a turning back on itself, not only of the nervous system, but of the entire being. On the contrary, what frightens us at first sight is to have to see that for this step to be taken it had to be made *all at once*. (HP, pp. 14–15)

VII   Art, Human Energy, and the Future

Teilhard once told his friend Ida Treat, paleontologist, journalist, and fiction writer, that his essays were an outlet for him. They were a release of energies that were overstimulated rather than absorbed by that part of his life turned toward God. That his essays were for him what music was for the musician, poetry for the poet, the novel for the novelist.

He dreamed, he said, of writing a "book of the Earth," where he could say at last what he thought, free from worrying about what it was acceptable to say, but allowing himself to become totally absorbed in translating as truthfully and faithfully as he could what was sounding deep inside him like a voice and a song, not of him but of the world in him. He would like to express the thoughts of someone who, finally having broken through the walls and ceilings of petty nations, coteries, and sects, emerges above all these categories and discovers that he is a child and citizen of the Earth. . . .[16]

"Art," he said in 1939 to students in Paris (this was during the period of his writing Part I of *Le phénomène humain*)—"Art brings that song, that cry, to the anxieties, hopes and enthusiasms of the human being. It gives them a body, and in some way materializes them. . . . If the work truly has issued from [the artist's] own depths, like a rich music . . . it will refract in iridescent light within the minds of those it touches. More primordial than any idea, beauty will reveal itself eloquently as the forerunner and generator of ideas.[17]

The Human Phenomenon has an inexhaustible coherence (light, energy). No one can imitate it, but, rather, it generates new vision, new work.

It must be read with utter attentiveness, heart delicacy. How we misread, mistranslate it if we hurry, if we utilize Teilhard's vision for an idea. The form of the book takes all life, thought, future for interpretation. It is itself a translation, a calling, a transforming of all things.

This book lies along our path. It draws all to it—mysteriously here for us, to pick up now, to learn to read again.

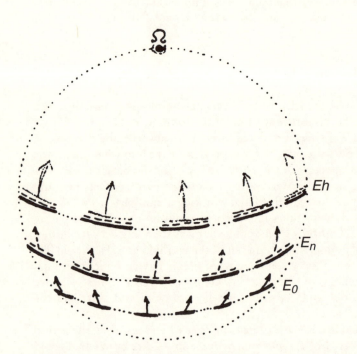

Teilhard's diagram, which did not appear in the 1955 French edition, or the 1959 English-language translation, shows the *global* development of energy in a universe of psychic stuff. Teilhard maintains that it is this global shape and motion which underlies the development of the *whole* of the human phenomenon. The reader should bear this perspective in mind, as it will make increasing sense in the flow of thought and diagrammatic material of the *Human Phenomenon* text which follows, and the explanatory material of the Appendix. Above, to the right, shows convergence in the vicinity of the whole (see Author's Note, p. 2, and text pp. 193–4).

THE HUMAN PHENOMENON

Pierre Teilhard de Chardin

In one way or another,
even in the eyes of a mere biologist,
it is still true that nothing resembles the
way of the Cross as much as
the human epic.

TEILHARD DE CHARDIN

AUTHOR'S NOTE

To be properly understood, the book I present here must not be read as a metaphysical work, still less as some kind of theological essay, but solely and exlusively as a scientific study. The very choice of title makes this clear. It is a study of nothing but the phenomenon; but also, the whole of the phenomenon.

Nothing but the phenomenon, first of all. Do not, therefore, look in these pages for an *explanation* of the world, but only an *introduction to an explanation*. What I have tried to do here, and this is all I have tried to do, is to establish around the human, chosen as center, a coherent order among consequents and antecedents; to discover not a system of ontological and causal relations among the elements of the universe, but an experimental law of recurrence that expresses their successive appearance in the course of time. It goes without saying that beyond this first *scientific* reflection, essential and ample room remains for the more advanced reflection of the philosopher and the theologian. I have carefully and deliberately avoided venturing into that profound domain of being at all times. At the very most, I trust that on the level of experience I have recognized with some accuracy the movement of the whole (toward unity) and marked at the right places the breaks that the subsequent approaches of philosophical and religious thought require for reasons of a higher order.*

But also the *whole* of the phenomenon. And although I may seem to contradict what I have just said, this is what threatens to give the *semblance* of a philosophy to the views I suggest. For some fifty years now, criticism of science has demonstrated in excessive detail that there is no such thing as a pure fact, but that all experience, however objective, is inevitably enveloped in a system of hypotheses as soon as the scientist attempts to formulate it. Now if this aura of subjective observation can remain imperceptible within a limited field of observation, it is inevitable that *in the case of a vision that extends to the whole* it will become almost

---

* See, for example, below, pp. 113–14*, 127*, 214*.

1

dominant. Just like meridians as they approach the pole, so science, philosophy, and religion necessarily converge in the vicinity of the whole. They converge, I repeat, but without merging, and never ceasing to attack the real from different angles and levels right to the end. Take any major book written about the world by one of the great modern scientists such as Poincaré, Einstein, Jeans, and the others. It is impossible to attempt a general scientific interpretation of the universe without *seeming* to intend to explain it right to the end. But only take a closer look at it, and you will see that this "hyperphysics" still is not metaphysics.

In the process of any effort such as this to give a scientific description of the whole, it is natural that the influence of certain initial presuppositions on which the entire future structure of the system depends will make their influence felt to the fullest extent. Especially in the case of this present essay, I would like to point out that two essential options combine to support and govern all developments. The first is the primacy accorded to the psyche and to thought in the stuff of the universe. And the second is the "biological" value attributed to the social fact around us.

The preeminent significance of the human in nature and the organic nature of humanity are two hypotheses that one might try to reject at the outset, but without them I do not see how it is possible for anyone to give a full and coherent representation of the human phenomenon.

PARIS, MARCH 1947

PROLOGUE: SEEING

These pages represent an effort *to see* and *to show* what the human being becomes, what the human being requires, if placed wholly and completely in the context of appearance.

Why should we try to see? And why turn our eyes more particularly toward the human object?

Seeing. One could say that the whole of life lies in seeing—if not ultimately, at least essentially. To be more is to be more united—and this sums up and is the very conclusion of the work to follow. But unity grows, and we will affirm this again, only if it is supported by an increase of consciousness, of vision. That is probably why the history of the living world can be reduced to the elaboration of ever more perfect eyes at the heart of a cosmos where it is always possible to discern more. Are not the perfection of an animal and the supremacy of the thinking being measured by the penetration and power of synthesis of their glance? To try to see more and to see better is not, therefore, just a fantasy, curiosity, or a luxury. See or perish. This is the situation imposed on every element of the universe by the mysterious gift of existence. And thus, to a higher degree, this is the human condition.

But if it is truly so vital and so exalting to know, why prefer to turn our attention once again toward the human? Has the human being not been described enough—to the point of tedium? And is not precisely one of the attractions of science that it at last takes our eyes off ourselves and allows them to rest on some other object?

By a double claim, of being twice center of the world, the human being is imposed on our effort to see as the key to the universe.

Subjectively, first of all, in relation to ourselves, we are inevitably the *center of perspective.* It was probably an inevitable naivete of science at its birth to imagine that it could observe phenomena in themselves, as if they happened apart from us. Instinctively at first, physicists and naturalists worked as if they looked down from above on a world their consciousness could penetrate without being influenced by it or changing it. Now they are starting to realize that their most objective observations are thoroughly steeped in conventions chosen at the outset, as well as in forms or habits of thought developed in the course of the historical development of research. Having reached the extreme limits of their analyses, they no longer can tell whether the structure they have reached is the essence of the material they study or rather the reflection of their own thought. And simultaneously they have become aware that, from the aftershock of their discoveries, they themselves are caught up body and soul in the mesh of relationships they thought to have cast over things from the outside: caught in their own net. A geologist would call it metamorphism and endomorphism.[1] In the act of knowledge, object and subject are wedded together and mutually transform each other. Whether we like it or not, from now on, as a human being, in everything we see, we find ourself and look at ourself.

This is surely a form of bondage, yet immediately compensated for by an incontestable and unique greatness.

It is only normal, but confining, for us to have to carry with us wherever we go the center of the landscape we are passing through. But what would happen to us, walking, if the chances of our journey brought us to a naturally advantageous panoramic point (an intersection of roads or valleys) from which not only our eyes looked out, but from which things themselves radiate? Then as the subjective point of view coincided with the objective distribution of things, perception would be established in its fullest. The landscape would become legible and illuminated from within. We would see.

This certainly seems to be the privilege of human knowledge.

It is not necessary to be a human being to perceive objects and surrounding forces "in the round." Every animal has reached that point as well as ourselves. Human uniqueness lies in the fact that we occupy a position in nature where the convergence of lines is not only visual, but structural. The following pages are written solely to verify and to analyze this phenomenon. By virtue of the biological quality and properties of thought, we find ourselves placed at a singular point, at a node,[2] that commands the entire fraction of the cosmos open to our experience at the present time. The center of perspective, we are at the same time the *center of construction* of the universe. It is therefore from this advantage as much as from necessity that all science must ultimately be related to the human. Truly, if to see is to be more, let us look at the human being and we shall have more life.

And to do this, let us focus our eyes correctly.

From the beginning of human existence, in our own eyes we humans have made a dramatic spectacle of ourselves. In fact, for ten centuries or so we have looked only at ourselves. Yet we have hardly begun to take a scientific view of our significance in the physical world. Such a slow awakening should not surprise us. Often nothing is more difficult to see than what "strikes the eye." Must not the infant be taught how to sort out the images that besiege its newly opened retina? For the human being to discover the human completely, a whole series of "senses" has been necessary, whose gradual acquisition, as we shall explain, covers and scans the very history of the struggles of the mind.

The sense of spatial immensity, the immensely great and the immensely small, disarticulating and spacing out the circles of objects rushing around us, at the interior of a sphere with an indefinite radius.

The sense of depth, laboriously pushing back events in an endless series over immeasurable temporal distances that a kind of heaviness continually tends to compress for us into a thin sheet of the past.

The sense of number, discovering and assessing with open eyes the staggering multitude of material or living elements involved in the slightest transformation of the universe.

The sense of proportion, somehow realizing the difference in physical scale that separates the dimensions and rhythms of the atom from the nebula, and the infinitesimal from the immense.

The sense of quality, or newness, managing to distinguish the absolute levels of perfection and growth in nature, without breaking the physical unity of the world.

The sense of movement, capable of perceiving the irresistible developments hidden in the immensely slow—the extreme agitation concealed under a veil of repose—the wholly new slipping into the heart of the monotonous repetition of the same things.

The sense, finally, of the organic, discovering the physical bonds and structural unity beneath the superficial juxtaposition of successions and collectivities.

If we lack these qualities of sight, no matter what anyone does to show us, the human being will indefinitely remain for us, what still is true for many minds, an erratic object in a disconnected world. But on the contrary, once the triple illusion of smallness, plurality, and immobility has vanished from our eyes, then the human being will effortlessly assume the central place we have just proclaimed, with the human as the momentary summit of an anthropogenesis, which itself crowns a cosmogenesis.

We humans cannot see ourselves completely except as part of humanity, humanity as part of life, and life as part of the universe.

From this stems the fundamental plan of my work: prelife, life, and thought—three events that outline in the past and command for the future (superlife!) one same single trajectory: the curve of the human phenomenon.

The *human phenomenon*—I repeat.

I have not picked this expression at random. I have chosen it for three reasons.

First of all, to affirm that the human is authentically a fact in nature, falling (at least partly) within the province of the requirements and methods of science.

Next, to make it clear that no fact among the facts offered for our understanding is more extraordinary or more illuminating.

Finally, to clearly stress the particular character of the essay I present.

My sole purpose, and my true strength, throughout these pages is simply, I repeat, to try *to see*; that is, to develop a *homogeneous* and *coherent* perspective of our general experience as it extends to the human being. A whole that unfolds.

Let no one look here for any final explanation of things—a metaphysics. And let no one mistake the degree of reality I attribute to the different parts of the film I present. When I attempt to project for myself the world before the origins of life, or life at the Paleozoic Era, I will not forget that it would be a cosmic contradiction to imagine the human as spectator of those phases that came before any appearance of thought on Earth. I therefore will not attempt to describe them as they really were, but as we must represent them to ourselves so that the world may be true for us at this moment; the past not in itself, but as it appears to an observer placed on the advanced summit where evolution has placed us. It is a safe and simple method, but one which, as we shall see, will serve to make surprising visions of the future spring up ahead of us by symmetry.

I need not say that, even reduced to these modest proportions, the views I attempt to express here are for the most part tentative and personal. Yet based on considerable effort of investigation and on prolonged reflection, they give one idea, based on an example, of the way the human problem poses itself for science today.

Studied narrowly and apart from everything else by anthropologists and legalistic minds, the human being is a trivial, even insignificant, thing. Human individuality, too pronounced, masks the totality from our sight, so that as we consider the human our mind tends to fragment nature and to forget the depth of its connections and the boundless horizons it has: entirely the wrong kind of anthropocentrism. From this stems the reluctance so many scientists still feel to accept the human being as an object of science in any other way than as a body.

The time has come for us to realize that to be satisfactory, any interpretation of the universe, even a positivistic one, must cover the inside as well as the outside of things—spirit as well as matter. True physics is that which will someday succeed in integrating the totality of the human being into a coherent representation of the world.

I only hope I can make it felt here that this attempt is possible, and that for those who desire and know how to go to the very heart of things, the preservation of our courage and our joy in acting depend on it.

I doubt whether there is truly any more decisive moment for thinking beings than when, as the scales fall from our eyes, we discover that we are not an element lost in the cosmic solitudes, but that within us a universal will to live converges and is hominized.

The human is not the static center of the world, as was thought for so long; but the axis and the arrow[3] of evolution—which is much more beautiful.

Part I
Prelife

Chapter I

THE STUFF OF THE UNIVERSE

Moving an object back into the past is equivalent to reducing it to its simplest elements. Followed as far as possible in the direction of their origins, the last fibers of the human composite are going to merge in our sight with the very stuff of the universe.

The stuff of the universe—that ultimate residue of the more and more advanced analyses of science. To know how to describe it properly, I have never developed the kind of direct and familiar contact with it that makes all the difference between someone who has read about it and someone who has experimented with it. I also know how dangerous it is to take as material for durable construction hypotheses conceived of as only meant to last a day, even in the minds of those who originate them.

The currently accepted representations of the atom are for the most part merely a simple, graphic, and transitory means in the hands of the scientist to accomplish the grouping and to verify the noncontradiction of the ever more numerous "effects" manifested by matter—many of which, moreover, as yet have no recognizable prolongation in the human being.

More naturalist than physicist, I will of course avoid unnecessarily expanding or dwelling on these complicated and fragile constructions.

On the other hand, from the variety of overlapping theories a certain number of characteristics do come to light that obligatorily reappear in every one of the proposed explanations of the universe. It is this body of "imposed" characteristics, insofar as they express the conditions inherent in every natural transformation, even living, that as a naturalist I must take as my point of departure, and about which I can speak legitimately when engaged in the general study of the human phenomenon.

1 ELEMENTARY MATTER

Observed from this particular angle, and, to start with, taken in its elementary state (I mean, taken at any given moment, point, and volume), the stuff of tangible things reveals itself to us with increasing insistence as radically particulate, yet basically connected, and finally, prodigiously active.

Plurality, unity, and energy are the three aspects of matter.

(a) Plurality, first of all

In the domain of our common experience the profound atomicity of the universe surfaces in visible form. We see it expressed in drops of rain and in the sands of the shore. It is prolonged in the multitude of the living and in the stars. And we even read it in the ashes of the dead. For humans no microscope or electronic analysis was needed to suspect that we lived surrounded and upheld by dust. But to count and describe the grains of this dust, it has taken no less than the clear discernment of modern science. The atoms of Epicurus were inert and indivisible. And the infinitesimally small worlds of Pascal were still seen to have their "mites" within them.[1] In certainty and precision we have now gone far beyond this stage of instinctive or inspired divination. Matter degrades endlessly. Like those minuscule carapaces of diatoms whose pattern resolves itself almost indefinitely under stronger magnifications into new patterns, each smaller material unit tends under the analysis of our physicists to be reduced to something more finely granulated than itself. And with each new step descending this way toward diminution into a larger number, the total configuration of the world is renewed, then blurs.

Beyond a certain degree of depth and dilution, the most familiar properties of our body (light, color, heat, impenetrability . . .) become meaningless.

In fact, our sense experience condenses and floats on a swarm of the indefinable. Dizzying in number and smallness, the substratum of the tangible universe continues on endlessly disaggregating toward what is below.

(b) Now the more we artificially cleave and pulverize matter, the more we can see its fundamental unity

In its most imperfect form, the simplest to imagine, this unity expresses itself in an astonishing similarity between the elements encountered. Whatever their degree of magnitude and whatever their name, these minuscule entities—molecules, atoms, electrons—manifest a perfect identity of mass and behavior (at least at the distance from which we observe them). They seem to be remarkably calibrated—and monotonous—in their dimensions and operations. As if all the surface excitement that delights our lives tends to be extinguished in the depths. As if the stuff of all stuff is reduced to one simple and unique form of substance.

There is a unity of *homogeneity*, therefore. But at the same time, unity of domain and of collectivity.[2]

Unity of domain. It would be natural for us to attribute to minute cosmic corpuscles[3] a radius of individual action as limited as their own dimensions. But it becomes evident that, on the contrary, each one of them can only be defined in function of its influence on everything around it. Whatever space we suppose each cosmic element to be placed in, it entirely fills that volume itself with its own radiation. However narrowly circumscribed is the "heart" of an atom, its domain is at least virtually coextensive with that of any other kind of atom. We shall meet this strange property again, further ahead, even in the human molecule!

And, as we added, *collective unity.* Even though the innumerable centers share a given volume of matter in common, for all that they are not independent from each other. Something binds them together that makes them mutually interdependent. Far from behaving like an inert receptacle, the space filled by their multitude influences them like an active medium of direction and transmission within which their plurality is organized. Atoms that are merely added together or juxtaposed still do not make matter. A mysterious identity incorporates them and binds them together, which goes against our mind, yet to which our mind will ultimately be forced to yield.

The sphere above the centers and enveloping them.

Throughout these pages, at each new phase of anthropogenesis we will find ourselves faced with the unimaginable reality of collective bonds, and we shall continually have to struggle against them, until we succeed in recognizing and defining their true nature. Here at the beginning, it is enough to include them under the empirical name science gives to their common initial principle: energy.

(c) Energy, the third aspect of matter

Under this word, which conveys the sense of psychological effort, physics has introduced the precise formulation of a capacity for action, or more exactly, for interaction. Energy is the measure of what is transferred from one atom to another in the process of their transformations. Energy, then, is a power of bonding; but also, because the atom seems to be enriched or depleted in the course of the exchange, a power of building up.

From the standpoint of energetics as it has been renewed by the phenomena of radioactivity, minute material particles can now be treated as transient reservoirs of concentrated power. Never, in fact, grasped in its pure state, but always more or less granulated (even in light!), for science energy currently represents the most primitive form of universal stuff. This is what accounts for our imagination's instinctive tendency to consider it as a kind of homogeneous primordial flux, of which everything that takes shape in the world is only a fleeting "vortex." From this point of view, the universe would find its consistency and ultimate unity *at the end of its decomposition. It would hold together from below.*

Let us keep the indisputable observations and measurements of physics. But let us avoid becoming attached to the perspective of final equilibrium they seem to suggest. A more complete observation of the movements of the world will gradually oblige us to turn this perspective around; I mean, to discover that if things hold, and are held together, it is only by reason of complexity, *from above.*

2   TOTAL MATTER

So far we have looked at matter "in itself," that is, in its qualities and at any given volume—as if we could legitimately detach a fragment of it and study this sample separately from the rest. It is time to point out that this process is a purely mental device. Considered in its physical, concrete reality, the stuff of the universe cannot be split apart. But taken in its totality, as a kind of gigantic "atom," it forms the only real indivisible there is (aside from thought where it centers and concentrates at the other end). The history of consciousness and its place in the world remain incomprehensible to anyone who has not seen beforehand that by the unassailable integrity of it as a whole, the cosmos in which we humans find ourselves engaged constitutes a *system*, a *totum*, and a *quantum*: a system in its multiplicity—a totum in its unity—a quantum in its energy; all three, moreover, within a boundless contour.

Let me explain what this means.

(a) System

The "system" in the world is immediately perceptible to anyone who observes nature.

The arrangement of the parts of the universe has always been a source of wonder for us. Now, in the degree to which a more precise and penetrating study of the facts becomes possible, the ordering of the parts of the universe is found to be more and more astonishing every day. The farther and deeper we penetrate into matter with our increasingly powerful methods, the more dumbfounded we are by the interconnection of its parts. Each element of the cosmos is woven positively from all the others; from below itself by the mysterious phenomenon of "composition" that gives it subsistence in the point of an organized whole, and from above by being subjected to the influence of unities of a higher order that encompass and dominate it for their own ends.

It is impossible to cut into this network, to isolate a piece, without all its borders fraying and coming undone.

The universe holds together by the whole of itself, as far as we can see around us. And there is really only one possible way to consider it. That is, to take it as a whole, as a unit.

(b) Totum

Now if we consider it more carefully, we quickly see that this unit is something entirely different from a simple tangle of articulate connections. When we speak of a fabric or network, we think of a homogeneous interlocking of similar units, which it may in fact be impossible to section, but if we only recognize the element and define its law, we have command of it as a whole and imagine the rest by repetition. We think of a crystal or an arabesque, where the same law is valid for filling up the entire space, but already entirely contained within a single mesh.

This structure has nothing in common with the structure of matter.

Matter never repeats itself in its combinations at different orders of magnitude. For expediency and simplicity we sometimes like to picture the world to ourselves as a series of planetary systems superposed on each other and placed at intervals from the infinitely small to the infinitely great—here again we find the two abysses of Pascal. This is only an illusion. The envelopes of which matter is composed are fundamentally heterogeneous in relation to one another. There is a circle, still nebulous, of electrons and other lower units. A circle, more clearly defined, of simple bodies, where the elements are distributed in periodic function of the hydrogen atom. A circle, farther on, of inexhaustible molecular combinations. Finally, by a leap or turn around from the infinitesimal to the immense, a circle of stars and galaxies. These multiple zones of the cosmos encompass but do not imitate one another—so that there is no way we can pass from one to the other by a simple change of coefficient. Here there is not a reproduction of the same motif on a different scale. The order and design appear only in the whole. The mesh of the universe is the universe itself.

Therefore it is not enough to affirm that matter is a unit or grouping.

Woven in a single piece according to a process that is one and the same, but that never repeats itself from point to point,* the stuff of the universe fits only one description: structurally it forms a whole.

---

* The process we shall later on call the "law of consciousness and complexity."

(c) Quantum

And now, if the natural unit of concrete space really does merge with the totality of space itself, we must try to redefine energy in relation to space as a whole.

And this leads us to two conclusions.

The first is that the radius of action of each cosmic element must then be prolonged to the outermost limits of the world. Since, as we said above, the atom is naturally coextensive with every space in which we situate it—and since, furthermore, as we have just seen, universal space is the *only space there is*—we have no choice but to admit that this immensity represents the domain of action common to all atoms. The volume of each one of them is the volume of the universe. The atom is no longer the microscopic and closed world we might perhaps have imagined. It is the infinitesimal center of the world itself.

On the other hand, let us extend our view to all of the infinitesimal centers that together share the universal sphere. However indefinable their number, by their multitude they constitute a grouping with precise effects. For since it exists, the whole must express itself in a global capacity for action whose partial resultant, moreover, we find in each one of us. In this way we are led to envision and conceive the world on a dynamic scale.

True, the world has apparently a boundless contour. To use different images, it behaves for our senses either like a progressively attenuated milieu that vanishes without a surface limit by some kind of infinite gradation; or like a curved or closed domain within which all the lines of our experience coil in on themselves—in which case, matter seems shoreless only because we cannot emerge from it.

That is no reason to deny the world its quantum of energy, which, incidentally, physicists already believe they are in a position to measure.

But this quantum assumes its full meaning only if we try to define it in relation to a natural and concrete movement, that is, in duration.

3   The Evolution of Matter

Physics was born in the last century under the double sign of fixity and geometry. Its youthful ideal was to find a mathematical explanation for a world conceived of as a system of stable elements in a closed equilibrium. And then, along with all the sciences of the real, it was irresistibly drawn by its own progress into becoming a history. Today positive knowledge of things is identified with study of their development. Further along, in the chapter on thought, we will be describing and interpreting the vital revolution brought about in human consciousness by the wholly modern discovery of duration. We only need to ask ourselves here how the introduction of this new dimension expands our view of matter.

The change brought about in our experience by what we shall soon call space–time essentially consists in this: everything that we regarded and treated until then as points in our cosmological constructions has become the momentary section of indefinite temporal fibers. From then on, to our opened eyes every element of things prolongs itself behind us (and tends to continue on ahead) as far as the eye can see. So that the whole immensity of space is no more than the slice "at time t" of a trunk whose roots plunge down into the abyss of an unfathomable past, and whose branches rise somewhere ahead in a future that, at first sight, seems boundless. From this new perspective, the world appears to be a mass in process of transformation. The totum and quantum of the universe tend to express and define themselves in a cosmogenesis.

In the eyes of the physicists at this moment, what form does this evolution of matter take (qualitatively) and what rules does it follow (quantitatively)?

(a) Form

Observed in its central and clearest part, the evolution of matter reduces itself, in current theory, to the gradual building up, by increasing complication, of the various elements recognized by physicochemistry. At the very bottom, to begin with, there is still unresolved simplicity, a kind of luminosity indefinable in terms of figures. Then abruptly (?)* a swarm of positive and negative elementary corpuscles (protons, neutrons, electrons, photons . . .), the list of which never stops growing. Then the harmonic series of simple bodies, spread over the notes of the atomic scale from hydrogen to uranium. And next the immense variety of compound bodies, where molecular masses continue to rise until they reach a certain critical value, above which, as we shall see, we go on to life. There is not a single term in this long series that, from valid experimental proofs, cannot be seen to be composed of nuclei and electrons. This fundamental discovery,

---

* A few years ago this first birth of corpuscles was imagined rather in the form of an abrupt *condensation* (like a saturated medium) of a primordial substance diffused throughout a boundless space. Now for various and convergent reasons (notably relativity, combined with the centrifugal flight of galaxies), physicists' preference is toward the idea of an explosion pulverizing a primitive quasi-atom in which space–time was strangled (at a kind of absolute natural zero) only several billions of years behind us. The two hypotheses are equivalent for the understanding of the pages that follow; in the sense that either one of them equally situates us at the heart of a corpuscular multitude we cannot escape from in any direction, either around or behind us—but perhaps ahead, through a singular point of enfolding and interiorization (see Part IV, ch. II and following).

that all bodies derive, *by arrangement,* from one initial corpuscular type is the flash that lights up the history of the universe for our eyes. From the beginning, matter has, in its own way, obeyed the great biological law of "complexification" (a law we shall return to again and again).

In its own way, as I said: because at the stage of the atom, many points in the history of the world still elude us.

First of all, to rise up in the series of simple bodies, do the elements have to pass through all the degrees of the scale successively (from the simplest to the most complicated) by a kind of onto- or phylogenesis? Or else do the atomic numbers only represent a rhythmic series of states of equilibrium, kinds of fixed compartments, into which nuclei and electrons fall abruptly assembled? And then, in either case, are we to picture the different combinations of nuclei to be immediately and equally possible? Or else are we to imagine the contrary, that, statistically, on the whole, heavy atoms appear only after light atoms and in a definite order?

It does not seem, as yet, that science can give any definite answer to these and other similar questions. At the present time, we are better informed about the evolution of preliving and living molecules than about the rising evolution of atoms (note I do not call it "disintegration"). The fact remains, meanwhile (and this is the only really important point for the subject we are concerned with here), that as far back as its most distant formations, we discover that matter is *in a state of genesis*—a genesis that allows us to catch sight of two of the aspects most characteristic of it in its subsequent periods. First of all, that matter begins with a critical phase, the phase of *granulation,* which abruptly gives birth (once and for all?) to the constituents of the atom, and perhaps to the atom itself. And next, that, at least from molecules onward, it pursues its course additively according to a process of growing complexity.

Nothing happens continually in the universe at any given moment. Nor does it happen everywhere.

In a few lines, we have just summarized the idea of the transformations of matter accepted by science today—but simply considering them in their temporal sequence and still without having situated them anywhere in the cosmic expanse. Historically, the stuff of the universe goes on concentrating in more and more organized forms of matter. But where, then, do these metamorphoses take place, at least from the construction of molecules onward? Is it just anywhere at all in space? Certainly not, as we all know, but uniquely at the core and on the surface of the stars. The fact of having considered what is elementary and infinitely small forces us, abruptly, to lift our eyes to the infinite greatness of the sidereal masses.

Sidereal masses. Our science is both troubled and fascinated by these colossal unities, which behave in some ways like atoms, but whose formation baffles us by its enormous and (seemingly?) irregular complexity. Perhaps the day will come when some arrangement or periodicity will be apparent in the distribution of the stars, in their composition as well as their position. Inevitably, is it not some kind of "stratigraphy" and "chemistry" of the heavens that prolongs the history of atoms?

We do not need to involve ourselves in these still hazy perspectives. However fascinating they may be, they are what surrounds, not what leads to the human being. On the other hand, we do need to notice and bear in mind the definite connection that associates the atom with the star genetically, because it has its consequences, even in the genesis of the mind. Physics may still hesitate for a long time about what structure to assign the astral immensities. In the meantime, one thing is certain enough to guide our steps along the pathways of anthropogenesis. And this is, that the fabrication of higher material compounds can only be carried out if there is a previous concentration of the stuff of the universe in nebulas and suns. Whatever overall shape the worlds may take, the chemical function of each one of them already has a definable significance for us. Stars are the laboratories where the evolution of matter is carried out in the direction of large molecules—and, moreover, according to well-defined quantitative rules, rules which we will deal with now.

(b) Numerical Laws

What ancient thought had glimpsed and imagined as a natural harmony of numbers, modern science has grasped and realized through the precision of formulas based on measurement. In fact, we owe our knowledge of the micro- and macrostructure of the universe to increasingly detailed measurements far more than to direct observation. And it is, again, ever bolder measurements that have revealed to us the calculable conditions to which every transformation of matter is subjected from the power it sets into play.

This is not the place for me to undertake a critical discussion of the laws of energetics. Let us simply summarize what is accessible and indispensable in them to everyone who attempts a history of the world. Considered from this biological perspective, they can be broadly reduced to the following two principles:[4]

First principle. In the process of physicochemical transformations, we detect no measurable appearance of new energy.

Every synthesis costs something. This is a fundamental condition of things, which as we know persists even into the spiritual zones of being. In every domain, to realize itself progress requires an increase of effort and therefore of power. Now where does this increase come from?

In the abstract, we might imagine that there is an internal increase in the resources of the world to meet the growing needs of evolution, an absolute augmentation of mechanical wealth throughout the ages. But in fact, things seem to happen in a different way. In no case does the energy of synthesis seem to add up from the accumulation of new capital, but from its expenditure. What is gained on one side, is lost on the other. Everything is constructed at the expense of an equivalent destruction.

Experimentally and at first sight, when we consider the mechanical functioning of the universe, it does not present itself to us as an open quantum, capable of encompassing in its angle an ever greater reality, but as a closed quantum, within which nothing progresses except by an exchange of what has originally been given.

This is the way it looks at first.

Second principle. But there is something more. Thermodynamics adds that in the process of every physicochemical transformation, a fraction of available energy is irremediably "entropized," lost, that is, in the form of heat. Of course it is possible to retain this dissipated fraction symbolically, in equations, so that nothing more is lost than is created in the operations of matter. This is a purely mathematical device. In fact, from the real evolutionary perspective, in the course of every synthesis something is definitively burned up to pay for it. The more the quantum of energetics of the world functions, the more it is used up. Within the field of our experience, the concrete material universe seems unable to continue on its course indefinitely. Instead of moving indefinitely in a closed cycle, it irreversibly describes a branch with a limited development. And through this it separates itself from abstract magnitudes, to take its place among the realities that are born, that grow, and that die. From time it passes into duration; and escapes geometry definitively, to become dramatically, in its totality and its elements, the subject of history.

Let us translate into images the natural significance of the two principles of the conservation and degradation of energy.

Qualitatively, as we said above, the evolution of matter manifests itself to us, *here and now*, as a process in the course of which the constituents of the atom are ultracondensing and intercombining. Quantitatively this transformation now appears to us to be a definite but costly operation, where the original impetus is slowly exhausted. Bit by bit and degree by degree, the atomic and molecular structures are laboriously becoming more complicated and rising. But the ascensional force is lost along the way. What's more, at the interior of each of the terms of synthesis (and the faster, the higher the terms), the same wearing out is at work that undermines the cosmos as a whole. Bit by bit the *improbable* combinations they embody come undone again into simpler elements that fall back and disaggregate into the amorphous state of *probable* distributions.

A rocket that rises following the arrow of time and bursts open only to be extinguished—an eddy rising in the midst of a current that descends. That is what our image of the world would be.

According to science. And I believe in science. But has science ever bothered until now to look at the world except from the *outside* of things?[5]

Chapter II

THE INSIDE OF THINGS

On the scientific plane, the quarrel between the proponents of materialism and spiritualism, and the propenents of determinism and finalism, is still very much alive today. After a century of dispute, each side still stands its ground and gives its adversaries solid reasons for remaining there.

From what I can understand of this struggle, in which I myself have been personally involved, it seems to me that it is prolonged not so much from the difficulties human beings experience in reconciling certain apparent contradictions in nature between mechanism and freedom, and death and immortality, as from the difficulties the two schools of thought have encountered in finding a common ground. The proponents of materialism, on the one hand, insist on talking about objects as though they consisted only of external actions in "transient" relationships. The proponents of the spiritual view, on the other, stubbornly refuse to go beyond a kind of solitary introspection, where beings are only seen as closed in on themselves in their "immanent" operations. They both fight on different planes, without meeting, and each only sees half the problem.

I am convinced that these two viewpoints need to be united, and that they soon will be, in a kind of phenomenology or generalized physics, where the internal face of things as well as the external face of the world will be taken into account. Otherwise, it seems to me that it would be impossible to cover the totality of the cosmic phenomenon with a coherent explanation, as science must aim to do.

We have just described the measurable connections and dimensions of matter from the *outside*. Now in order to advance further in the direction of the human, we must extend the base of our future constructions to the *inside* of this same matter.

Things have their *interior*, their "reserve," one could say. And that interior appears either in direct *qualitative* or *quantitative* relationship to the developments of cosmic energy recognized by science. These three assertions form the three sections of this new chapter.

Treating them as I must do here will force me to go beyond prelife and to somewhat anticipate life and thought. But is not the distinctive feature and difficulty of every synthesis that its end is already implied in its beginning?

1 EXISTENCE

If any single perspective has been clearly brought out by the latest advances in physics, surely it is that in the unity of nature there are different types of spheres (or levels) for our experience, each one characterized by the dominance of certain factors that become imperceptible or insignificant in the neighboring sphere or level. On the middle scale of our organisms and constructions, speed does not seem to alter the nature of matter. We now know today that at the extreme values reached by atomic movements, speed profoundly modifies a body's mass. Among "normal" chemical elements, stability and longevity appear to be the rule. And now suddenly this illusion has been destroyed by the discovery of radioactive substances. On our human scale of existence, the mountains and stars appear to be models of unchanging majesty. We now see that observed over a great depth of duration, the Earth's crust goes on endlessly modifying under our feet, while the heavens are sweeping us along in a cyclone of stars.

In every one of these instances and others like them, there is no absolute appearance of a new magnitude. *Every* mass is modified by its speed. *Every* body radiates. At speeds slow enough, *every* movement is veiled in immobility. But on a different scale or at a different intensity, a particular phenomenon becomes apparent that invades the horizon, blots out the other nuances, and lends its particular tonality to the whole spectacle.

The same applies to the "inside" of things.

For a reason that will soon become obvious, in the domain of physicochemistry objects are manifested only by their external determinism. In the eyes of the physicist, there is legitimately nothing but an "outside" of things (at least until now). For the bacteriologist, whose cultures are treated (obviously, with major difficulties) as reactive substances of the laboratory, the same intellectual attitude is still permissible. But in the world of plants, it already presents many more difficulties. In the case of the biologist concerned with the behavior of insects or coelenterates, to take this attitude is to attempt the impossible. In the case of vertebrates, it appears to be simply futile. And in the human, in whom the existence of an interior is inescapable, it finally fails completely, because it becomes the object of direct intuition and the stuff of all knowledge.

The apparent restriction of the phenomenon of consciousness to higher forms of life has long served science as a pretext for eliminating it from its constructions of the universe. To dismiss it, thought has been classed as a bizarre exception, an aberrant function, an epiphenomenon. But what would have become of modern physics if it had done no more than to classify radium among "abnormal" substances? Clearly the activity of radium was not and could not have been disregarded because, being measurable, it forced its way into the exterior tissue of matter— whereas to integrate consciousness into a system of the world requires us to envision the existence of a new face or dimension of the stuff of the universe. We shrink from the effort. But anyone can see that the problem for those who do research is identical in each case and that it must be solved by the same method: that is, *to discover the universal underlying the exceptional*.

Recently, our experiments have shown this too often for us still to have any doubt: a natural anomaly is always the exaggeration until it becomes perceptible of a property that is spread everywhere in the imperceptible state. By virtue of the world's fundamental unity, once a phenomenon has been clearly observed, even only at a single point, its value and roots are simultaneously present everywhere. Where does this rule lead us if we apply it to human "self-consciousness"?

"Full evidence of consciousness appears only in the human," we had been tempted to say, "therefore it is an isolated case and of no interest to science."

"Evidence of consciousness appears in the human," we must begin again, correcting ourselves, "therefore half-seen in this single flash of light, it has cosmic extension and as such takes on an aura of indefinite spatial and temporal prolongations."

The conclusion is fraught with consequences. And yet in sound analogy with the rest of science, I can see no way to escape it.

Indisputably, deep within ourselves, through a rent or tear, an "interior" appears at the heart of beings. This is enough to establish the existence of this interior in some degree or other everywhere forever in nature. Since the stuff of the universe has an internal face at one point in itself, its structure is necessarily *bifacial*; that is, in every region of time and space, as well, for example, as being granular, *coextensive with its outside, everything has an inside*.

Although disconcerting for our imagination, the picture of the world that logically follows from this is in fact the only one our reason can absorb. Taken at its lowest point, exactly where we placed ourselves at the beginning of these pages, matter at its origins is something more than the particulate swarming so marvelously analyzed by modern physics. Beneath this initial mechanical sheet we must conceive the existence of a "biological" sheet, thin in the extreme, but absolutely necessary to explain the state of the cosmos in the times that follow. Inside, consciousness,* and spontaneity are three expressions of one and the same thing, and we can no more legitimately set an experimental absolute beginning for them than for any other of the lines of the universe.

In a coherent perspective of the world, life inevitably presupposes a prelife before it, as far back as the eye can see.†

But then, as the proponents of both the spiritual and material views will object together, if everything in nature is fundamentally living, or at least preliving, how, then, is it possible for a mechanistic science of matter to have been built up and for it to prevail?

Outwardly determinate and inwardly "free," would the two faces of objects be irreducible and noncomparable? And if this is the case, what is your solution?

The answer to this difficulty is already implicitly contained in the observations made above on the diversity of "spheres of experience" superposed at the interior of the world. It will be more clearly apparent when we have seen the qualitative laws governing the growth and variation of the manifestations of what we have just called the "inside" of things.

2   THE QUALITATIVE LAWS OF GROWTH

The sole purpose of this present study, we must not forget, is to harmonize objects in time and space, without presuming to fix the conditions that

---

* Here as elsewhere in this book the term "consciousness" is taken in its broadest sense to designate every kind of psyche, from the most rudimentary forms of interior perception conceivable to the human phenomenon of reflective consciousness.

† These pages had been written for some time when I was surprised to find their substance in a few masterful lines recently written by the great biologist J. B. S. Haldane. "We find no obvious traces of either thought or life in so-called inert matter," the great English biochemist said. "And as a result we naturally studied these properties where they are most completely manifested. But if the perspectives of modern science are correct, we shall ultimately find them, at least in rudimentary forms, all through the universe." And he even adds these words, which my readers can recall further along, when (with all due reservations and corrections) I evoke the perspective of the "Omega Point": "If the cooperation of some thousands of millions of cells in our brain can produce our capacity for consciousness, the idea becomes vastly more plausible that some kind of cooperation of humanity as a whole, or a fraction of it, may determine what Comte called a Great Superhuman Being" (J. B. S. Haldane, "Science and Ethics," in *The Inequality of Man*, Harmondsworth: Pelican Editions, ser. A 12,1937:114–15). What I say is therefore not absurd. Beside the fact that every metaphysician should be glad to observe that even in the eyes of physics the idea of absolutely brute matter (that is, of something purely "transient") is only a first and rough approximation of our experience.[1]

might govern the depths of their being. To establish an experimental chain of succession in nature, not an ontological causal connection. In other words, "to see," and not to explain.

From this perspective, and concerned only with phenomena (which is *the* perspective of science), is there any way to go beyond the position where we stopped our analysis of the stuff of the universe? We have just recognized that everywhere in the stuff of the universe there necessarily exists an internal conscious face lining the external "material" face habitually the only one considered by science. Can we go further and define the rules according to which this second, most often hidden, face comes to shine through, then to emerge in certain areas of our experience?

It seems they can be defined, and even very simply, provided that we put end to end three observations, which any one of us could have made, but whose true value can be seen only if we think of linking them together.

(a) *First observation.* We have just admitted the reality of an inside, even in the nascent forms of matter. Considered in its prevital state, the inside of things should not be imagined to form a continuous layer, but to be affected by the same granulation as matter itself.

We shall soon return to this major point. As far back as we begin to catch a glimpse of the *first living beings*, in their size and number they manifest themselves to our experience as kinds of "mega-" or "ultra-molecules," an overwhelming multitude of microscopic nuclei. This means that, for reasons of homogeneity and continuity, we may suppose that below the horizon the preliving being is an object participating in the *corpuscular* structure and properties of the world. Looked at from the inside as well as observed from the outside, the stuff of the universe thus tends equally to resolve itself behind us into a dust of particles that (1) perfectly resemble each other (observed, at least, from a great distance); (2) are each coextensive with the totality of the cosmic domain; and (3) finally, are mysteriously bound together by an energy of the whole. Point by point, at these depths the external and internal faces of the world correspond so well that in the definition of the partial centers of the universe given above (Part I, ch. 1, sec. 1(b)),[2] we can switch from one to the other on the simple condition that we replace "mechanical interaction" with "consciousness."

Atomicity is a property shared by the inside and the outside of things.

(b) *Second observation.* Practically homogenous among themselves at the origin (exactly like the elements of matter they support), the elements of consciousness continue to complicate and differentiate their nature in the course of duration. From this perspective and considered purely from the experimental angle, consciousness is manifested as a cosmic property of variable magnitude, subject to global transformation. Taken as it rises, this enormous phenomenon, which we shall follow throughout the stages of life and as far as thought, has ended up seeming ordinary. Followed in the opposite direction, as we already observed above, it leads us to the less familiar concept of lower states that become more and more indistinct and almost "distended."

Refracted back in evolution, consciousness spreads out qualitatively behind us in a spectrum of variable shades whose lower terms are lost in darkness.

(c) *Third observation.* Finally, from two different regions of this spectrum let us take two particles of consciousness that have reached unequal stages of evolution. As we just saw, corresponding to each of them by construction, there is a certain definite material grouping of which they form the inside. Let us compare these two external groupings to each other and ask ourselves how they are arranged among themselves and in relation to the parcel of consciousness they each respectively envelop.

The answer comes immediately.

Whatever situation we can visualize we can be certain that each time the richer and better organized construction corresponds to the most developed consciousness. The simplest protoplasm is already a substance of unheard-of complexity. The degree of complication augments in geometric proportion from the protozoan to higher and higher forms of the metazoan. And always and everywhere the same can be said for the rest. Here again the phenomenon is so obvious that we ceased to be amazed by it a long time ago. And yet it has decisive importance. In fact, thanks to it we have a tangible "parameter" allowing us to connect both the external and internal layers of the world, not only *in position* (point by point), but *in movement* as we shall verify later on.

We can say that the concentration of a consciousness varies in inverse ratio to the simplicity of the material composition that it lines. Or again: the richer and better organized the material edifice it lines, the more perfected is the consciousness.

*Spiritual perfection (or conscious "centricity") and material synthesis (or complexity) are merely the two connected faces or parts of a single phenomenon.**

And here we have by the fact itself reached the solution of the problem we posed. We were looking for a qualitative law of development capable of explaining from sphere to sphere first the invisibility, then the appearance, and then the gradual dominance of the inside in relation to the outside of things. This law reveals itself once the universe is conceived of

---

* From this perspective one could say that each being is constructed (on the plane of phenomena) like an *ellipse* on two conjugated foci: a focus of material organization and a focus of psychic centration—the two foci varying mutually independently and in the same direction.

as passing from *state A*, characterized by a very large number of very simple elements (that is, having a very impoverished inside), to *state B*, defined by a smaller number of very complex groupings (that is, having a richer inside).

Because they are at once very numerous and extremely lax in state A, the centers of consciousness are only manifested by effects of the whole, *submitted to the laws of statistics*. They therefore collectively obey mathematical laws. This is the particular domain of physicochemistry.

In state B, on the contrary, since these elements are less numerous* and at the same time better individualized, bit by bit they escape the slavery of large numbers. Their fundamental and nonmeasurable spontaneity shines through. We can begin to see them and to follow them one by one. And from then on we have reached the world of biology.[3]

The rest of this essay will, in short, be nothing but this history of the embattled struggle in the universe between the unified multiple and the unorganized[4] multitude, the application throughout of the great law of *complexity and consciousness*, a law that itself implies that the world has a *psychically convergent structure and curvature*.

But let us not go too fast. And since all we have to concern ourselves with here is prelife, let us merely keep in mind the fact that from a *qualitative* point of view there is no contradiction in admitting that a universe is built of "freedoms" even though it outwardly appears to be mechanical—provided that these "freedoms" are contained within a great enough state of division and imperfection.

To go on, now, in conclusion, to the more difficult point of view of *quantity*, let us see if it is possible to define the energy this kind of universe would contain in a way that does not conflict with the accepted laws of physics.

3   SPIRITUAL ENERGY

No concept is more familiar to us than spiritual energy. And yet nothing remains more obscure to us scientifically. On the one hand, the objectivity of the effort and work of the psyche is so certain that the whole of ethics resides in it. And on the other, the nature of this interior power is so impalpable that the whole of mechanics could be built up without it.

The difficulties we still have in grouping spirit and matter together in the same rational perspective are nowhere more obvious. And nowhere, either, do we more tangibly see the urgency for making a bridge between

---

* Despite the specifically vital mechanism of *multiplication*, as we shall see.

the physical and moral shores of our existence if we want the spiritual and material aspects of our activity to mutually enliven each other.

Science has provisionally taken the stance of ignoring the question of how to link the two energies of body and soul together in a coherent way. And it certainly would be convenient to do the same. But caught here as we are, for better or for worse, in the logic of a system where the inside of things has just as much or even more value as their outside, the difficulty confronts us. It is impossible to avoid the encounter: we must move ahead.

Of course the considerations that follow do not presume to provide a truly satisfactory solution. Their purpose is simply to show, from one example, what line of research in my opinion should be adopted by an integrated science of nature and what type of explanation this science should pursue.

(a) The Problem of the Two Energies

Since the internal face of the world comes to light and reflects upon itself in the very depths of our human consciousness, it would seem that all we need to do is look at ourselves in order to understand what the dynamic relationships of the outside and inside of things are at any given point of the universe.

In fact, it is the most difficult of all readings to perform.

We certainly *feel* the two opposing forces combine in our concrete acts. The engine runs. But we do not manage to decipher the play of it, which seems to be contradictory. What is most irritating for our reason about the problem of spiritual energy is the continual and acute sense we have inside us, simultaneously, of the dependence and independence of our activity in relation to the power of matter.

Dependence, first of all. The obvious fact of this dependence is both depressing and magnificent. "To think we must eat." A whole economy is expressed in this blunt formula that, according to our purpose when we look at it, turns into the tyranny or else, on the contrary, the spiritual power of matter. The highest speculation and the most burning love are coupled with, and must be paid for by, an expenditure of physical energy, as we know too well. Sometimes we need bread; sometimes wine, sometimes the infusion of a chemical element or hormone; sometimes the stimulus of color; sometimes the magic of sound passing through our ears as a vibration and emerging in our brain in the form of an inspiration.

There is no doubt that material energy and spiritual energy hold together and are prolonged *by something*. Ultimately, *somehow or other* there must be only a single energy at play in the world. And the first idea that comes to mind is to see the "soul" as a center of transmutation, where through all the avenues of nature the power of bodies converges in order to become interiorized and sublimated in beauty and truth.

Now hardly have we grasped this seductive idea of a *direct* transformation of one of these two energies into the other, when we must give it up. For as soon as we try to link them together, we see their mutual independence as clearly as their connection.

"To think we must eat," once again. But on the other hand, so many different thoughts come out of the same piece of bread! Just like the letters of an alphabet, which can produce incoherence as well as the most beautiful poem ever heard, the same calories seem to be as indifferent as they are necessary to the spiritual values they nourish.

The two energies—physical and psychical—spread respectively through the external and internal layers of the world behave on the whole in the same way. They are constantly associated and somehow flow into each other. But it seems impossible to establish a simple correspondence between their curves. On the one hand, only an infinitesimal fraction of "physical" energy is used in the highest developments of spiritual energy. And on the other, once this minimal fraction is absorbed, it is expressed on the inner table in the most unexpected oscillations.

Such a quantitative disproportion is enough to reject the too simple idea of "change of form" (or of direct transformation) and consequently the hope of ever finding any "mechanical equivalent" for will or thought. That there are dependencies between the energetics of the inside and the outside of things is incontrovertible. But they can probably only be expressed by a complex symbolism described in terms of a different order.[5]

(b) One Line of Solution

To escape a fundamental, impossible and antiscientific dualism—and at the same time to safeguard the natural process of complication of the stuff of the universe—I will therefore propose the following description to serve as a foundation for all the developments that follow.

We shall assume that all energy is essentially psychic. But we shall add that in each individual element this fundamental energy is divided into two distinct components: a *tangential energy* making the element interdependent with all elements of the same order in the universe as itself (that is, of the same complexity and same "centricity"); and a *radial energy* attracting the element in the direction of an ever more complex and centered state, toward what is ahead.*

* Note, by the way, that the less centered an element is (that is, the weaker its radial energy), the more its tangential energy is shown through powerful mechanical effects. Between strongly centered particles (that is, particles with a high radial energy), the tangential seems to become "interiorized" and to disappear, in the eyes of physics.

From this initial state, and supposing that it has a certain free tangential energy at its disposal, it is clear that the particle thus constituted is in a position to augment to a certain value its internal complexity as it associates with neighboring particles, and as a result (since its centricity is automatically increased) to raise its radial energy accordingly—this radial energy will in its turn then be able to react in the form of a new arrangement in the tangential domain. And so on.

The only difficulty with this perspective, where tangential energy represents the abbreviated view of "energy" habitually considered by science, is to explain the play of tangential arrangements so that it is in harmony with the laws of thermodynamics. Now on this subject, we can make the following observations.

(1) First of all, given that the variation of radial energy in function of tangential energy works, by virtue of our hypothesis, *through the intermediary of an arrangement*, it follows that as large a value as you like of the first could be linked to as small a value as you like of the second; since an extremely perfected arrangement can only require an extremely slight amount of work. And this thoroughly takes the observed facts into account (see p. 30, par. 3).

(2) Next, in the system proposed here we are paradoxically led to assume that cosmic energy is constantly increasing, not only in its radial form (since the centricity of the elements augments)[7] but also, much more important, in its tangential form (since with their very centricity the tension between elements augments); and this seems to be in direct contradiction with the principle of the conservation of energy in the world. But let us notice that this increase of the tangential of the second kind, which is the only kind that becomes a problem for physics, becomes perceptible only with very high radial values (in the case of the human, for example, and with social tensions). Below, and for an approximately constant number of initial particles in the universe, the sum of cosmic tangential energies remains practically invariable statistically in the course of transformations. And this is all that science needs.

(3) And finally, since in our scheme the entire fabric of the universe in the process of centration is constantly supported in all its phases by its primary arrangements, it is clear that its completion remains conditioned right to its highest stages by a certain primordial quantum of free tangential energy, which gradually keeps being exhausted, as entropy requires.

There is probably some auxiliary principle of solution to explain the apparent conservation of energy in the universe (see (2) below). It is probably necessary to distinguish *two* sorts of tangential energy: one of *radiation* (the maxima for very small radial values—as in the case of the atom); the other of *arrangement* (perceptible only for higher radial values—in the case of living beings, and the human).[6]

Taken as a whole, this picture satisfies the requirements of reality.

However, three questions are yet to be resolved:

(1) First of all, what is the special energy by virtue of which the universe is propagated as it follows its principal axis in the less probable direction of higher forms of complexity and centricity?

(2) Next, is there a definite limit and term to the elementary value and to the sum total of radial energies developed in the course of transformation?

(3) Finally, if it exists, is this ultimate form and resultant of radial energies subject to and destined to reversibly disaggregate one day, in conformity with the requirements of entropy, until, through the exhaustion and gradual leveling off of the free tangential energy contained in the successive envelopes of the universe from which it has emerged, it falls back indefinitely into the preliving centers and below?

These three questions can only receive a satisfactory answer much further ahead, when the study of the human has led us to take into consideration a higher pole of the world—the "Omega Point."

Chapter III

THE JUVENILE EARTH

Some thousands of millions of years before this, not, it seems, through any regular process of stellar evolution, but as the result of some incredible chance (stars brushing against each other? rupture from within? . . .), a fragment of matter formed of particularly stable atoms broke away from the surface of the sun. Without cutting the ties attaching it to the rest of things and at just the right distance from the parent star to feel its radiation at moderate intensity, this fragment agglomerated, coiled in on itself, and took shape.*

One more star has just been born—this time, a planet—imprisoning the human future within its globe and motion.

Until now, we have let our eyes wander over the boundless layers in which the stuff of the universe is displayed.

From now on let us restrict our attention and concentrate on this minimal, obscure, but fascinating object that has just appeared. *It is the only point in the world* still given to us to follow the evolution of matter in its ultimate phases and as far as ourselves.

Let us look at the juvenile Earth,[1] balancing there in the depths of the past, so fresh and charged with nascent powers.

1   THE OUTSIDE

What arouses the interest of the physicist in this new globe, born it would seem by some stroke of luck in the cosmic mass, is the presence of chemically compound bodies observable nowhere else.† At the extremes of

---

* Once again astronomers seem to be returning to the more Laplacean idea of planets born from the effect of "nodes and loops" in the midst of the cloud of cosmic dust that originally floats around each star.
† Except very fleetingly in the planets closest to ours.

temperature prevailing in the stars, matter can subsist only in its most dissociated states. Only simple bodies exist on these incandescent stars. On the Earth this simplicity of elements is still maintained on the periphery in the more or less ionized gases of the atmosphere and stratosphere and probably also deep inside in the metals and the "barysphere." But between these two extremes, stretching out in successive zones, is a long series of complex substances, hosts and exclusive products of "extinct" stars, that in their beginning manifest the powers of synthesis included in the universe. The zone of silicon, first of all, preparing the solid armature of the planet. And the zone of water and carbonic acid next, surrounding the silicates with an unstable, penetrating, and mobile envelope.

Barysphere, lithosphere, hydrosphere, atmosphere, and stratosphere.

This fundamental composition could have varied in detail and been much more complicated. But the outlines of it must have been established from the beginning. And from this composition the progress of geochemistry is going to develop in two different directions.

(a) The Crystallizing World

From its origins, terrestrial energy tended to be exhaled and released in a first, and by far the most common, direction. The essential oxides, silica, water, and carbonic gas were formed by burning and neutralizing the affinities of their elements (either alone or in association with other simple bodies). According to this protracted plan the rich variety of the "mineral world" was progressively born.

The mineral world . . .

This is a much more supple and changing world than earlier science could have suspected, for we now know that, remotely symmetrical to the metamorphosis of living beings, there is a perpetual transformation of mineral species in the most solid rocks.

Yet it is a world whose combinations are relatively impoverished because the internal architecture of its elements is so narrowly limited (at last count, in all we only know of some hundreds of silicates in nature).

What is characteristic of mineral species "biologically," one might say, is that, like so many incurably fixed organisms, they have taken a path that prematurely closes them in on themselves. By innate structure, their molecules are incapable of growing larger. To grow and expand they therefore must somehow get out of themselves and resort to a purely external subterfuge of association: sticking to one another and linking together atom to atom, without actually combining or uniting. Sometimes they are set in lines, as in jade. Sometimes they spread out in planes, as in mica. Sometimes they form into solid quincunxes, as in garnet.

In this way regular groupings are born whose composition is often highly advanced, yet does not correspond to any properly centered unity. There is simply a juxtaposition of relatively uncomplicated atoms, or groupings of atoms, in a geometrical lattice. An indefinite mosaic of small elements, as in the structure of crystals, which thanks to X-rays we can now read photographically. And it is this simple and stable organization that the condensed matter around us must have adopted from its origin.

Considered in its principal mass, the Earth is veiled in geometry as far back as we can see it. It crystallizes.

(b) The Polymerizing World

In the course, and by very virtue, of the initial advance of terrestrial elements toward the crystalline state, an energy was constantly emitted and freed (just as it is happening around us at this moment within humanity from the effect of the machine). This energy kept increasing from the energy constantly provided by the atomic decomposition of radioactive substances. It continually grew from the energy poured out by solar rays. But where could this now available power flow on the surface of the juvenile Earth? Was it simply to be lost around the globe in obscure emanations?

The spectacle of the world at present offers us another, much more probable hypothesis. Although the free energy of the nascent Earth was from now on too weak to escape in incandescence, it had on the other hand become capable of coiling back into itself in a work of synthesis. Thus then, as today, with the absorption of heat it flowed into the building up of certain hydrogenized, hydrated, and nitrogenous carbonic compounds similar to those that astonish us with their power of indefinitely increasing the complication and instability of their elements. It flowed into the realm of *polymerization,** where, grouping and exchanging, particles link together at the summits of theoretically endless networks, as in crystals, *but this time molecule to molecule so as to form each time, through a closed or at least limited association, an ever larger and more complex molecule.*

We are constructed in and of this world of "organic compounds." And we have grown used to thinking of it only in direct connection with life that is *already constituted* because this association of the world of organic compounds with already constituted life exists right before our eyes. What's more, because its incredible richness of forms, which is far greater than the variety of mineral compounds, involves only a tiny part of

---

* Allow me here (as later, in the case of orthogenesis) to take this term in the plainly generalized sense: that is, covering (in addition to polymerization in the *strict sense* used by chemists) the entire process of "additive complexification" giving birth to large molecules.

terrestrial substance, we have instinctively come to attribute to it only a subordinate position and significance in geochemistry—the same as we do for the ammonia and nitrogen oxides[2] enveloping the lightning flash.

If we wish later on to establish the human's place in nature,[3] it is essential, it seems to me, that we restore the actual antiquity and physiognomy of this phenomenon.

Whatever the quantitative disproportion of the masses affected by mineral chemistry and organic chemistry, these two functions are and can only be the two inseparable faces of the same total telluric operation! Consequently, it is not just the former but also the latter that we must think of as having been under way from the springtime of the Earth. And this is the meaning of the motif upon which this whole book is built: "Nothing could ever burst to light in the world as final one day through the different thresholds (no matter how critical) successively crossed by evolution if it has not existed at first in some obscure primordial way." If the organic had not begun to exist on Earth from the first possible moment, it never would have begun later.

Around our nascent planet, in addition to the first outlines of a metallic barysphere, silicated lithosphere, hydrosphere, and atmosphere, there is thus room to consider the first features of a special envelope—the antithesis, one might say, of the first four: a temperate zone of polymerization, where water, ammonia, and carbonic acid already float, bathed in solar rays. To neglect this tenuous mist would be to deprive the juvenile planet of its most essential adornment. For in it soon, if we trust the perspectives I have just developed above, the "inside of the Earth" is gradually going to concentrate.

2   THE INSIDE

Understand that by the "inside of the Earth" I do not mean here the material depths a few kilometers under our feet where the chemical nature and exact physical conditions of the internal regions of the globe are hidden, which is one of the most vexing mysteries of science. With this expression, as in the preceding chapter, I refer to the "psychic" face of the portion of the cosmic stuff encircled by the narrow radius of the juvenile Earth in the beginning. Within this newly isolated fragment of sidereal substance, just as everywhere else in the universe, an interior world inevitably lines the exterior of things point by point. This we have already shown. But here the conditions have changed. Matter no longer stretches before our eyes in indefinable and diffuse layers. It has become wrapped within itself *in a closed volume. What will be the reaction of its internal sheet to this bending back on itself?*

A first point to consider is that from the very fact of the individual-ization of our planet, a certain mass of elementary consciousness becomes imprisoned in terrestrial matter at the beginning. Scientists have felt they were obliged to attribute the power of seeding the cooling stars to some interstellar germs. Without explaining anything, this hypothesis distorts the magnitude of the phenomenon of life as well as its noble corollary, the human phenomenon. In fact it is quite useless. Why look in space for incomprehensible principles of fertilization of our planet? In its initial chemical composition, the juvenile Earth itself, in its totality, is the incred-ibly complex germ we need. I would dare say that it carried prelife within it congenitally, and in a definite quantity. The whole question is to explain how all the rest has come from this essentially elastic and primitive quantum.

To conceive of the first phases of this evolution, we only need to compare term by term, on the one hand, the general laws we thought we were able to establish for the development of spiritual energy, and on the other, the physicochemical conditions recognized on the new Earth a moment ago. We have said that, by nature, the "radial" value of spiritual energy increases positively, absolutely, and without any ascribable limit, according to the growing chemical complexity of the elements whose internal lining it represents. But as we have just recognized in the preceding section, the chemical complexity of the Earth increases, in conformity with the laws of thermodynamics, in the particular surface zone in which its elements polymerize. Let us bring these two propositions together. They unequivocally confirm and clarify each other. They agree in saying that hardly was prelife enclosed in the nascent Earth when it woke from the torpor it seemed to have been condemned to by its dif-fusion in space. In rhythm with the awakening of the forces of synthesis included in matter, its activities, dormant until then, were set in motion. And at the same time over the entire periphery of the newly formed globe, the tension of internal freedoms began to rise.

Let us look more closely at this mysterious surface.

A first characteristic to be noticed is how it resolves into an incalcu-lable number of extremely small particles. Over kilometers of thickness, in the water, the air, and the deposits of mud, ultramicroscopic grains of protein densely cover the surface of the Earth. Our imagination rebels at the idea of counting the flakes of this snow. And yet if we have under-stood that prelife has already emerged in the atom, is it not these myriads of large molecules that we should have expected?

But there is still something else to consider.

What is even more remarkable in a sense, and just as important to keep in mind for future developments of this multitude, is the unity that links the primordial dust of consciousnesses together in itself by their very genesis. I repeat that what fundamentally allows these elementary freedoms to grow is the increase in synthesis of the molecules they subtend. But I also repeat that this synthesis itself would not operate at all if the globe as a whole did not bend back the layers of its substance at the interior of a closed surface.

In this way, whatever point we consider on Earth, the growth of the inside can only take place thanks to a *double, conjugated enfolding*, the enfolding of the molecule on itself, and the enfolding of the planet on itself.* The initial quantum of consciousness contained in our terrestrial world is not formed simply from an aggregate of parcels fortuitously caught in the same net. It represents an interdependent mass of infinitesimal centers structurally interconnected by their conditions of origin and their development.

Once again the fundamental condition reappears that already characterized original matter, but this time seen over a domain that is more clearly defined and brought to a new order: the condition of unity in plurality. The Earth was probably born by chance. But in conformity with one of the most universal laws of evolution, hardly had that chance appeared when it was immediately used and recast into something naturally directed. By the very mechanism of its birth, the film in which the inside of the Earth is concentrating and deepening emerges for our eyes in the form of an organic whole where no element can any longer be separated from the elements surrounding it. A new indivisible has appeared at the heart of the great indivisible, the universe. Truly, a *prebiosphere*.

It is this envelope that we shall devote ourselves to from now on—solely and entirely.

Still bending over the abysses of the past, see how its shades are changing.

From age to age its colors intensify. Something is going to burst out on the juvenile Earth.

Life! See, it is life!

---

* These are exactly the conditions we shall find prevailing at the genesis of the "noosphere" much further ahead, at the other end of evolution.

38

Part II
Life

Chapter I

THE APPEARANCE OF LIFE

After what we have just acknowledged about the germinal powers of the juvenile Earth, it might seem that there is nothing left in nature to mark a beginning of life, and there might be some objection to the title of this new chapter. From the middle scale of our human organisms, if we look at the mineral and animal worlds massively and in their extreme forms, they seem to be two antagonistic creations; but if we force ourselves, either by spatial analysis or going back in time (which amounts to the same) to the microscopic scale and even lower, to the infinitesimal, they seem to be a single mass gradually melting on itself.

At these depths do not all distinctions fade? At the level of single cell beings there is no longer any clearcut boundary between animal and plant (as we have known for a long time). And it is becoming more and more uncertain that there is any barrier between "living" protoplasm and "dead" proteins at the level of very large molecular masses (we will return to this below). These unclassified substances are still referred to as "dead." But have we not recognized that they would be incomprehensible if they did not already possess some kind of rudimentary psyche deep within?

Therefore it is true, in a sense, that from now on we cannot establish an absolute temporal zero for life as we once thought we could, anymore than for any other experimental reality. On the experimental and phenomenological plane, for a given universe and for each of its elements only one same duration is possible, which has no other shore behind. By what makes it most itself, therefore, each thing prolongs its structures and thrusts its roots into an ever more distant past. By some very attenuated extension of itself, everything has begun from the beginning. There is nothing to be done directly to counter this fundamental condition of our knowledge.

But to have clearly recognized and definitively accepted the necessity and the fact that every new being has a *cosmic embryogenesis* does not at all suppress the reality of its *historical birth*.

In every domain, when the magnitude of something has increased enough it abruptly changes its appearance, state, or nature. The curve doubles back, the surface reduces to a point, the solid crumbles, the liquid boils, the egg segments, intuition bursts upon the accumulated facts. There are all kinds of leaps *in the course* of development—critical points, changes of state, levels of grade; this from now on is the *only*, but still true, way for science to conceive of a "first moment" and to detect it.

Even after (and precisely after) what we have said about prelife, it is in this more developed and new sense that we still need to consider and define a beginning of life.

For untold but certainly immense durations, the Earth, now cool enough for chains of carbonaceous molecules to form and to subsist on its surface—and probably enveloped in a watery layer where only the first buds of future continents were emerging—would have seemed deserted and lifeless to an observer equipped with our most modern instruments of research. Its waters collected at that period would not have relinquished a single moving particle to our finest filters. All they would have shown are inert aggregates, even in the field of our strongest magnifications.

And then later, after a long enough time, at a given moment these same waters must have begun in places to team with minuscule beings. And from this initial proliferation has come the astonishing mass of organized matter, whose complex matting constitutes at present the last (or rather next-to-last) of our planet's envelopes to appear: the biosphere.

We will probably never—at least history alone will never—directly find the material vestiges of this emergence of the microscopic out of the molecular, the organic out of the chemical, the living out of the preliving (unless perhaps tomorrow's science manages to reproduce the phenomenon in the laboratory). But one thing is certain: a metamorphosis such as this can never be explained by a merely continuous process. By analogy with everything the comparative study of natural developments tells us, at this particular moment in terrestrial evolution we must locate a maturation, a transformation, a threshold, a crisis of the first magnitude: the beginning of a new order.

Let us try to find out what the nature of this passage must have been, on the one hand, and on the other, the spatial and temporal modalities of it so as to meet both the conditions presumed to have existed on the juvenile Earth and the requirements now contained in the modern Earth.

1 THE STEP OF LIFE

Materially speaking and viewed from the outside, the most we can say specifically at this moment about life as such is that it *begins with the cell*.

For centuries, the more science has concentrated its efforts on this chemically and structurally ultracomplex unit, the more evident it has become that hidden there is the secret whose knowledge would establish the felt yet still unrealized link between the world of physics and the world of biology. The cell is the *natural grain of life*, just as the atom is the natural grain of unorganized matter. If we specifically want to measure what the step of life consists in, then clearly it is the cell that we must try to understand.

But to understand it, how should we look at it?

Volumes already have been written about the cell. Whole libraries can no longer contain all the meticulously accumulated observations on its texture, the relative functions of its "cytoplasm" and its nucleus, the mechanisms of its division, and how it relates to heredity. Yet, taken in itself, it still remains as enigmatic and closed to our sight as ever. It seems as though having reached a certain depth of explanation, we are now circling around some kind of impenetrable fortress, without making any progress.

Could this mean that histological and physiological methods of analysis have presently given all that we can expect of them, and that in order to make any advance we must adopt a new angle of attack?

Actually and for obvious reasons, up to now cytology has been constructed almost entirely from the biological perspective, with the cell considered as a microorganism or protoliving being that is to be interpreted in relation to its highest forms and associations.

Yet in doing this, we have quite simply left half of the problem in the shadows. Like a planet in its first quarter, the object of our inquiry is illuminated by the face it turns toward the summits of life. But on the layers of what we have called prelife, it continues to float in the dark. Scientifically speaking, this is probably what has so unnecessarily prolonged its mystery for us.

Just like anything else in the world, however marvelous it seems to be in isolation from the other constructions of matter, the cell can only be *understood* (that is, incorporated into a coherent system of the universe) when it is put back again between a future and a past along an evolutionary line. We are much too absorbed in its differentiations and its development. If we want to put our finger on the real essence of its novelty, now is the time for us to make our research converge on its origins, that is, on the roots it thrusts into the unorganized.

Contrary to what experience has taught us in every other domain, we are too accustomed or resigned to thinking of the cell as an object without antecedents. Let us try to see what it becomes if we look at it as we should, treating it *both* as something long prepared for and profoundly original, that is, as something *born*.

(a) Microorganisms and Megamolecules

And first of all, the preparation of the cell.

In every effort made to observe initial life in relation to what precedes rather than what follows it, an immediate result has been to bring to light a peculiarity that strangely enough had never struck our eyes before: I mean, that in and through the cell it is the molecular world "in person" (so to speak) that rises to the surface, passes, and is lost in the midst of the higher constructions of life.

Let me explain.

When we look at a bacterium, we always have the higher plants and animals in mind. And that is what dazzles us. But let us take another approach. Let us shut our eyes to the more advanced living forms of nature at present. As it seems appropriate, let us also put aside most of the protozoans, whose outlines are almost as differentiated as those of the metazoans. And in the metazoans let us forget the nerve, muscle, and reproductive cells, which are often huge and in any case overspecialized. In this way let us thus limit our sight to the more or less independent and exteriorly amorphous or polymorphous elements that proliferate in natural fermentations, that circulate in our veins, and that accumulate in our organs in the form of connective tissue. In other words, let us restrict our field of vision to the cell taken in its simplest and thus most primitive appearances as we can still observe it in nature at present. And then, having done this, let us look at that corpuscular mass in relation to the matter it covers. Now I ask you, who can fail even for a moment to recognize the obvious kinship in its composition and its behavior linking the protoliving world to the physicochemical world? Such simplicity of cellular form, such symmetry of structure, such minuscule dimensions, such exterior identity of characteristics and ways of behavior—are these not unmistakably the traits and habits of the granular? That is, at this first level of life, are we not still, although not at the heart, at least fully inside the borders of "matter"?

It is no exaggeration to say that just as the human group, in the eyes of the paleontologist, blends anatomically into the mass of the mammals that precede it, so the cell, *taken as it descends*, is qualitatively and quantitatively drowned in the world of chemical structures. Prolonged immediately behind itself, it visibly converges with the molecule.

Now the evidence for this is beyond mere intellectual intuition.

Only a few years ago what I have just said here about the gradual change from the grain of matter to the grain of life would have seemed just as suggestive, but also as gratuitous as the first treatises on transformism[1] by Darwin or Lamarck. But things are changing now. Since the times of Darwin and Lamarck numerous findings have come to light to establish the existence of the transitional forms postulated by the theory of evolution. So also, recent advances in biochemistry are beginning to establish the reality of molecular aggregates that certainly seem to reduce and mark out the supposedly gaping abyss existing between protoplasm and mineral matter. If we accept that certain measurements (indirect, it is true) are correct, the molecular weight of certain natural protein substances such as the viruses—so mysteriously associated with microbial disease in plants and animals—must perhaps be estimated *in the millions*. Even though they are much smaller than all bacteria, so small, in fact, that no filter has yet been able to retain them, nevertheless, compared to the molecules usually treated in organic chemistry, the particles that form these substances are colossal. And it is profoundly suggestive to note that, although they cannot be mistaken for a cell, still they do possess certain properties already heralding those of organized beings in the strict sense (particularly their power of multiplying in contact with living tissue).*

It is due to the discovery of these gigantic corpuscles that the predicted existence of *intermediate states* between living microscopic and "inanimate" ultramicroscopic beings enters into the domain of direct experimentation.

From positive indications as well as intellectual necessity, it is already possible to affirm, therefore, that in conformity with our theoretical presuppositions about the reality of a prelife, there actually is some natural function linking the microorganic to the megamolecular in their successive appearance and present existence.

And now this first observation allows us to take one more step toward a better understanding of life's preparations and therefore of its origins.

(b) A Forgotten Era

From the mathematical perspective, I am not in any position to evaluate either the basic validity or the limitations of the physics of relativity. But speaking as a naturalist I am obliged to recognize that the only way we have found so far to explain the distribution of the material and living substances around us is by taking into account a dimensional milieu where space and time are organically combined. In fact, the more our knowledge of the natural history of the world advances, the more we discover that the distribution of objects and forms at any given moment can only be

---

* Since in the powerful magnifications of the electron microscope, viruses have been seen to be like fine rods that are asymmetrically active at both their extremities, the prevailing opinion seems to hold that they must be classified among bacteria rather than "molecules." But is not the study of enzymes and other complex chemical substances beginning to prove precisely that molecules have a *form* and even a great diversity of forms?[2]

explained in terms of a process whose temporal length varies in direct ratio to the spatial (or morphological) dispersion of the beings considered. Every distance in space and every morphological divergence presupposes and expresses a duration.

Let us take the particularly simple case of the vertebrates living today. Since the time of Linnaeus the classification of animals as a whole has advanced far enough to show that they have a definite structure as a group, which is expressed in orders, families, genera, etc. Yet the naturalists of that time did not offer any scientific rationale for this arrangement. We now know today that Linnaean systematics represents merely a cross-section made at the present time of a divergent bundle of lineages (*phyla*) that have appeared successively in the course of the ages,* so that in each instance the zoological divergence between the various living types we see before us reveals and measures a difference of age. Thus in the constellation of species, every existence and every position entails a certain past and a certain genesis. In particular, every time a zoologist meets a type that is more primitive than any known before (the *Amphioxus*,[3] let us say), the result is more than just to extend the range of animal forms a little further. Such a discovery implies by the very fact itself a stage, a verticil,[4] another ring added on the trunk of evolution. For example, the only way we can make a place for the *Amphioxus* in nature is by imagining an entire phase of life in the past below the fishes, a "protovertebrate" phase.

In biological space–time the introduction of a supplementary morphological term or stage immediately requires its translation into a correlative lengthening of the axis of durations.

Keep this principle in mind. And let us return to the giant molecules just discovered by science.

It is possible (although not very probable) that at present these enormous particles form only an exceptional and relatively restricted group in nature. But however rare we might suppose them to be, or even however modified we might imagine them to be by secondary association with the living tissue whose parasites they are, there is no reason to make them into monstrous or aberrant beings. On the contrary, whether in the survival or residual state, everything indicates that we should see them as representing a particular stage in the constructions of terrestrial matter.

It necessarily follows that a zone of the megamolecular squeezes its way in between the molecular and cellular zones we thought bordered each other. But by this very fact also, as a result of the relationships we recog-

---

* For the discussion of this subject, see ahead, ch. II, section 3 "The Tree of Life."

nized above between space and duration, a *supplementary* period is discovered and inserts itself behind us in the history of the Earth. One more circle on the trunk—therefore, one more interval to count in the life of the universe. Not only does the discovery of viruses or other such elements enrich our series of states or forms of matter by a significant period of time, but it obliges us to intercalate an era forgotten until then (an era of the "sub-living") in the series of ages that measure our planet's past.[5]

And so by starting with and descending from initial life, we find again, in a well-defined terminal form, that phase and aspect of the juvenile Earth we had been led to conjecture above, when we climbed the slopes of the elementary multiple.

Clearly we cannot yet say anything precise about the length of time required to establish this megamolecular world on the Earth. But even if we cannot think what number to give it, there are several considerations to guide us toward some evaluation of its order of magnitude. For three reasons among others, the phenomenon that concerns us could only have proceeded extremely slowly.

In the first place, its appearance and development were clearly dependent on the general transformation of chemical and thermal conditions on the surface of the planet. Unlike life, which seems to propagate at its own speed in a material medium that has become practically stable in relation to itself, megamolecules could only have been formed to the *sidereal* rhythm of the Earth (that is, at an incredibly slow rate).

In the second place, once the transformation had begun and before it could form the necessary basis for an emergence of life, it had to extend over a mass of matter significant and widespread enough to constitute a zone or envelope of telluric dimensions. And this also must have required much time.

In the third place, megamolecules most likely bear in themselves the traits of a long history. Is it really conceivable that they could have been constructed suddenly and remain that way once and for all, like the simpler corpuscles? Their degree of complication and their instability, somewhat like those of life, suggest rather that a long additive process was carried out through successive increases over a series of generations.

For these three reasons, we can roughly estimate that the time necessary for the formation of proteins on the terrestrial surface represents a duration perhaps greater than all the geological ages since the Cambrian.[6]

And so the abyss of the past deepens behind us by a level, that abyss which an invincible weakness of intellect would have us compress into an ever-thinner slice of duration, whereas the analysis of science is forcing us to extend it more and more.

And in this way the necessary basis is provided for the representations that follow.

Without a long period of maturation, no profound change can come about in nature. On the other hand, given such a period, it is inevitable that something *entirely new* takes place. To add a terrestrial era of the megamolecular to our table of durations is not just to add a supplementary term. Much more importantly, it requires the advent of a critical point to conclude it and bring it to a close. This is exactly what we needed in order to justify the idea that there is an evolutionary break of the first order at the level marked by the appearance of the first cells.

But having said all this, how can we imagine what the nature of this break will be?

(c) The Cellular Revolution
(1) External Revolution

From the external perspective, which is the position normally taken by biology, the fundamental originality of the cell seems to be in its having found a new method of incorporating a larger mass of matter into a unified whole. It was a discovery that had probably been long prepared for by the experimentation that had given birth to the megamolecules, but sudden enough and revolutionary enough to have immediately met with prodigious success in nature.

We still are far from being able to define the actual principle of cellular organization (probably luminously simple). Yet we have learned enough about it to be able to measure the extraordinary complexity of its structure and the no less extraordinary fixity of its fundamental type.

Its *complexity*, first of all. We learn from chemistry that cellular construction is based on albuminoids, which are nitrogenous organic substances ("amino acids") with enormous molecular weight (up to 10 thousand and more). In association with fatty bodies, water, phosphorous, and all kinds of mineral salts (potassium, soda, magnesium, and various metal compounds . . .), these albuminoids constitute a "protoplasm," an organized sponge of innumerable particles where the forces of viscosity, osmosis, and catalysis play an appreciable part, forces that are characteristic of matter having reached its higher degrees of molecular grouping. But this is still not all. In the midst of this complex, in most cases a nucleus enclosing "chromosomes" stands out against a background of "cytoplasm," which is perhaps itself composed of fibers or rods ("mitochondria"). The higher the microscopic magnification and the more distinctly the different colors can be seen, the more new structural elements also appear in the foreground or background of this complex. It is a triumph of multiplicity organically gathered in a minimum of space.

Fixity, next. However indefinite are the possibilities of modulating its fundamental theme—however inexhaustible is the variety of forms in nature that it in fact clothes, in every case the cell remains fundamentally the same. We have already mentioned this. Faced with the cell, our mind hesitates to look for its analogies either in the "animate" or the "inanimate" world. Do not cells resemble each other more like molecules than animals? We have every reason to regard them as the first living forms. But is it not just as true to think of them as representing *another state* of matter: something in its own order as original as the electronic, atomic, crystalline, or polymeric states? A new type of material for a new stage of the universe?

In short in the cell, simultaneously so one, uniform, and complicated, we see the stuff of the universe reappearing again with all its characteristics—but this time raised to a subsequent level of *complexity* and, as a result, at the same time (if the hypothesis guiding us throughout these pages is valid) to a higher degree of *interiority*, that is, of consciousness.

(2) Internal Revolution

Usually there is general agreement that psychic life "begins" in the world with the early stages of organized life. By placing a decisive step in the progress of consciousness on Earth at this particular stage of evolution I thus join the commonly held view and way of stating things.

But because I have assumed an origin that is much more ancient and primordial in the true sense for the first features of immanence in matter, the burden is on me to explain what specific modification of internal ("radial") energy corresponds to the external ("tangential") establishment of the cellular unit. If we have already placed the obscure and distant roots of free elementary activity within the long chain of atoms, then the molecules, and then the megamolecules, it is not by an absolute beginning but by a *metamorphosis* that the cellular revolution must be psychically expressed. But how are we to represent the leap (or even find a place for the leap?) of the preconsciousness included in prelife to the consciousness of the first truly living being, however elementary? Are there thus several ways for a being to have an inside?

I must admit that it is difficult to be clear about this point. Further ahead, in the case of thought, a psychic definition of the "human critical point" will seem to be possible right away because the step of reflection possesses something definitive in itself and also because to measure it, we need only to look into the depths of ourselves. In the case of the cell compared to the beings that precede it, on the contrary, introspection can only guide us by repeated and distant analogies. What do we know about the "mind" of animals, even those closest to us? At such distances below and behind us we must resign ourselves to vague speculations.

In these conditions of obscurity and marginal approximation, three observations remain at least possible—enough to establish in a useful and coherent way, the position of the *cellular awakening* in the series of psychic transformations preparing for the appearance of the human phenomenon on Earth. *Even*, and *above all* , I will add, in the perspectives assumed here, namely that a rudimentary kind of consciousness precedes the eclosion[7] of life: (1) such an awakening or leap *was able* to occur—much better, it (2) *must* have occurred; and (3) this is the partial explanation for one of the most extraordinary renewals the surface of the Earth has ever undergone historically.

First of all, it is perfectly conceivable that a fundamental leap is possible between two states or forms even of lower consciousness. Returning to the doubt we formulated above in order to take it up again in these same terms, I will say that there are in fact many different ways for a being to have an inside. A *closed* surface that is irregular at first can become *centered*. A circle can augment its order of symmetry by becoming a sphere. Whether by arrangements of parts or acquisition of another dimension, there is nothing to prevent the degree of interiority possessed by a cosmic element from varying to the point of rising abruptly to a new level.

That such a psychic mutation precisely must have accompanied the discovery of the cellular combination follows immediately from the law we recognized above that regulates the mutual relationships of the inside and the outside of things. An increase in the state of synthesis of matter: therefore correlatively, as we said, an augmentation of consciousness for the medium synthesized. A *critical* transformation in the innermost arrangement of elements, we must now add: therefore, by the very fact itself, a change *in the nature* of the state of consciousness of the parcels of the universe.[8]

And now, in light of these principles, let us take a new look at the astonishing spectacle presented by the definitive eclosion of life on the surface of the juvenile Earth. Such a spurt forward in spontaneity. Such a luxuriant unleashing of fantastic creations. Such unbridled expansion. Such a leap into the improbable. Is this not exactly the event the theory could have led us to expect? The explosion of internal energy consecutive and proportionate to a fundamental superorganization of matter?

The external realization of an essentially new type of corpuscular grouping that permits the more supple and better-centered organization of an unlimited number of substances taken at all degrees of particulate size; and simultaneously the internal appearance of a new type of conscious activity and determination: it is by this double and radical metamorphosis that we can reasonably define what is specifically original in the critical passage from molecule to cell—the step of life.

Before taking up the consequences this has for the rest of evolution, we still need to study more closely the conditions of the historical realization of this step, first of all in space and then in time.

This will be the subject of the following two sections.

2   THE INITIAL APPEARANCES OF LIFE

Since the appearance of the cell is an event that took place at the frontiers of the infinitesimal and since it occurred in elements of utmost delicacy, now dissolved in sediments transformed long ago, there is, as I said, no chance of our ever finding any traces of it. And so right from the start we come up against that fundamental condition of experience by virtue of which the beginnings of all things tend to become materially imperceptible for us: the law universally encountered in history that we will call, further along, the "automatic suppression of evolutionary peduncles."[9]

Fortunately, for our minds there are several different ways of attaining reality. When something escapes the intuition of our senses, we still have the resource of circling around it and defining it approximately through a series of indirect steps. If we wish to arrive at a possible representation of newborn life by taking this roundabout route—it is the only route open—then we can proceed in the following way, through the following stages.

The Milieu

To begin with, by going back perhaps as much as a billion[10] years in time, we must erase most of the material superstructures that presently give the surface of the Earth its particular physiognomy. Geologists are far from being in agreement about what our planet could have looked like at these distant periods. Personally I find no difficulty in picturing it as covered by a shoreless ocean (perhaps our Pacific Ocean is a vestige of it) where continental protrusions were just beginning to emerge from volcanic eruptions at several isolated points. Certainly these waters were warmer than those of our time—and also more charged with all the free chemistry that was to be absorbed and fixed by the ages. It is in this type of heavy and active solution—in any case, inevitably in a liquid medium[11]—that the first cells must have formed. Let us try to distinguish them.

At this distance we can only see their form indistinctly. The only analogy we can find in nature at present with which to represent for our imaginations the least altered traits of this primordial generation is that of grains of protoplasm, with or without an individual nucleus. But if the contours and individual construction remain indecipherable, certain other kinds of precise characteristics assert themselves, which have no less value although they are quantitative: I mean their incredibly small size, and as a natural consequence, the staggering numbers of them.

Smallness and Number

Having reached this point, it is necessary that we practice one of those "efforts to see" I mentioned in my preface. Year after year we can look at the sky dense with stars without even once making a *real* effort to calculate the distance and consequently the enormous size of the sidereal masses. In the same way, however familiar our eyes are with the microscopic field, we risk never actually "realizing" the disconcerting decrease in dimension that separates the world of humanity from the world of a drop of water. We speak accurately about beings measurable in hundredths of a millimeter. But have we ever tried to put them on their own scale in the context in which we live? Yet it is indispensable for us to make this effort of perspective if we want to penetrate the secrets, or simply the "space" of nascent life—which could only have been a *granular life*.

There can be no doubt that the first cells were minuscule. This is required by the way they originated from megamolecules. And inspection of the simplest beings we still encounter in the living world establishes this directly. When we lose bacteria from sight, they are no more than 0.2 thousandths of a millimeter long!

Now a natural relationship between size and number seems positively to exist in the universe. Whether it results from a relatively larger space being open in front of them or whether it is to compensate for a diminution in their effective radius of individual action, the smaller beings are, the more they surge in crowds. Measurable in the microns, the first cells must have numbered in the myriads. The closer we pursue life to its point of issue, the more it is seen to be *simultaneously microscopic and innumerable*.

There is nothing surprising in itself about this double characteristic. Surely it is only natural that life just emerging from matter arises *still streaming with the molecular state*? But already it is not enough only to look behind us.[12] For we now need to understand the function and future of the organized world. At the source of its progression we encounter number—an immense number. How are we to represent the historical modalities and evolutionary structure of this innate multiplicity?

The Origin of Number

Life teemed from the moment it was born (at the distance from which we see it).

To explain why this plurality exists right from the start of the evolution of animate life, and also to clarify its nature, there are two lines of thought open to us.

Either we can suppose that although they appeared at one or a small number of points, the first cells nevertheless multiplied almost instantaneously, the way crystallization propagates in a supersaturated solution. For had not the juvenile Earth been in a state of biological supertension?

Or on the other hand, we can also think that arising from and due to these very conditions of initial instability, the passage of megamolecules to the cell was made at a great number of points almost simultaneously. Is this not how great discoveries are made even in humanity itself?

As "monophyletic" or as "polyphyletic"? What is the most suitable way to represent the bundle of living beings at its base? As very narrow and simple in its origin, but opening out with extreme rapidity? Or, on the contrary, as relatively broad and complex from the beginning, but then dilating at moderate speed?

Throughout the entire history of terrestrial organisms, we encounter fundamentally the same problem at the origin of each zoological group: is there a single stem? or a bundle of parallel lines? And just because beginnings always escape our direct vision, time after time we experience the same difficulty in opting for one or the other of two almost equally plausible hypotheses.

To be of two minds this way is upsetting and irritating.

But do we really need to choose—here at least? However slender the initial peduncle of terrestrial life is supposed to have been, it must have contained an appreciable number of fibers thrusting into the enormous dimensions of the molecular world. And conversely, however wide we picture the section to have been, like all nascent physical reality it must have shown an exceptional aptitude for unfolding into new forms. Basically, the only difference between the two perspectives is the relative importance given to one or the other of two factors (their initial complexity and their "expansibility"), which are the same in both cases. Both of them, moreover, imply a *close* evolutionary *kinship* between the first living beings within the juvenile Earth. Therefore let us ignore their secondary oppositions in order to focus our attention on the essential fact they clarify in common. This fact, in my opinion, can be expressed in the following words.

"From whatever angle we look at it, we discover that the *nascent* cellular world is already infinitely complex. Whether this is because of the multiplicity of its points of origin, or as a result of a rapid diversification from several focal points of emergence, or, we must also add, because of regional differences (climatic or chemical) in the aqueous envelope of the Earth, we come to understand that, taken at the protocellular stage life is an enormous bundle of polymorphous fibers. Already, even at these depths, the vital phenomenon can fundamentally only be treated as an organic problem of masses in motion."

It is an organic problem of masses or multitudes, I repeat; and not a simple statistical problem of large numbers. What does that difference mean?

Interconnections and Shape

Here again we see the threshold that stands between the worlds of physics and biology, but this time on the collective scale. As long as it was only a question of mixing molecules and atoms together, we were content to use the numerical laws of probability to account for the ways in which matter behaves. But the moment the monad[13] tends to become individualized at the heart of the pleiad as it acquires the dimensions and higher spontaneity of the cell, a more complicated arrangement takes shape in the stuff of the universe. For two reasons at least, it would be inadequate and erroneous to imagine that life is a kind of fortuitous and amorphous teeming, even at its granular stage.

In the first place, from the very first moment, the initial mass of cells must have been subject from inside to a form of interdependence that was no longer only a simple mechanical adjustment, but the beginning of a "symbiosis," or life in common. However thin it might have been, the first veil of organic matter spread over the Earth could neither have established nor maintained itself without some network of influence and exchange that made it biologically *connected* as a whole. Therefore from the beginning, in spite of its internal multiplicity, the cellular nebula necessarily represented a kind of diffuse superorganism. Not just a *foam of lives*, but to a certain extent a *living film*. This, after all, is simply the reappearance in a higher form and order of the much more ancient conditions we saw already presiding over the birth and equilibrium of the first polymerized substances of the surface of the juvenile Earth. It is also a simple prelude to the much more advanced evolutionary interdependence, whose existence, so evident in higher living beings, will gradually oblige us to admit the specifically organic nature of the connections that unite them in a whole within the *biosphere*.

In the second place (and this is more surprising), the innumerable elements that compose the beginnings of the Earth's living film do not seem to have been assembled either exhaustively or randomly. But their admission into this primordial envelope gives rather the impression of having been guided by a mysterious prior selection or dichotomy. Biologists have observed that, depending on which chemical group they belong to, molecules incorporated into living matter are all asymmetrical in the same way—that is, if a beam of polarized light passes through them, they all make the plane of this beam turn *in the same direction*: they are all right-rotating or all left-rotating, depending on the case. And even more remarkable: all living beings, from the lowest bacteria to the human, contain (among so many possible chemical forms!) the same complicated types of vitamins and enzymes—just as the higher mammals are all "trituburculates," or the walking vertebrates are all "tetrapods." Now does not such similarity of living substance, in arrangements that *do not seem to be necessary*, suggest an original choice or triage? In this chemical uniformity of protoplasm at accidental points some have wanted to find proof that all organisms existing at present are descended from a single ancestral group (the case of the crystal falling into a supersaturated medium). Without going this far, we could say that it only establishes the fact of certain initial cleavage—between the right-rotating and left-rotating molecules, for example (depending on the case)—in the enormous mass of carbonaceous matter that has reached the threshold of life (the case of the discovery made at *n* points simultaneously).[14] In short, it is not important. What is interesting is that in both of these hypotheses, the living terrestrial world takes on the same curious appearance of a totality re-formed from a *partial* grouping; whatever the complexity of the original main shoot could have been, it exhausts only a *part of what might have been*! Taken as a whole, the biosphere thus represents only a simple *branch* in the midst of, and above other less progressive or fortunate proliferations of prelife. What else can this mean but that considered globally, the appearance of the first cells already poses the same problems as the origin of each of the later stems that we will call "phyla." The universe had *already begun to ramify*, and it probably goes on ramifying indefinitely, *even below the tree of life*!

In short, seen from afar, elementary life appears to be a variegated multitude of microscopic elements, a multitude large enough to cover the Earth and yet closely related and selected enough to form a structurally and genetically interdependent whole.

These observations, as I said, apply exclusively to general traits and to characteristics of the whole. We must resign ourselves to this and be patient; it was to be expected. Following all the dimensions of the universe, in our field of vision one law of perspective inexorably shades out the depths of the past and distant backgrounds of space. What is very far away and very small can only be blurred.[15]

For our sight to penetrate further into the secrets of the phenomena accompanying its appearance, life would have to* continue to spring up somewhere on Earth right in front of our eyes.

---

* As we wait (who knows?) for chemists to succeed in triggering the reproduction of the phenomenon in the laboratory.

Now it is precisely this chance that has not been given to us, and this is the final point to consider before bringing the present chapter to a close.

3   THE SEASON OF LIFE

A priori, we are perfectly able to imagine that the mysterious transformation from megamolecules to cells that began millions of years ago is still being carried on around us imperceptibly at the frontiers of the microscopic and the infinitesimal. So many of the forces thought to be slumbering in nature forever, on more minute analysis have proved to be still active. The terrestrial crust is still endlessly lifting or sinking under our feet. Mountain chains are still rising on our horizon. Granites continue to feed and nourish the shelves of continents. The organic world itself is endlessly burgeoning with new buds on the surface of its enormous branching structure. If extreme slowness succeeds in masking motion, why should not extreme smallness create a similar effect? In itself there is nothing to prevent living substance from continuing to be born in infinitesimal masses right in front of our eyes.

But in fact nothing seems to indicate and, on the contrary, everything seems to dissuade us from thinking this is so.

We all know about the famous controversy nearly a hundred years ago that created a division between the proponents and the opponents of "spontaneous generation." It would seem at the time that they tried to draw more conclusions from the results of the battle than were justified: as though Pouchet's defeat scientifically ended any hope of giving an evolutionary explanation for the first origins of life.[16] But today there is universal agreement on one point, and that is, if life never appears in the laboratory in a medium from which all germs have been previously removed, we cannot conclude, contrary to all kinds of general evidence, that the phenomenon has not occurred in other conditions at other ages. The experiments of Pasteur could not, nor can they prove anything against a birth of cells on our planet in the past. On the other hand, their success, which has been forever confirmed by the universal use of the methods of sterilization, clearly seems to demonstrate one thing: I mean that within the field and limits of our investigations, *protoplasm is no longer being formed directly* today from the unorganized substances of the Earth.*

* The objection could always be raised against Pasteur's experiments that, in addition to the living germs it seeks to eliminate, the brutality of sterilization threatens to destroy "preliving" germs, the only ones from which life could have come. Fundamentally, the best proof that life has appeared only once on Earth is provided by the profound structural unity of the tree of life (see below, ch. II).

To begin with, this forces us to revise certain overly absolute ideas we might hold about the value and use, in the sciences, of explanations *"from present causes"*.[17]

As I mentioned a moment ago, many terrestrial transformations that we would have sworn had stopped, and for a long time, are still going on in the world around us. Influenced by this unexpected observation, which caters to our natural preference for palpable and manageable forms of experience, our mind gradually tends to think that there has never been anything absolutely new under the sun in the past, nor will there be in the future. One more step, and we would restrict the full reality of consciousness only to events in the present. Fundamentally is not everything except the present mere "conjecture"?

We need to fight at all costs against this instinctive limitation of the rights and domain of science.

No, it is exactly the conditions imposed by the "present" that the world would not fulfill—it would not be the great world of mechanics and biology—if we were lost in it like insects whose ephemeral existence knows nothing beyond the limits of a season. By very virtue of the dimensions of the universe revealed to us by the scale of the present, all kinds of things must have happened in the universe that never had a human witness. Long before the awakening of thought on Earth, manifestations of cosmic energy must have occurred that are unparalleled at this moment. Alongside the group of immediately recordable phenomena, there is thus a particular class of facts to consider in the world—the most important kind, because they are the most significant and rarest; facts which arise neither from observation nor direct experimentation, but which only that very authentic branch of "physics" can reveal: *the discovery of the past*. And judging from our repeated failure to find its equivalents around us or to reproduce it, the initial appearance of living bodies seems to be precisely one of the most sensational of these events.

Assuming this to be true, let us advance a little further. There are two possible ways in which something in time does not coincide with our vision. Either we miss it because it recurs only at such long intervals that our entire existence is contained between two of its appearances. Or else it even more radically escapes us, because once it has taken place it is never again repeated. After the discoveries of Pasteur, which of these two categories of the experimental (or rather the praeter-experimental) is the proper one in which to put the initial formation of cells from matter, the birth of life? Is it a cyclical phenomenon over a very long period (the kind so familiar to astronomy), or a strictly unique phenomenon (such as Socrates or Augustus in human history)?

There is no lack of facts to support the idea that organized matter might germinate on the Earth *periodically*. Further along, when I sketch in the tree of life, I will need to mention the coexistence in our living world of certain large groupings (protozoans, plants, polyps, insects, vertebrates . . .), whose badly dissolved contacts can be explained satisfactorily enough by heterogeneous origins. Something like those successive intrusions of a single magma rising at different ages, whose interlaced veins form the eruptive complex of the same mountain. The hypothesis of independent vital pulsations would conveniently account for the morphological diversity of the principal subkingdoms recognized by systematics. And it would not, in fact, run into any difficulty with regard to chronology. In any case, the length of time separating the historical origins of two successive subkingdoms is generally greater than the age of humanity. Consequently, it is not surprising that we live under the illusion that nothing is happening anymore. Matter seems dead. But in reality, is not the next pulsation slowly being prepared everywhere around us?

I must point out and even defend, to a certain extent, this concept of the spasmodic birth of life. Yet this does not mean that I have settled on it. Actually, a decisive objection does arise against the thesis of several successive and different vital thrusts on the surface of the Earth; I mean the fundamental similarity of organized beings.

In the present chapter we have already mentioned the very curious fact that all molecules of living substances are asymmetrical *in the same way* and that they contain exactly the same vitamins. Now the more complicated organisms become, the more evident their inherent kinship. This is suggested by the absolute and universal uniformity of cellular type. It is above all apparent in animals in the identical solutions brought to various problems of perception, nutrition, and reproduction: everywhere there are vascular and nervous systems; everywhere some form of blood; everywhere gonads; and everywhere eyes. It is carried on in the similarity of methods used by individuals to associate together in higher organisms or to socialize. And finally, it stands out brilliantly in the general laws of development ("ontogenesis" and "phylogenesis") that give to the living world, taken as a whole, the coherence of a single outpouring.

Even though certain of the multiple analogies might be explained by the adjustment of a single "preliving magma" to identical terrestrial conditions, it does not seem as though we can consider that their combined bundle expresses a simple parallelism or "convergence." Even if there were only one general solution on Earth to the physical and physiological problem of life, this general solution inevitably leaves a host of particular accidental determinants undecided, which it would be impossible to conceive of as *twice the same*. Now it is just in these accessory modalities that all living beings resemble each other, even among very distant groups. For this reason the oppositions observable at present between zoological subkingdoms lose much of their significance (are they not merely the result of an effect of perspective combined with a progressive isolation of living phyla?), and for the naturalist the conviction is growing that the eclosion of life on Earth belongs to the category of events that are absolutely *unique*, events which once they are accomplished are never repeated again. This is a more likely hypothesis than it might seem at first—however incorrect an idea we may have of what lies hidden beneath the history of our planet.

The current mode in geology and geophysics is to attach a preponderant importance to periodic phenomena. The rising and falling of seas, the lifting and sinking of continental shelves. The intersecting and leveling of mountains. The advance and retreat of glaciers. The accumulation of radioactive heat in the depths, then venting at the surface. These majestic "ebbs" and "flows" are all we hear of in the treatises describing the episodes of the Earth.

This predilection for the rhythmic in events goes along with the preference for present causes. And both alike are explained by precise rational needs. Whatever repeats itself remains at least virtually observable. We can make it the subject of a law. We find reference points in it for the measurement of time. I am the first to recognize the scientific quality of these advantages. But I cannot help but think that an exclusive analysis of the oscillations recorded by the terrestrial crust or the movements of life would precisely omit the principal subject of geology from its research.

For the Earth, after all, is not merely a kind of great breathing body. It rises and sinks. But more important than that, at some moment it must have begun; it passes through a linked succession of moving equilibriums; and in all likelihood it tends toward some final state. It has a birth, a development, and, no doubt, a death ahead of it. Deeper, therefore, than any pulsation expressible in geological eras, there must be some kind of process of the whole in course around us, which is not periodic, and which defines the *total* evolution of the planet: something chemically more complicated and intrinsic to matter than the "cooling down" once spoken of; but still something that is irreversible and continuous. A curve that never descends, whose points of transformation, as a result, are never repeated. A single rising tide beneath the rhythm of the ages. Now I imagine that it is on this basic curve, and in relation to this fundamental rising, that the phenomenon of life must be situated.

If one day life was able to isolate itself in the primitive ocean, this is probably because the Earth at that time, as a result of the distribution and global complexity of its elements (which is exactly what made it juvenile), was then in a general privileged state that allowed and favored the building up of protoplasms.

And if, as a result, life is no longer being formed directly at present from elements contained in the lithosphere or hydrosphere, this seems to be because the very fact of the appearance of a biosphere so disrupted, impoverished, and relaxed the primordial chemistry of our fragment of the universe that the phenomenon could never again be reproduced (unless, perhaps, artificially).

From this perspective, which seems to me to be the right one, the "cellular revolution" is therefore seen to express *a critical and singular point of germination* on the curve of telluric evolution—an unparalleled moment. Protoplasm was formed only once on the Earth, just as nuclei and electrons were formed only once in the cosmos.

This hypothesis has the advantage of providing a reason for the profound organic similarity that marks all living beings from bacteria to man, at the same time as it explains why we never anywhere come upon the formation of the least living grain except through generation. And that was the problem.

But this hypothesis still has two other notable consequences for science.

First of all, by extricating the phenomenon of life from the host of other periodic and secondary terrestrial events to make it one of the principal reference points (or parameters) of the sidereal evolution of the globe, it rectifies our sense of proportion and of values, and thus renews our perspective of the world.

Next, by the very fact that it shows us that the origin of organized bodies is linked to a chemical transformation without precedent and never repeated in the course of terrestrial history, it makes us tend to see the energy contained in the living layer of our planet as though it develops from and at the interior of a kind of closed "quantum," which is defined by the amplitude of that primordial emission.

Life was born and propagates itself on the Earth as a solitary pulsation.

We must now follow the propagation of that unique wave, right up to the human being and, if possible, beyond.[18]

Chapter II

THE EXPANSION OF LIFE

When a physicist wants to study the development of a wave, he begins by calculating the pulsation of a single particle. Then reducing the vibrating medium to its principal characteristics and directions of elasticity, he generalizes the results found in the case of the element to the scale of these. In this way he obtains a fundamental shape, which is as close as possible to the movement of the whole he sought to determine.

Faced with the task of describing the rise of life, the biologist is forced to resort to a similar method, using his own means. It is impossible to put any order into this enormous and complex phenomenon without first analyzing the processes life has imagined to advance in each of its elements taken in isolation. And it is impossible to isolate the general ways taken by the multitude of the sum total of these individual processes without selecting the most expressive and luminous traits of their resultant.

In the following sections I intend to develop a simplified but structural representation of terrestrial life in evolution. A vision whose truth springs from the pure and irresistible effect of homogeneity and coherence. With no minor details, no argument. Again and always, a perspective to see and to accept—or not to see.

Three main headings contain and define the substance of what I want to say:

1. The Elementary Movements of Life
2. The Spontaneous Ramifications of the Living Mass
3. The Tree of Life.

All this will be seen, to begin with, from the exterior and surface point of view. Only in the following chapter will we try to fathom things from inside.

1   THE ELEMENTARY MOVEMENTS OF LIFE

<u>A</u>. *Reproduction*

The entire process by which the envelope of the biosphere is woven around the Earth is based on the characteristically vital mechanism of reproduction. At a given moment, every cell divides (by "scissiparity" or "karyokinesis"[1]) and gives birth to a new cell like itself. At first there is only a single center; then two. Everything in the subsequent movements of life derives from this elementary and powerful phenomenon.

In itself, cellular division seems to be provoked simply by the living particle's necessity to remedy its molecular fragility and by the structural problems related to the continuity of its growth, the necessity for it to rejuvenate and to become lighter. The limited groupings of atoms, the micromolecules, have an almost indefinite longevity (but a corresponding fixity). But because the cell is continually doing the work of assimilation, it must divide itself in two to continue to exist. This is the reason why reproduction initially appears to be a simple process nature has imagined to assure the permanence of what was unstable in the case of vast molecular constructions.

But as always happens in the world, what began only as a stroke of luck or means of survival is immediately transformed and used as a tool of progress and conquest.[2] At the start, life seemed to have reproduced itself only in self-defense. Now by this very act it was preparing for its invasions.

<u>B</u>. *Multiplication*

For once introduced into the stuff of the universe, the principle of duplication of living particles knew no limitations other than the quantity of matter available for its functioning. It has been calculated that simply by division of itself and its descendants a single infusorian would cover the Earth in several generations. No volume, however large, can withstand the effects of geometric progression. And this is not purely mental extrapolation. By the single fact that it doubles itself, and that nothing can prevent it from doubling itself continually, life possesses a force of expansion as invincible as that of a body that dilates or vaporizes. But whereas for so-called "inert" matter the increase in volume soon reaches its point of equilibrium, for living substance there seems to be no evidence of slackening. The more the phenomenon of cellular division spreads, the more virulent it becomes. Once the play of scissiparity has been unleashed, nothing from inside can stop this constructive and devouring fire, because it is spontaneous. And as a result nothing from outside is great enough to extinguish it by satiation.

C. Renewal

Now multiplication is still only a first result, and quantitative side, of the operation in process. Reproduction doubles the mother cell. And thus by a mechanism the inverse of chemical disaggregation, *it multiplies without fragmenting*. But at the same time, moreover, it transforms what it only aimed to prolong. Shut in on itself, the living element sooner or later reaches a state of immobility. It becomes trapped and fixed in its evolution. At that moment, by the play of reproduction, it regains the faculty of interior readjustment and as a result takes on a new shape and orientation. It pluralizes in form as well as number. The elementary wave of life issuing from each individual does not spread as a monotonous circle formed of other individuals exactly like itself. It diffracts and becomes iridescent in an indefinite spectrum of diverse tonalities. By the very fact that the living being is a center of irresistible multiplication, it constitutes a focal point of just as irresistible diversification.

D. Conjugation

And then it would seem that to enlarge the breach made in the wall of the unorganized by its first wave, life discovered the marvelous process of conjugation. It would take an entire work in itself to establish and appreciate how the duality of the sexes grew and became sublimated in the evolution from cell to man. In its beginnings, where we will consider it here, the phenomenon appears to be primarily a means of accelerating and intensifying the double effect of multiplying and diversifying that was achieved first of all through asexual reproduction, just as it still functions in so many lower organisms and even in each of the cells of our own bodies. By the first conjugation of two elements (however little differentiated they were into male and female) the doors were opened to those modes of generation where a single individual can pulverize itself into a myriad of germs. And simultaneously an endless game was set into play: the combination of "characters" whose analysis is minutely pursued by modern genetics. Instead of simply radiating out from each center in process of division, from then on the rays of life began to anastomose,[3] exchanging and varying their respective wealth. We never think to be astonished in the presence of this prodigious invention, anymore than we do before fire, bread, or writing. And yet how many chances and attempts—consequently, how much time—it must have taken for this fundamental discovery we have come from to ripen! And how much more time still for it to find its natural complement and culmination in the even more revolutionary innovation of association!

E. Association

On first analysis, without touching prematurely on deeper factors, it is almost an inevitable consequence of their multiplication that living particles group into complex organisms. Cells tend to agglomerate because they press against each other, or they are even born in clusters. But this purely mechanical opportunity or necessity of drawing close together finally germinated and brought forth a definitive method of biological improvement.

All the stages of that, *still unended*, advance toward the unification or synthesis of the constantly accumulated products of living reproduction seem to survive in nature right before our eyes. At the very bottom, we see the simple *aggregate*, such as it exists among bacteria and lower fungi. At a higher level, the fused *colony*, with its elements more distinctly specialized but still not centralized: such as higher plants, and bryozoa and polyparies.[4] Higher still, the *metazoan*,[5] veritable cell of cells, in which, through a kind of prodigious critical transformation, as if from an excess of compression, an autonomous center is established over the organized group of living particles.[6] And to conclude, even further on, at the present limit of our experience and life's experimentations, we find *society*, those mysterious associations of free metazoa, within which it seems the formation of hypercomplex units is being attempted along more or less successful lines, through "megasynthesis."

The last part of this book will be specifically devoted to the study of that ultimate and supreme form of grouping attained at present, where matter's effort to become organized perhaps culminates in the self-reflective society.[7] But let us merely note here that considered at every degree, association is not a sporadic or accidental phenomenon among animate beings. On the contrary it represents one of the most universal, constant, and therefore significant mechanisms used by life for its expansion. Two of its advantages are immediately obvious. Thanks to it, first of all, living substance succeeds in constituting itself in voluminous enough masses to escape the innumerable exterior constraints (capillary adhesion, osmotic pressure, chemical variation of medium, etc.) that paralyze the microscopic being. In biology as in navigation it requires a certain physical size to make certain movements possible. And thanks to it as well (and always owing to the augmentation in volume it allows), the organism finds the necessary space inside itself to accommodate the multiple parts born progressively and *additively* from its differentiation.

F. *Directed Additivity*

Reproduction, conjugation, association. However prolonged they might be, these various movements in themselves only determine a surface deployment of organisms. Reduced to their resources alone, life would always spread and diversify at the same level. It would be like an airplane running over the ground, never able to take off. It would not rise.

This is where the phenomenon of *additivity* enters, playing its role of vertical component.

In the course of biological evolution, there is certainly no lack of examples of transformations that operate on the horizontal, purely by crossing of characters. These are the so-called "Mendelian" mutations. But more generally and at a deeper level, the renewals made possible by each reproduction do more than replace each other; they *add* to one another, their sum increasing *in a definite direction*. Dispositions are accentuated, or else organs fit together or are superposed. In one place there is growing diversification and in another growing specialization, of terms that form a single genealogical succession. In other words, insofar as it is a natural unit distinct from the individual, the *hereditary line* appears. *Directed complication* is the law in which, from the micromolecules, then megamolecules, the very process ripened that gave birth to the first cells, and to it biology has given the name *orthogenesis.**

Orthogenesis[8] is the only complete and dynamic form of heredity. What reality and what energizing forces on the cosmic scale lie hidden in this term? We shall gradually come to find this out. A first point already seems clear at this stage of our investigation. Thanks to the additive power that characterizes it, living substance (contrary to the matter of the physicist) becomes "weighted" with complication and instability. It falls, or more exactly it rises, toward more and more improbable forms.

Without orthogenesis, life would only spread out; with orthogenesis, life has invincibly some sort of ascent.

Corollary. The Ways of Life

Now let us stop for a moment. And before we attempt to discover what will happen when we extend the laws that we saw regulating the

---

* On the pretext that this term, "orthogenesis," has been used in various questionable or limited senses, or else that it has a metaphysical flavor, certain biologists would simply like to suppress it. My firm conviction is that, on the contrary, it is an essential and irreplaceable word to indicate and affirm the obvious property living matter possesses of forming a system "within which terms *succeed each other* experimentally according to constantly increasing values of centro-complexity."

movements of the isolated particle to the whole of life, let us try to distinguish the general behaviors or attitudes that, in accordance with these elementary laws, are going to characterize life in movement at all levels and occurrences.

These attitudes or ways of doing things can be reduced to three: profusion, ingenuity, and (judging from our own point of view as individuals) indifference.

(a) *Profusion*, first of all, which is born from the boundless process of multiplication.

Life proceeds by mass effects, from multitudes hurled ahead seemingly at random. Billions of germs and millions of adults pushing each other, shoving each other aside, devouring each other over who will occupy the most and best space. We see all the apparent waste and ruthlessness, all the mystery and the scandal, but at the same time also, to be accurate, all the biological efficiency of the *struggle for life*. In the course of the implacable game that forces one block of living substance to confront another in the process of their irresistible dilation, the individual is certainly pushed to the limits of its possibilities and efforts. Emergence of the fittest and natural selection are not at all empty terms, provided we do not use them to imply any ultimate ideal or final explanation.

But it is not the individual that seems to count for most in the phenomenon. Deeper than the series of single combats, a conflict of chances develops in the struggle to be. By reproducing itself beyond count, life arms itself against fatal blows. It increases its chances to survive. And at the same time it multiplies its chances to advance.

And here is where the fundamental technique of *trial and error* continues on, reappearing at the level of animate particles, that specific and invincible arm of every expanding multitude. Trial and error, where the blind fantasy of large numbers and the precise orientation of a pursued goal are combined. Not simply chance, as we often think, but *directed chance*. Filling everything to try everything, trying everything to find everything. Fundamentally, is not profusion nature's way of seeking, so to speak, to develop this action, which grows all the more enormous and costly the more extensive it becomes?

(b) *Ingenuity*, next. This is the indispensable condition, or more precisely the constructive side, of additivity.

To accumulate characters in stable and coherent assemblages, life is lead to deploy a tremendous skillfulness. It has to imagine parts and combine them within a minimum of space. Like an engineer, it must put together supple and simple machinery. Now for the structure of organisms (the more so the higher they are) this implies and entails a property that we must never forget.

What is put together comes apart.

At the first stage of its discoveries, biology was surprised and fascinated to observe that no matter how perfect, or more perfect, even, was the spontaneity of living beings, they could always be dissected into an endless chain of closed mechanisms. Then from this it thought that it could conclude a universal materialism. But it had forgotten the essential difference between a natural whole and the products of its analysis.

True, by construction any organism can always and necessarily be taken apart into well-ordered pieces. But it does not follow at all from this circumstance that the adding of these pieces together would in itself be automatic or that some specifically new value might not emerge from the sum of them. The fact that what is "free" is found to be pan-analyzable into something determinate, even in the human being, does not prove that the world is not fundamentally free (as I maintain here). It is simply the result, and triumph, of life's ingenuity.

(c) *Indifference*, finally, toward individuals.

So many times art, poetry, and even philosophy have depicted nature as a woman, blindfolded, trampling down a dust of crushed existences. In life's profusion we find the first traces of this apparent hardheartedness. Like Tolstoy's grasshoppers, life passes over a bridge of accumulated corpses. And this is a direct effect of multiplication. But orthogenesis and association also work in this same "inhuman" way each in its own fashion.

By the phenomenon of association, the living particle is torn away from itself. Captured in a whole vaster than itself, it becomes partly a slave of the whole. Its life is no longer its own.

And what organic or social incorporation does to distend it in space, its accession to a hereditary line accomplishes no less inexorably in time. By the force of orthogenesis the individual is caught up in the network. From being the center, it becomes the intermediary, the link. It no longer is; it transmits. Life is more real than lives, as it has been said . . .

Here lost in number. There torn apart in the collective. There again, in a third direction, stretched out into becoming. The dramatic and perpetual opposition in the course of evolution between the element born of the multiple and the multiple constantly being born of the element.

Insofar as the general movement of life becomes more ordered, in spite of periodic resumptions of the offensive the conflict tends to resolve itself. Yet it is still cruelly recognizable right to the end. Only from the spirit, where it reaches its *felt* paroxysm, will the antinomy clear; and the world's indifference to its elements be transformed into an immense solicitude—in the sphere of the person.

But we are not there yet.

As a result of its elementary mechanisms, life rises with these three traits: groping profusion, constructive ingenuity, indifference toward what is not future and totality. And with still a fourth, enveloping them all: *global unity*.

We had already found this last condition in primordial matter, then on the juvenile Earth, then at the eclosion of the first cells. Here it manifests itself once again, even more clearly. However vast and multiform the proliferations of animate matter may be, these increases will always extend in *mutual interdependence*. Continuous adjustment coadapts them from without. A profound equilibrium balances them from within. Taken as a whole, from the first stages of its evolution, the living substance spread over the Earth forms the features of a single, gigantic organism.

At the end of each of the stages that bring us to the human being, I will repeat this same thing again and again, like a refrain. But only because if we forget it, we will never understand.

To catch a glimpse of life we must never lose sight of the unity of the biosphere covering over the fundamental plurality and rivalry of individual existences. A unity that is still diffuse at the start. A unity of origin, framework, and diffused impulse rather than an ordered grouping. But a unity that from now on, to the extent in which life rises, will continually become more defined, bend back on itself, and ultimately center itself before our eyes.

2 THE RAMIFICATIONS OF THE LIVING MASS

Now let us take these various movements whose shape we have just analyzed in the case of isolated cells or groupings of cells and study them over the entire expanse of the living Earth. We might imagine that raised to these dimensions, their multitude is going to blur and generate nothing but hopeless confusion. Or we might expect, to the contrary, that the sum of them would harmonize and create merely a kind of continuous wave, like the wave spreading over the calm surface of water where a stone has fallen. But in fact, a third thing happens. Observed in the form in which we see it at this very moment, the front of rising life is neither confused nor continuous. Rather it seems to be a grouping of fragments that are simultaneously divergent and tiered: classes, orders, families, genera, species—the whole range of groups, whose variety, order of magnitude, and interlinkings modern systematics tries to express through its system of names.

Taken as a whole, life segments as it advances. Through expansion, it spontaneously breaks into broad, natural units that are hierarchical. *It ramifies*. Now is the moment for us to concern ourselves with this particular phenomenon, which is as essential to large animate masses as "karyokenesis" is to cells.

There are many different factors that contribute, each one in its own way, to the formation and accentuation of the branching structure of life. Here again I will reduce them to three, as follows:

(a) the aggregations of growth, giving birth to "phyla"
(b) the unfolding (or disjunctions) of maturity, periodically producing "verticils"
(c) the effects of distance, suppressing "peduncles" from sight.

A. *The Aggregations of Growth: The Phylum*

Let us return to the living element in process of reproduction and multiplication. We have seen how due to orthogenesis different lineages radiate from this element as their center, each one recognizable by the accentuation of certain characteristics. These lines diverge in their construction and tend to separate from each other. Everything still suggests that through their encounter with lineages stemming from neighboring elements they will do nothing but intermingle until their union forms an impenetrable maze.

By "aggregation of growth," I refer to the new and unexpected fact that just where the play of chance would most lead us to fear a complicated tangle, a *simple type* of dispersion occurs. Spreading over the ground, a sheet of water quickly channels into rivulets, then into clearly defined streams. In the same way, influenced by a variety of causes (native parallelism of elementary orthogeneses, attraction and mutual adjustment of lineages, selective action of environment), the fibers of a living mass in the process of diversification tend to draw together, group, and agglutinate in a few dominant directions. Caught at its beginning stages, this concentration of forms around several privileged axes is indistinct and blurred: there is simply an increase in the number or density of lineages in certain sectors. And then, gradually, the movement asserts itself. Actual veins begin to form, but without yet breaking the limbus of the leaf in which they have appeared. At that moment the fibers still manage to partly escape the network that would capture them. From vein to vein they still can join each other, anastomose, and cross. The grouping remains at the racial stage, a zoologist would say. And it is then, depending upon the point of view we take, that aggregation or final disjunction both occur. Having reached a certain degree of mutual connection, the lineages are isolated into a closed sheaf, impenetrable from then on to neighboring sheaves. From this point, their association continues to evolve on its own, as something autonomous. The species has become individualized. The phylum has been born.

The phylum. The living fascicle, lineage of lineages. So many still refuse to see this mesh of life in evolution, or to admit that it is real. But that is because they do not know how to focus their eyes or to look properly.

The phylum is first of all a collective reality. To distinguish it clearly, it is therefore essential to place oneself high enough and far enough away. Focused on from too close in space, it fragments into a confusion of irregularities. You cannot see the forest for the trees.

Next, the phylum is something polymorphous and elastic. Resembling the molecule in this, which attains all sizes and degrees of complication, it can be as small as a species or as vast as a subkingdom. There are simple phyla and phyla of phyla. Phyletic unity is not so much quantitative as structural. Therefore, it is necessary to know how to recognize it at any dimension whatsoever.

The phylum, finally, is a dynamic kind of reality. It can therefore only be seen clearly over a certain depth of duration, that is, in movement. Immobilized in time, its features are lost, the life of it as well. A snapshot kills motion.

Viewed without these precautions, the phylum appears to be just another artificial entity cut from the living continuum for purposes of classification. Yet observed in the proper magnification and light, it on the contrary proves to be a perfectly well-defined structural reality.

What defines the phylum in the first place is its "initial angle of divergence," that is, the particular direction in which it groups and evolves as it separates from neighboring forms.

What defines it in the second place is its "initial section." There is still everything to learn about this last point (which we have already touched on in regard to the first cells and which will assume such importance in the case of the human). One thing at least is already certain. Just as a drop of water must exceed a certain volume to condense physically, or just as there must be a certain quantity of matter for a chemical reaction to begin, so also a phylum must have a large enough number and variety of possibilities grouped within itself from the outset to succeed in establishing itself biologically. We now see that if it does not offer enough consistency and initial richness (as well as a wide enough divergence at the start), a new branch will never succeed in becoming individualized. The rule is clear. But how are we to imagine the way this rule functions and expresses itself concretely? As the diffuse segregation of a mass within a mass? As a contagious effect propagated around a narrowly limited zone of mutation? In what form are we to represent the *surface* aspect of the birth of a species? We still are not sure, and the question may entail a variety of answers. But is the problem not almost solved when we can put it clearly?

Finally, and in conclusion, what not only completes the definition of the phylum, but moreover puts it in a category with other *natural units* of the world, is its "power and specific law of autonomous development."

Without metaphor, although certainly in its own way, the phylum behaves like a living thing: it grows and it unfolds.

_B_. The Unfolding (or Disjunctions) of Maturity: The Verticil

By virtue of analogies that stem from a profound natural bond, as we will discover further ahead, the development of the phylum strangely parallels the successive stages through which a human invention passes.[9] We well know these stages from having constantly observed them around us for over a century. First of all, the idea takes shape approximately, in a theory or provisional mechanism. Then there comes a period of rapid modifications, with a continual touching up and adjustment of the rough sketch, until it almost reaches its final form. Having reached this state of completion, the new creation then enters its phase of expansion and equilibrium. Qualitatively, it reaches its "ceiling," changing only in a few secondary details. Quantitatively, on the other hand, it spreads out and acquires its full consistency. That is the history of all modern inventions, from bicycle to airplane, from photography to film and broadcasting.

From the naturalist's viewpoint, the curve of growth followed by the living branches is formed in exactly the same way. At the start, the phylum corresponds to the "discovery" through experimentation of a new, viable, and advantageous organic type. But this type does not achieve its most economical or well-adapted form all at once. For an indefinite period of time, it devotes its whole strength, one might say, to experimenting on itself. Trial follows trial, and not one is definitively accepted. Then finally it approaches perfection. From that moment, the rhythm of change slows down; and having reached the limits of what it can yield, the new invention enters its phase of conquest. Stronger than its less-perfected neighbors, the newly born group spreads out, while at the same time establishing itself. It multiplies, but without further diversification. It has just entered both its maximum size and stability.[10]

This is how a phylum develops by _simple dilation_, or by means of a simple thickening of its initial stem. Except in the case of a branch that has reached the limits of its evolutionary power, this elementary case is never strictly realized. Actually, however decisive and victorious is the solution the new form has brought to the problems raised by existence, this solution in fact allows for a certain number of variants, and because the variants each offer their own advantages, they have no reason or power to reciprocally eliminate each other. This explains the fact that the more a phylum grows the more it tends to dissociate into secondary phyla where each one corresponds to a variant or harmonic of the fundamental type. It somehow breaks along the whole length of its widening front. Qualitatively it subdivides, while quantitatively it spreads out. Disjunction has begun again. Sometimes the new subdivisions seem only to correspond to superficial diversifications, to be effects of chance or exuberant fantasy. Sometimes, on the other hand, they represent precise adaptations of the general type to particular needs or habitats. This is how the rays ("radiations") appear that are so clearly marked in the case of the vertebrates, as we shall see below. And within each ray, the mechanism inevitably tends to come into play all over again in a more attenuated form. These rays, in their turn, also soon show signs of resegmentation into fans. And the process is theoretically endless. In fact, experience proves that the phenomenon soon dies out. Fairly quickly the formation of fans stops; and terminal dilation of the branches occurs, with no further appreciable division.

Ultimately, the fully opened phylum generally looks most like a *verticil*[11] *of consolidated forms.*

And it is then, giving its final touch to the whole phenomenon, that the profound tendency toward socialization is discovered at the heart of each component of the verticil. I must repeat here for socialization what I said above generally holds true for association. Because definitive groupings of individuals or organized and differentiated colonies are found relatively rarely in nature (termites, hymenopterans, human species[12] . . .), there is a risk that we might see them only as an exceptional trait of evolution. Contrary to this first impression, on more careful observation we quickly recognize that they reveal one of the most fundamental laws of organized matter. Is it the ultimate method employed by the living group for augmenting by coherence its resistance to destruction and its power of conquest? Is it above all the ultimate[13] method it has imagined for multiplying its internal wealth by pooling its resources in common? Whatever the reason behind it, the fact is before us. Once the elements of a phylum have reached their definitive form at the end of each verticillate ray, as surely as the atoms of a solid body tend to crystallize, they tend to draw together and to socialize.

Once this final progress has been realized in the reinforcement and individualization of the extremities of its fan, a phylum can be said to have reached its full maturity. From now on it is going to last until it is thinned out and finally eliminated by internal weakening or external competition. Then, except for the accidental survival of a few permanently fixed lineages, its history is closed—unless at one or another of its points it begins again to thrust out a new bud through a phenomenon of self-fertilization.

To understand the mechanism of this revival, we must continually return to the idea, or symbol, of experimentation. The formation of a verticil, as we said, is explained first of all by the phylum's necessity to pluralize itself in order to meet a variety of needs or possibilities. But by the very fact that the number of rays continues to increase and that moreover as each ray spreads out it augments the number of individuals, these "trials" and "experiments" are going to multiply as well. A fan at the end of a phylum is a forest of exploring antennas. If one of these antennas chances to encounter the fissure, the formula, giving access to a new compartment of life, then at that point, instead of becoming fixed or leveling out in monotonous diversifications, the branch regains all its mobility. *It undergoes mutation.* A pulsation of life sets out again through the open pathway, and, influenced by the combined forces of aggregation and disjunction, is soon led in its turn to divide into verticils. A new phylum appears, which grows and which, without necessarily suffocating or exhausting the main branch on which it was born, unfolds above it. Perhaps waiting for a third branch to germinate from itself, and then a fourth—if the direction is still favorable and the general equilibrium of the biosphere allows it.

C. *The Effects of Distance: The Suppression of the Peduncles*

And so in this way, through the very rhythm of its development, each line of life continues alternately contracting and dilating. It forms a string of "nodes" and "loops,"[14] a succession of narrow peduncles[15] and spreading leaves.

But this schematic representation of what happens is still only theoretical. For it to be *seen* exactly as it is would mean presupposing the simultaneous existence of a terrestrial witness throughout its entire duration, and an observer such as this could only be a freak of the imagination. In reality, as things are, what we see of life can only be grasped in a very short instant: that is, through an enormous thickness of *elapsed* time. What is given to our experience, what consequently the "phenomenon" consists in, is not, therefore, the evolutionary movement in itself; it is this movement corrected according to its alteration by the *effects of distance.* Now how is this alteration going to express itself? Simply in the accentuation (rapidly increasing with distance) of the fan structure born of the phyletic radiations of life; this, moreover, brought about in two different ways: first by the exaggeration of the apparent dispersion of the phyla; and next by the apparent suppression of their peduncles.

The exaggeration of the apparent dispersion of the phyla. This first effect of perspective, visible to all, derives from the decline and "decimation" of living branches as a result of aging. Only an infinitesimal number of the organisms that have successively sprouted on the trunk of life still survive before our eyes in nature today. And in spite of the diligent efforts of paleontology, there are many extinct forms that will forever remain unknown to us. As a result of this destruction, holes are continually created in the foliage of plant and animal forms. And these blank spaces become more and more gaping the further we descend toward the origins. Dry branches break off. Leaves fall—with the disappearance of an equal number of morphological forms, whose absence so often makes the surviving lineages look like leafless and solitary stems. The same duration that multiplies its creations ahead with one hand works just as effectively with the other to thin them out behind. By this act, it separates them and isolates them more and more in our view—and meanwhile, through another more subtle process, gives us the illusion of seeing them floating like clouds, rootless, over the abyss of past ages.

The suppression of the peduncles. Since the epic times of Lamarck and Darwin, the preferred tactic against transformists has always been to remind them how powerless they are to prove the *birth* of a species from *material traces.* "There is no doubt that you show us the succession of various forms in the past," they are told, "and, granted, within certain limits, even the transformation of these forms. But however primitive they are, your first mammal is already a mammal, your first equid already a horse, and this holds true for the rest besides. Perhaps then there is some evolution within a type. But no type appears through evolution." The survivors of the *fixed-species* school, who are more and more rare, still continue to talk this way.

Independently of any arguments drawn from the continual accumulation of paleontological evidence, as we shall see, there is an even more radical response to be used against this objection (rather, a categorical end to nonacceptance): that is, to deny its presuppositions. Basically what antitransformists demand is to be shown the "peduncle" of a phylum. But this demand is both unreasonable and futile. For to satisfy it would require changing the very order of the world and the conditions of our perception.

Nothing is more delicate and fleeting in its nature than a beginning. As long as a zoological group is young, its characteristics lack definition. Its structure is soft. Its dimensions faint. It is made up of relatively few individuals, and they change rapidly. The peduncle of a living branch (or the terminal bud, which amounts to the same thing), corresponds to a minimum of differentiation, expansion, and resistance both in space and in duration. How then will time act on this weak zone? Inevitably, to destroy every vestige of it.[16]

Anyone who deals with history must be highly conscious of the disturbing, yet fundamental, fragility of all beginnings.

In every domain when something truly new begins to break through around us, we do not distinguish it—for the good reason that we would have to see its unfolding in the future to notice its beginnings. And after that very same thing has grown, when we turn back to find the germ and first sketches of it, these first stages in their turn are hidden—destroyed or forgotten. Where are the first Greeks and the first Romans, those so close to us? Where are the first looms, the first carts, and first hearth-stones? Where, already, are the first models of automobiles, of airplanes, of cinemas? In biology, in civilization, in linguistics—everywhere—time like an eraser in the hands of the artist wipes out each weak line in the drawings of life. By a mechanism whose details seem so inevitable and accidental in each case, but whose universality proves that it reflects a fundamental condition of our knowledge, embryos, peduncles, all initial phases of growth, whatever they are, continually vanish from view behind us. Except for fixed maxima and for consolidated achievements, there is nothing left (neither witness, nor trace) of what has existed before us. In other words, it is only the terminal enlargements of the fans that prolong themselves into the present through their survivors, or their fossils.

And so there is nothing surprising in the fact that retrospectively things seem to arise *ready-made.** Automatically, through the selective absorption of the ages, what moves tends to disappear from our perspective only to resolve itself in the whole domain of phenomena into a discontinuous succession of levels and stabilities.†

Thus it is through the destructive effect of the past superimposed on a constructive effect of growth that the ramifications of the tree of life are finally drawn and emerge in the eyes of science.

Let us try to see this tree in its concrete reality, and to measure it.

---

* If our machines (autos, airplanes, etc.) were to be buried and "fossilized" by some cataclysm, when future geologists discovered them they would have the same impression we have when faced with a pterodactyl. It would seem to them as though these products of our invention, represented solely by their latest models, had been created without any evolutionary phase of experimentation—completed and fixed from the start.

† As I note later in regard to "monogenism" (p. 127, note*), there is the nonfortuitous impossibility we find ourselves in (for fortuitous reasons each time, cf. Cournot.[17]) of going beyond a certain limit of precision (of "separation") in our perception of the far distant past. In every direction (toward what is very ancient and small, but also toward what is very large and very slow) our sight is blunted, and beyond a certain radius we can no longer distinguish anything at all.[18]

3 THE TREE OF LIFE

A. The Main Outlines

(a) A Quantitative Evolutionary Unit:
The Layer of the Mammals

The immediate result of the preceding observations is that to see the tree of life properly, we must begin by "staring hard" at that part of its branching structure where the corrosive action of time has had only a moderate effect. Not too close, to avoid being blocked by the leaves, not too far, to keep in sight the branches where the leaves are still thick enough.

Where can we find this privileged region in nature today? In the large family of the mammals, of course.

We know positively through geology, and a simple inspection of its internal structure is enough to prove it, that although humanity still represents an "immature" group, the mammals themselves as a whole form a group that is both mature and *fresh*. Having fully unfolded only in the course of the Tertiary[19] their assemblage still allows us to see an appreciable number of its most delicate appendages. That is why it has been from the start, and still is today, the preferred domain for the awakening and development of transformist ideas.

So let us look at the main outlines of it here (FIGURE 1);[20] however, limiting our field of investigation at first to its youngest and most progressive part: the placental mammals.*

From the evolutionary (we could even say "physiological") perspective, taken as a unit the placental mammals constitute what I will call here conventionally a *biota*. By this I mean a grouping of verticils whose elements are not only related by birth, but also support and mutually complete each other in the effort to stay alive and to propagate.

To begin to understand this important point, which the American school of paleontology[22] has a partiality for bringing to the fore, we only need to observe in its proper light the distribution of the animal forms most familiar to us. Here we have the herbivores and the rodents who feed directly on the plant branch of life, and there the insectivores who are similarly parasitic of the "arthropod" branch. Here again the carnivores who live on one another—and there the omnivores who feed at all tables at

---

* This term, as opposed to aplacentals (or marsupials), is applied to mammals in whom the embryo, protected and nourished by a special membrane called *placenta*, can remain inside the womb of its mother until it is fully mature.[21]

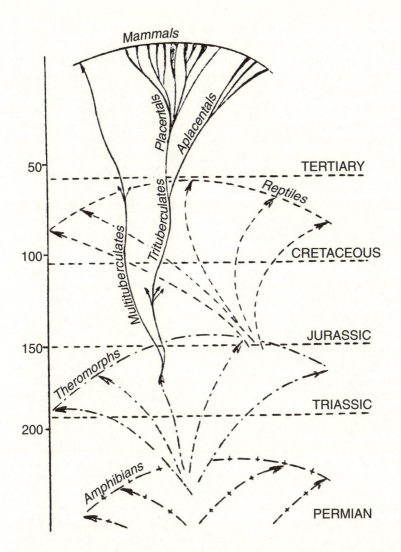

FIGURE 1   Diagram symbolizing the development of the tetrapods in layers (birds omitted). The numbers on the left refer to *millions* of years. For details, see text.

once. These are the four principal *radiations*[23] that substantially coincide with the generally accepted division of phyla.

Let us now consider these four radiations or sectors separately, one after the other. Each one is going to subdivide and cleave perfectly easily into subordinate units. This is true, for example, of the ray that from our present perspective is the most thickly provided among them, the herbivore ray. According to the two different methods chosen for transforming the extremities of their limbs into feet for running (by the hyperdevelopment of two fingers, or else of the single middle finger), we see two broad families emerge, the artiodactyls and the perissodactyls,[24] each one formed of a bundle of broad and distinct lineages. Here in the perissodactyls we have the obscure crowd of tapirids; the short-lived but astonishing branch of titanotheres;[25] the chalicotheres with claws for burrowing—which man perhaps still may have seen; the unspined or horned tribe of rhinocerotids; and finally the solid-hooved equids, mimicked in South America by an entirely independent phylum. And there within the artiodactyls, the suids,[26] the camilids, the cervids, and the antilopids—not to mention other stems that are less vigorous but just as individualized and interesting from the perspective of paleontology. To say nothing of the dense and powerful group of proboscideans. . . . In conformity with the rule of "the suppression of peduncles," the base of each of these units is drowned in the mists of the past. But once they have appeared, we can also follow each and every one of them in the principal phases of their geographical expansion; in their almost indefinite successive subdivisions into subverticils; and finally, in the exaggeration by orthogenesis of certain bony characteristics of tooth or skull—which usually ends up making them into something monstrous or fragile.

But this is still not all. Superposed on this flowering of genera and species born of the four fundamental radiations, we distinguish another network that corresponds to the attempts made here and there to abandon terrestrial life and to inhabit the air, the water, or even deep under the ground. Along with forms built for running, we see arboreal and even flying forms, swimming forms, and burrowing forms. Some of them (cetaceans and sirenians[27]) are derived, with apparently surprising speed, from the carnassials and the herbivores. Others (chiropterans[28] and moles and mole rats[29]), generally richly provided with the most ancient elements of the placental group, are derived from the insectivores and rodents, two groups as old as the end of the Secondary.[30]

We need only to look at this functional whole in itself, so elegantly balanced, for the inescapable evidence that it represents an organic and natural grouping in a *class of its own*. This conviction grows even stronger when we realize that the grouping does not correspond to an exceptional and isolated case, but that other units like it have periodically appeared throughout the history of life. Let us cite only two examples, still remaining within the mammals.

From geology we learn that during the Tertiary a fragment of the placental biota, then at the height of its evolution, was cut off by the sea and imprisoned within the southern half of the American continent. Now how did this "cutting" react to being isolated? Just like the plant, that is, by reproducing on a smaller scale the pattern of the trunk from which it had been separated. It began to grow its pseudoproboscideans, pseudorodents, pseudohorses, and pseudomonkeys (the platyrrhines[31])—an entire biota on a reduced scale (a subbiota) inside the first!

Here is the second example, provided for us by the marsupials.

Judging from their relatively primitive mode of reproduction and also by their geographical distribution at present, which is obviously discontinuous and residual, the marsupials (or aplacentals) represent a separate stage at the base of the mammals. They must have unfolded sooner than the placentals and formed their own biota ahead of them. On the whole, except for a few odd types (such as the pseudo-*Machairodus** recently discovered in fossil form in Patagonia), this marsupial biota has disappeared without a trace. On the other hand, one of its subbiotas, which was accidentally developed and preserved, again by isolation, from before the Tertiary in Australia, still amazes naturalists by the clarity of its contours and its perfection. When Australia was discovered by Europeans, it was only inhabited, as we all know, by marsupials,† but by marsupials of all sizes, habitats, and forms: running herbivore marsupials, carnassial marsupials, insectivore marsupials, rat marsupials, mole marsupials, etc. It is impossible to imagine any more striking example of the power inherent in every phylum to differentiate into a kind of closed and physiologically complete organism.

Having clearly seen this, let us raise our eyes to look at the vast system formed[33] by the placental and aplacental biotas taken together. Very quickly zoologists noticed that the molar teeth in all the forms making up these two groups consist essentially of three tubercules[34] with top and bottom jaws meshing together. This is a seemingly insignificant trait in itself, but all the more intriguing for its constancy. How can the universality of such an accidental characteristic be explained? The key to the puzzle has been provided for us by a discovery made in certain Jurassic terrains of England. In the mid Jurassic, in a flash, we catch a glimpse of a first pulsation of mammals[35]—a world of small creatures no larger

---

* *Machairodus*, or "saber-toothed tiger." This large feline, very commonly found at the end of the Tertiary and beginning of the Quarternary, is oddly mimicked by the Pliocene carnassial marsupial of South America.[32]

† Except for a group of rodents and, the last to arrive, humans along with their dog.

than rats or musaraignes.[36] Now, among these minuscule animals, which are already so extraordinarily varied, the dental type was not yet fixed as it is in nature at present. The tritubercular type can already be recognized among them. Yet alongside this type all kinds of other different combinations are observed both in development and in the way the tubercules are opposed to the molars. And these other combinations have long since been eliminated! This forces us to a conclusion. Except perhaps for the ornithorhynchus[37] and echidna (those paradoxical egg-producing forms thought to have been a prolongation of the "multituberculates"[38]), all living mammals today derive from a strictly unique bundle. Taken as a whole they represent (in the unfolded state) only one of the multiple rays into which the Jurassic verticil of the mammals was divided: the *trituberculates*.*

With this point, we have just about reached the limits of what the opacity of the past allows us to see. Below, except for the probable existence of still another verticil right at the very end of the Triassic, to which the multituberculates would be attached, the history of the mammals is lost in darkness.

All around and toward the top, at least, their group, naturally isolated by the rupture of its peduncle, stands out with enough clarity and individuality to allow us to take it as a *practical unit* of "evolutionary mass."

Let us call this unit a *layer*.

We will need to put it to use right away.

(b) A Layer of Layers: The Tetrapods

When it is a question of measuring the distances of nebulas, astronomers use light years. If we in our turn want to enlarge and prolong our view of the tree of life downward from the mammals toward what is below, we have to count in layers.

And to begin with, the reptile layer of the Secondary.

When we lost sight of the branch of the mammals below the Jurassic period, it does not evaporate into a kind of void. It is enveloped and covered over by a thick living foliage with an entirely different look: by dinosaurians, pterosaurians, ichthyosaurians, crocodilians, and so many other monsters less familiar to those who have not been initiated into paleontology. The zoological distances between forms inside this grouping are distinctly greater than the distances between orders of mammals. Yet we are immediately struck by three characteristics. First, that we are dealing

---

* Which we could also call the "septem-vertebrates," since, by a coincidence just as unexpected and significant, whatever their neck length they all have *seven* cervical vertebras.

here with a ramified system. Next, that the branches in this system are seen to have already reached a very advanced, or even terminal, stage of unfolding. And finally, that taken broadly, the entire group represents nothing but an immense, and perhaps complex, biota. Here, we see the herbivores, which are often gigantic. There, their satellites or tyrants, the massive or leaping carnivores. And there again, the long-flight birds, with their bat membranes or bird feathers. Last of all, the swimmers, as sleek as dolphins.[39] At a distance, the reptile world looks more compressed than the world of the mammals. Yet, measured by its final expansion and complication, we can only imagine it to be at least of equal longevity. In any case, it vanishes in its depths in the same way. Toward the mid Triassic, dinosaurians are still recognizable. But they are just then emerging from another layer—itself about to reach its decline—the Permian reptiles, who are characterized above all by the theromorphs.[40]

Thick and deformed, rare also in our museums, the theromorphs are much less popular than the *Diplodocus*[41] and the iguanodons. This does not keep them from acquiring increasing importance on the horizons of zoology. Although at first they were seen to be unique and atypical beings, narrowly confined to South Africa, they have now been definitively identified as the sole representatives of a complete and individual stage of continental vertebrate life. At a given moment, before the dinosaurians and before the mammals, they were the ones who occupied and possessed all the ground not covered by water; or rather, standing firmly, as they already were, on their strongly articulated limbs, and often provided with molariform teeth, they must be said to be the first quadrupeds solidly settled on dry land. When we catch a glimpse of their presence, horned, crested, armed with tusks, they already abound in strange forms, which (as always!) indicates that they are a group whose evolution has come to an end. Beneath its superficial strangeness, in fact it is a somewhat monotonous group—and as a result, the nervures of a true biota are not yet clearly distinguishable. It is a fascinating group, nevertheless, because of the spread of potentialities of its verticil. At one extreme, we have the immutable tortoises. And at the other, types whose agility and cranial structure are extremely advanced, and it is here among them that we have every reason to think the long dormant stem of the mammals has sprung up.

And then, we find a new "tunnel." At these distances, the sections of duration are rapidly compressed under the weight of the past. When, at the base of the Permian and below, we discern another inhabited surface of the Earth, it is now populated solely by amphibians slithering in the mud. The amphibians are a burgeoning of thickset or serpent-shaped bodies, where it is often difficult to distinguish the adult from the larval forms; they are bare-skinned or armor-plated, with vertebras that are tubular or a mosaic of osselets. Here again, according to the general rule, all we manage to grasp is a world that is already highly differentiated—a world almost coming to an end. Throughout the thickness and immeasurable history of sediments that we still discern so poorly, how many of these layers do we still confuse within that teeming? One thing at least is certain: at this stage we catch a glimpse of an animal group in the process of emerging from the nutritive waters in which it had been formed.

Now at this extreme beginning of their subaerial life, the vertebrates show us a surprising characteristic that warrants reflection. In every one of them, the skeletal formula is the same and (aside from marvelous cranial homologies) identical, especially in the number and plan of limbs for walking. What is the reason for this similarity?

The fact that the amphibians, reptiles, and mammals all have four legs, and only four, could, strictly speaking, be explained by pure convergence[42] toward a particularly simple mode of locomotion (nevertheless, the insects always have as many as six legs . . .). But how can an exact structural similarity between the four appendages be justified on mechanical grounds alone? In front, we have the single humerus, then the two bones of the forearm, then the five rays of the hand? Is this not still another example of those accidental combinations that could have been discovered and realized *only once*? Here again, therefore, our mind is forced to reach the same conclusion as it was in the case of the tritubercularity of the mammals. In spite of their extraordinary variety, terrestrial animals with lungs merely represent variations built on a particular one of life's solutions.

Extended back toward its origins, the immense and complex fan of walking vertebrates thus folds up and shuts again into a single ray.

One single peduncle, bringing to a close and defining the base of a *layer of layers*: the *world of tetrapodism*.

(c) The Main Branch of Vertebrates

In the case of the mammals, we have been able to grasp the verticil from which the "trituberculate" ray isolated itself and thrust upward. Science has made less progress on the origins of the amphibians. We are certain, however, about the single region of life, where, among other tentative combinations, tetrapodism could have been formed. It must have germinated somewhere in the midst of the fishes with lobed and "limbform" fins whose once-resistant layer survives today only in a few living fossils: the dipnoids (or lunged fishes) and the totally recent surprise, a *Crossopterygian*[43] from the southern seas.

Although superficially "homogenized" by mechanical adaptation to swimming, the assemblage of the fishes (it would be better to speak of them as pisciforms) is terribly complex. Here most of all, how many layers have been accumulated and confused under one term? Relatively young layers that developed in the oceans during the same period when the tetrapod layers fanned out on the continents. And even more numerous still, ancient layers terminating far below, toward the Silurian[44] in a fundamental verticil from which we see two principal rays diverging, the jawless single-nostril pisciforms, represented in nature at present solely by the lamprey; and the jaw-mouthed two-nostril pisciforms, *from which everything else has come.*

After what I said above about the interlinking of terrestrial forms, I am not going to try to resurrect this other world and take it apart. Rather I am going to draw our attention to a fact of another kind, which we encounter here for the first time. The most ancient fishes we know are for the most part heavily, even abnormally, armored.* But concealed beneath this first apparently fruitless attempt at outer consolidation was an entirely cartilaginous skeleton. The further we follow the vertebrates downward, the less and less interiorly ossified they appear to be. This explains the fact that we have completely lost trace of them, even in the sediments that have remained intact throughout the ages. Now in this particular instance we encounter a general phenomenon that is extremely important. Whatever living group we might consider, in its depths it always ends up being drowned in the *domain of the soft.* The infallible way for a peduncle to disappear. . . .

Below the Devonian, therefore, the pisciforms enter a kind of fetal or larval stage—nonfossilizable. If it were not for the accidental survival of the strange *Amphioxus,*[45] we would have no idea at all of the multiple stages in which the chordate type must have been built, to the point where it was ready to fill the waters, waiting to invade the land.

Thus, brought to a close and marked off at its base by a major blank, we have the enormous edifice of all the quadrupeds and all the fishes—a main branch, of vertebrates.

(d) The Rest of Life

In the *main branch,* we now hold the vastest type of assemblage that systematics has yet recognized and defined within the biosphere. In addition to the vertebrates, there are two, and only two, other main branches that contribute to form the main branching structure of life: the worm and arthropod branch and then the plant branch. The first consolidated by chitin or calcareous matter and the second hardened by cellulose, they, too, have succeeded in breaking out of the prison of water

---

* Without these ossified integuments, precisely, nothing would have been left of them and we would know nothing of them.

and spreading powerfully into the atmosphere. And that is why in nature today the plants and insects are entangled and struggle with the boned animals over who will occupy more of the world.

It would be possible to repeat for each of these two other main branches the same analysis I have made of the vertebrates, but there is no need to do so. At the top are fresh groups, rich with slender verticils. Deeper down, layers of boughs that are more sharply defined but less dense.[46] At the very base, everything vanishes in a world of chemically inconsistent forms. The general shape of development is the same. But because the main branches are clearly older, we find increased complication; and in the case of the insects, extreme forms of socialization.

There seems to be every good reason to believe that in the abysses of time these various lines converge toward some common pole of dispersion. But well before the chordates, the annelids[47] and the plants join (the first two main branches apparently among the metazoans—the metazoans and the plants only at the level of single cell animals), with their respective trunks disappearing in a complex of positively strange forms—the sponges, echinoderms[48] and the polypoids—with all of them just so many sketches made of responses to the problem of life. A bush of aborted main branches.

All this certainly emerges (but we cannot tell how, for the break created by the effects of duration has become so deep) from another incredibly old and multiform world: infusorians, the various protozoans, and bacteria—naked or carapaced free-living cells, in whom the kingdoms of life become indistinguishable and systematics no longer has any sure foothold. Are they animals or plants? These words are meaningless now. Are they a piling up of layers and main branches—or a "mycelium"[49] of tangled fibers like the fungus? We no longer know. Nor can we tell anymore what all this has germinated from. Beginning with the Pre-Cambrian, the single cell beings themselves in their turn entirely lose their siliceous or calcareous skeleton. And at the same pace, the roots of the tree of life are definitively lost from sight in the softness of tissues and the metamorphosis of primeval sediments.

_B_. The Dimensions

So here in miniature we have the completed table of the forms collected and classified by the patient labor of naturalists since Aristotle and Linnaeus. In the process of describing the world we have sought to resurrect, we have already tried to give a sense of its enormous complexity. Yet, faced with the whole of it together, in a final effort of vision, we still must make ourselves more explicitly aware of how tremendous these dimensions are. Left to itself, not only does our mind constantly tend to clarify the realities it touches (which is its function), but to shrink and to isolate them. It bends wearily under the weight of distances and crowds. After having in some way depicted the expansion of life, it is therefore important for us to restore the elements of our diagram to their true dimensions.

Let us try.

Their number, first of all. For simplicity's sake we had to sketch the animate world in large, collective sections: families, orders, biotas, layers, and main branches. But did we really suspect what multitudes we were actually dealing with as we worked with these various units? For someone who wishes to think or write about evolution, before all else it is important to wander through one of the four or five great museums in the world, where an army of travelers has managed to squeeze the entire spectrum of life into a few rooms (the costly, heroic, and spiritual value of these efforts will someday be understood). And on entering, not to bother with names, but just to look—to let oneself be permeated by all that is around. In one place, we come upon the universe of the insects, where "good" species[50] figure in the tens of thousands. In another, we see the mollusks, more thousands of them, with their inexhaustible varieties of marbling and coiling. And then, the fishes, as unpredictably capricious and varie-gated as the butterflies. And then, equally fantastic, the birds, with all types of shapes, beaks, and colors. The antelopes, with all kinds of coats, bearings, and crowns. And so on, and on. Such multiplicity, such impetus, such effervescence dwells in each one of these names, names that bring to our imagination only a dozen really sound forms! And besides, all we see before us are only the survivors. What would it be like if we could see the rest . . . ? For all eras of the Earth, for all stages of evolution, other museums would have recorded the same kind of teaming luxuriance. Put end to end, the hundreds of thousands of names written in the catalogues of our systematics do not represent even a millionth of the leaves that have sprouted on the tree of life up to this time.

Now *their volume*. By this I mean, what quantitatively is the relative importance of the different natural zoological and botanical groups? Materially, what portion of the general assemblage of organized beings falls to each one of them?

To give a brief idea of the relative proportions, I reproduce here (FIGURE 2) the expressive table where the great naturalist Lucien Cuénot liked to draw a map of the animal kingdom and its principal regions according to the most recent findings of science. A map that indicates position more than structure, but that precisely answers the questions I am asking.[51]

Let us take a look at this diagram.[52] At first glance, does it not give our minds a shock—the kind of shock felt when an astronomer shows us the

FIGURE 2   The "tree of life" (in its present form) according to Cuénot. On this symbolic diagram, each principal lobe (or cluster) is equivalent to a layer at least as important (morphologically and quantitatively) as the layer formed by the whole of the mammals taken together. Below line AB, the forms are aquatic; above, they live in the open air.

solar system as a simple star—and all our stars as a single Milky Way—
and our Milky Way as an atom among other galaxies? And what about
the mammals, who commonly embody for us the idea and image of the
"animal"? Here we see them as a meager little lobe, born late on the trunk
of life. And all around them, beside them, and below, on the other hand?
Such an abundance of rival types, whose existence, immensity, or masses
we never even suspected! Mysterious creatures that we have glimpsed
from time to time leaping among the dry leaves or crawling on a beach—
never asking what they meant or where they came from. Creatures
insignificant in size and today perhaps in number. These discounted forms
now appear to us in their true light. Given the wealth of their modalities
and the time it must have taken for nature to produce them, each one of
them represents a world as significant as our own. *Quantitatively* (I
emphasize this) we are just one among them, and the last to come.

Their duration, finally. And as usual, this is the most difficult thing for
our imagination to reestablish. Even more invincibly than the horizons of
space, as I have already pointed out, the levels of the past become
compressed and "telescoped" in our perspective. How can we manage to
separate them?

To bring the depths of life into true relief, it will be useful, to begin
with, for us to return again to what above I have called the layer of the
mammals. Because this layer is relatively young, we have some idea of
the time required for its development, starting from the moment when it
clearly emerges above the reptiles at the end of the Cretaceous. The whole
of the Tertiary and a little more—about 80 million years. Now let us
assume that the layers form periodically along the axis of the same zoological main branch, like boughs along the trunk of a conifer, so that in
the case of the vertebrates their points of maximum unfolding (the only
clearly recordable ones) succeed each other at distances of 80 million
years. To obtain the relative size of duration of a zoological interval, we
only need to multiply the number of layers observed in the interval under
consideration by 80 million years; three layers at the very least, for
example, between the mammals and the base of the tetrapods. The figures
become imposing. But they coincide well enough with the idea geology is
tending to develop now about the immensity of the Triassic, the Permian,
and the Carboniferous periods.

More approximately, there is another method we can attempt to
follow from one main branch to another. At the interior of a single layer
(let us take the mammals again), we are able to roughly estimate the
average spread between one form and another—this dispersal, I repeat,
required some 80 million years to occur. Once having done this, let us
compare the mammals, the insects, and the higher plants to each other.
Unless the three main branches at the end of which these three groups

flourished did not diverge exactly from the same stock, but germinated separately on a single "mycelium" (something that is possible), think what durations it must have required, and what an accumulation of periods, to create these gigantic rifts between one type and another! This time, it seems to be zoology's figures that defy geology's facts. After having measured the percentage of lead in a radiferous mineral of the Precambrian, physicists have decided that only fifteen hundred million years have passed since the time of the most ancient traces of carbon in sediments. But are not the first organisms still earlier than these vestiges? And then, in case of conflict, which of these two chronometers shall we rely on to count the years of the Earth: how slowly radium disintegrates, or how slowly living matter aggregates?

If it takes a simple *Sequoia*[53] five thousand years to reach its full growth (and no one has yet seen a *Sequoia* die a natural death), then what can be the total age of the tree of life?

C. *The Evidence*

And now the tree is planted there before us. Surely it is a strange tree. We could call it the negative of a tree, since in the inverse of what happens for the giants of our forests, its branches and its trunk reveal themselves to our sight only through gaps of ever-widening diameter. A tree, also, that looks as if it were frozen, since the buds we shall never know more than half open seem to take so long to unfold. But a tree that nevertheless is clearly delineated by the layered tufts of its foliage of visible species. In its main outlines and its dimensions, we see it towering above us, covering the Earth. Before we attempt to penetrate the secret of its life, let us take a good look at it. For we still have a lesson and evidence to draw, simply from contemplating its exterior forms: *the feeling that it is there*.

There still are some thinkers around who remain suspicious or skeptical about evolution. Knowing nature and naturalists solely through books, they believe that the transformist battle is still going on as in the time of Darwin. And because biology still has a question about some of the mechanisms by which species have most likely been formed, they imagine that biology could still doubt, without committing suicide, the fact and reality of such a development.

But the situation is already quite different.

It might have seemed surprising that in the course of this chapter devoted to the interlinking of the organized world I have not yet made any reference to the still active disputes over the distinction between "soma" and "germ plasm,"[54] the existence and function of "genes," and the transmission or nontransmission of acquired characteristics.[55] But at this point of my inquiry these questions are of no direct concern to me.

Actually, in order to prepare a natural framework for anthropogenesis and a cradle for the human being—to guarantee, I mean, the substantive objectivity of evolution—one thing and one thing only is necessary: that we come to recognize the general phylogenesis of life (whatever its process and driving force might be, moreover) as clearly as we recognize the individual ontogenesis[56] through which we see each living being pass as a matter of course.

Now it is impossible to escape the quasi-mechanical proof of this global growth of the biosphere forced[57] on our mind by the material pattern we end up with every time we make a new attempt to fix the contours and nervures of the organized world point by point.

No one would think of doubting the giratory origin of the spiral nebulas; or the successive aggregation of particles in a crystal or stalagmite; or the concrescence of woody bundles around the axis of a stem. Certain geometrical dispositions, which to our eyes are perfectly stable, are the trace and irrefutable sign of a kinematics.[58] How is it possible, even for an instant, to doubt the evolutionary origins of the Earth's living layer?[59]

Through our efforts of analysis, life peels apart. It disarticulates indefinitely[60] into an anatomically and physiologically coherent system of overlapping fans.* Of faintly sketched microfans of subspecies and races. Of already broader fans of species and genuses. Of more and more enormous fans of biotas, and then of layers, and then of main branches—until we have, at last, the whole assemblage of animals and plants, forming by association just one single gigantic biota, perhaps rooted as a simple ray in some verticil drowned in the depths of the megamolecular world. With life as a simple main branch on something else. . . .

From top to bottom, from smallest to largest,[61] the same structure is visible, whose pattern, reinforced by the very distribution of its shadows and gaps, is accentuated and prolonged (*beyond all hypothesis!*) by the quasi-spontaneous ordering of the unforeseen elements each day brings. Each newly discovered form finds its natural place—in reality, not one of them is absolutely "new" within the framework already traced.[62] What more do we need to be convinced that all this *was born*—that it *has grown*?

---

* Clearly it would be possible to trace the continuity in this interplay of fans in another way from mine—specifically, by giving a larger place to parallelisms and convergence. For example, the tetrapods could be seen as a bundle composed of several rays that have issued from different verticils but also ended up in the quadruped formula. In my opinion this polyphyletic scheme does not account as well for the facts. But it would not in any way alter my fundamental thesis; namely, that life presents itself as an organically articulated whole that clearly reveals a phenomenon of growth.

After that, we can still continue to argue for years about how this enormous organism could have arisen. The more clearly we are able to see the staggering complexity of its parts, the more overwhelmed we are. How can this persistent growth be reconciled with molecular determinism, the blind play of chromosomes, and the apparent incapacity of individual acquisitions to be transmitted through generation? How, in other words, are we to reconcile the external "finalistic" evolution of *phenotypes* with the internal "mechanistic" evolution of *genotypes*?[63] Because we have taken it apart, we now fail to understand how the machine can go forward. True, perhaps. But while we wait, the machine stands before us—and it works. Because chemistry still stumbles over its description of the way granites might have been formed, can we deny the fact that the continents are continually in the process of granitization?[64]

Like all things in a universe where time has definitively been established as a *fourth dimension* (I will return to this), life is, and can only be, a magnitude of evolutionary nature and dimensions. Physically and historically, it corresponds to a specific function X, which defines the position of every living thing, in space, duration, and form. This is the fundamental fact that requires an explanation, but the *evidence* of it is from now on above all verification as well as safe from any further refutation by experience.

At this level of generality, we can say that the question of "transformism" no longer exists. It has been definitively settled. From now on, to shake our conviction that biogenesis is real, we would have to uproot the tree of life—undermining the entire structure of the world!*

---

* In fact, insofar as evolutionism merely expresses that it is experimentally impossible for us to perceive any being (living or nonliving) except as engaged in a tempero-spatial series, it has ceased to be a hypothesis a long time ago and has become a (dimensional) condition that all hypotheses in physics and biology must satisfy from now on. Currently, biologists and paleontologists still argue about modalities—and above all about the mechanism of life's transformations—about the preponderance of (Neo-Darwinian) chance or the (Neo-Lamarckian) play of invention in the appearance of new characteristics. But I say that all scientists are now in agreement about the general and fundamental fact that there is organic evolution in the case of life considered globally, as well as in the case of any living being taken individually—and for the good reason that they could not be scientists if they thought otherwise. The only regrettable (and somewhat surprising) thing is that despite the clarity of the facts, unanimity has not yet extended far enough to recognize that the "galaxy" of living forms outlines (as these pages assume) a vast "orthogenic" movement of enfolding, upon ever-increasing complexity and consciousness (see the "Summary or Postface" at the end of this work).[65]

Chapter III

MOTHER EARTH (DEMETER)

Demeter! Mother Earth! A fruit? What kind of fruit? Is it seeking to be born on the tree of life?[1]

Throughout the previous chapter, we spoke of growth to express the way life behaves. To some extent we were even able to recognize the principle behind this thrust, linked, as it seemed to us, to the phenomenon of a *directed additivity*. By its continuous accumulation of properties (whatever the exact mechanism of this heredity might be), life has a "snowball" effect. It heaps character on character in its protoplasm. It continually grows more and more complicated. But as a whole, what does this movement of expansion represent? A working and contained explosion like that of an engine? Or a disorderly release in every direction like that of a blast?

As I said, all scientists are now in agreement about the general fact that there is *an* evolution. But whether or not this evolution is *directed* is quite another matter. Ask a biologist today if he accepts that life is going *somewhere* in the process of its transformations, and nine times out of ten he will answer no—even vehemently. "Anyone can see that organized matter is in continual metamorphosis," he will tell you, "and even that, with the passage of time, this metamorphosis makes it move toward more and more improbable forms. But is it possible to find any kind of scale on which to appraise the absolute, or simply relative, value of such fragile constructions as these? By what right, for example, can we say that the mammal—even if it is a human—is more advanced and perfect than the bee or the rose? Starting with the first cell we can to some extent rank beings in larger and larger circles according to their distance from each other in time. But then, when all these diverse elucubrations of nature reach a certain degree of differentiation, it becomes scientifically impossible to establish any priority among them. Although the solutions are diverse, they are equivalent. In all azimuths around the center of a sphere, every radius is valid. Nothing seems to be going anywhere."

At this moment, because our minds hesitate to recognize that there is *one* precise *orientation* and a privileged *axis* of evolution, the rise of science, and even the advance of humanity, as I will show, is at a standstill. Weakened by this fundamental doubt, our research is scattered and we lack the will to decide to build the Earth.

All anthropocentrism and anthropomorphism aside, I would like to explain here why I believe I see that a direction and line of progress do exist for life—a direction and a line that are even so clearly marked that I am convinced their reality will be universally accepted by the science of tomorrow.

1   ARIADNE'S THREAD

Then to begin with, since it is a matter of degrees of organic complication, let us try to find an order in the complexity.

If we approach the assemblage of living beings without some kind of guiding thread, we must admit that qualitatively it forms an inextricable labyrinth. What is happening, and where are we going, throughout this monotonous succession of fans? True, over the centuries living beings multiply the number and sensitivity of their organs. But they also reduce them by specialization. And then, what does the term "complication" really mean? There are many ways for an animal to become less simple. Is it by differentiation of limbs? of integuments? of tissues? of sense organs? All kinds of distributions are possible, depending on your point of view. Among these multiple combinations, is any one really more *true* than the others—I mean, does it give a more satisfactory coherence to living things as a whole, whether in relation to itself or to the world in which life is engaged?

To answer this question, I believe we must turn back to the observations made above, where I tried to establish the mutual relationship between the outside and inside of things. As I said then, the essence of reality could well be represented by the amount of "interiority" the universe contains at a given moment; and in this case, evolution would be fundamentally nothing but the continual increase in the course of duration of that "psychic" or "radial" energy beneath the mechanical or "tangential" energy that is practically constant on our scale of observation (see p. 30). What, moreover, I added, is the particular function linking both the radial and tangential energies of the world together *experimentally* in their respective developments? Clearly, it is *arrangement*: whose successive progressions are interiorly lined, as we can observe, with a continuous growth and deepening of consciousness.

Now let us turn this proposition around (not in a vicious circle, but simply by an adjustment of perspective). From among the innumerable complications undergone by the boiling up of organic matter are we not at a loss to distinguish the merely surface diversifications from those (if there are any) corresponding to a grouping that renews the stuff of the universe? Well, then, let us simply attempt to recognize among all the combinations life has tried whether or not there are some that might be organically associated with a positive variation in the psyche of those who possess it. If so, and if my hypothesis is correct, then in the equivocal mass of ordinary transformations, certainly these are the ones that represent the complications of paramount importance and the fundamental meta-morphoses. Let us seize them and follow them. They may possibly lead us somewhere.

Put in these terms, the problem is solved immediately. A preferred mechanism for the play of consciousness certainly does exist in living organisms, and to become aware of it all we need to do is look inside ourselves; it is the nervous system. There is only one interiority we can positively grasp in the world—our own directly; and at the same time, by an immediate equivalence, thanks to language, that of other human beings. But we have every reason to think that some interiority exists in animals as well, which can be measured approximately by the perfection of their brain. Therefore let us try to distribute living beings according to their degree of "cerebralization." What happens? An order is established, the very order we wanted—and automatically.

To begin with, let us again take up that region in the tree of life that we know best because it is still particularly vigorous today and because we belong to it: the main branch of the chordates. A first characteristic of this grouping appears, brought to light by paleontology a long time ago: *from layer to layer*, in massive leaps, the nervous system is continually in the process of developing and concentrating. Who is not familiar with the example of those enormous dinosaurians, in whom the ridiculously small cerebral mass formed only a narrow string of lobes with a diameter less than that of the marrow in the lumbar region? These conditions are remin-iscent of the conditions prevailing below in the amphibians and in the fishes. But if we move now to the stage above, what a change we find in the mammals!

In the mammals, that is, *in the interior of the same layer* this time, the brain is on the average much more voluminous and folded than in any other group of vertebrates. And yet if we look at the layer in more detail, again what differences there are, and above all, what organization in the distribution of differences! There is first of all a gradation according to the position of biotas; cerebrally, the placentals have overtaken the mar-supials in nature today. And next, within the interior of the same biota, there is a gradation according to age. In the lower Tertiary, the brains of the placentals (except for a few primates) can be said to be always relatively smaller and less complicated than from the Neogene onward. The same can be definitely observed on the extinct phyla, such as the dinocerates, horned monsters whose cranial box did not much exceed in the smallness and spacing of lobes the stage reached by the reptiles of the Secondary. Such, also, as the condylarths. But this same thing can still be observed right *within the interior of the same lineage.* The brain in the Eocene carnassials, for example, when it is still at the marsupial stage, is smooth and well separated from the cerebellum. And the list could easily be extended. Generally speaking, whatever ray is chosen on any verticil, if the ray is long enough, only rarely can we observe that it does not, in time, end up in more and more "cephalized" forms.

Let us skip now to another main branch, the branch of the arthropods and the insects. We find the same phenomenon. Here the values are not so easy to estimate, because we are dealing with another type of consciousness. Yet our guiding thread still seems to hold true. From group to group and age to age, these forms themselves, which are psychologically so different from us, like us are subject to the influence of cephalization. Nerve ganglions curl up. They become localized and enlarged forward in the head. And at the same pace instincts become more complicated. At the same time as well, extraordinary phenomena of socialization are exhibited (we will come back to this).

It would be possible to pursue this analysis indefinitely. I have said enough about it here simply to indicate that once we have grasped the right thread, the tangle is unraveled. In classifying organized forms, naturalists, for obvious reasons of convenience, are led to use certain variations of ornamentation, or also certain functional modifications of bony apparatus. Guided by orthogenesis as it affects wing coloration and venation, or disposition of limbs or pattern of teeth, their classification sorts out the fragments, or even the skeleton, of a structure in the living world. But because the lines drawn in this way express only the secondary harmonics of the evolutionary movement, the system does not take on shape or motion as a whole. On the contrary, the moment that the measure (or parameter) of the evolutionary phenomenon is sought in the elaboration of the nervous system, not only does the multitude of genera and species fall into place; but the entire network of verticils, layers, and main branches lifts up like a trembling spray. Not only does the distribution of animal forms according to their degree of cerebralization exactly follow the contours imposed by systematics; but it also confers on the tree of life a depth, a sharpness of feature, and an impetus in which it is impossible not to see the sign of truth. Such coherence—and I may add, such ease, inexhaustible fidelity, and evocative power of coherence—could never be an effect of chance.

Among the infinite modalities in which the complications of life are dispersed, the differentiation of nervous substance stands out as a significant transformation, the way our theory foresaw it would. *It provides a direction—and consequently proves that the evolutionary movement has a direction.*

This is to be my first conclusion.

Now this proposition has its corollary. In living beings the brain is the sign and measure of consciousness (this was our starting point). In living beings, we added just now, the brain proves to be continually perfecting itself over time, to the point where a certain quality of brain seems to be fundamentally bound to a certain phase of duration.

The final conclusion emerges by itself—a conclusion that both verifies the basis of my account and governs what follows. Since the natural history of living things, in its totality and along each branch, outlines *exteriorly* the gradual establishment of a vast nervous system, this means that it corresponds *interiorly* to the installation of a psychic state in the very dimensions of the Earth. Fibers and ganglions on the surface. Consciousness deep within. All we sought was a simple rule to organize the tangle of appearances. Now we possess (fully in accordance with our initial assumption that the nature of the evolutionary movement was ultimately psychic) a fundamental variable capable of following the true curve of the phenomenon in the past, and perhaps even of defining it in the future.

Does this solve the problem for us?

Yes, almost. But clearly on one condition, a condition that will seem hard for certain scientific prejudices: that by a change or reversal of level, we leave the outside in order to move to the inside of things.

2   THE RISE OF CONSCIOUSNESS

Let us go back then to the "expansional" movement of life as we saw it in its main outlines. But this time, instead of getting lost in the maze of arrangements affecting the "tangential" energies of the world, let us try to follow the "radial" progress of its internal energies.

Everything becomes definitively clear—in value, in function, and in hope.

(a) Thanks to this simple change of variable, what we see, to begin with, is *what place the development of life occupies in the general history of our planet.*

Above, after having discussed the origin of the first cells, we estimated that if their spontaneous generation occurred only once in the course of time, this was apparently because the initial formation of protoplasm had been linked to a state through which the general chemistry of the Earth passed only once. We then said that the Earth must be seen as the seat of some global and irreversible evolution, more important for science to consider than any other of the current oscillations on its surface; and that the primordial emergence of organized matter marks a point (a critical point!) on the curve of this evolution.

After that, the phenomenon seemed to be lost in a proliferation of branching structures. We almost forgot about it. Now it emerges again. With and in the tide (duly registered by nervous systems) that carries the living wave toward ever more consciousness, we see the great fundamental movement reappear, and we now grasp its sequel.

Just like the geologist absorbed in enumerating breaks and folds in rock, the paleontologist in determining the temporal position of animal forms risks seeing the past as only a series of monotonous and homogeneous pulsations. The tables show the mammals succeeding the reptiles and the reptiles the amphibians, just as the Alps succeed the Cimmerian chains and these the Hercynian mountains. From now on we can and must free ourselves from such shallow perspectives. What we are dealing with is no longer the creeping sinusoidal curve, but the spiral springing up in a helix. From one zoological layer to the next, *something is passed on, in successive bursts, and never stops growing in the same direction*. And it is physically the most essential thing in the celestial body that bears us. There are many transformations other than the vital movement that sound a continuous note beneath the rhythms of the Earth: the evolution of simple bodies by the process of radioactivity, the granitic segregation of continents, and perhaps the isolation of internal envelopes within the globe. But since life has separated out at the heart of matter, these various processes have lost the quality of being the supreme event. With the birth of the first albuminoids, the essence of the terrestrial phenomenon has decisively migrated, and it has become concentrated in the film of the biosphere that seemed to be so insignificant. From now on the axis of geogenesis passes and is prolonged through biogenesis. And this finds its definitive expression in a psychogenesis.

From an internal perspective, and verified by the ever-increasing harmonies we shall see, these are the different subjects of our science arranged in their true perspective and proportions. Life is at the head—with the whole of physics subordinate to it. And at the heart of life, to explain its progression, the driving force of a rise of consciousness.

(b) *The driving force of life*. This question has been bitterly debated among naturalists since the knowledge of nature has come to mean understanding evolution. True to its analytical and deterministic methods, biology continues to try to find the principle of life's developments in external stimuli or statistics; in the struggle for survival and natural selection. From this perspective the animate world would rise (insofar as it really rises at all!) only through the automatically regulated sum of its attempts to remain itself.

Far be it from me, I repeat here once again, to deny the important, even essential, role of this historical play of material forms. Do we not each feel it in ourselves, simply from the fact of being alive? Exterior emergencies or shocks are indispensable to force individuals out of their natural laziness and set routines—and also to periodically break the collective frameworks that imprison them. What would we do without our enemies? It seems that for its creative combinations, life, which is capable of regulating in a supple way the blind movement of molecules within organized bodies, manages also to use the vast reactions born fortuitously in the world among material currents and animate masses. It seems to play with collectivities and events as skillfully as with atoms. But what could that ingenuity and its stimuli do if it were applied to a fundamental inertia? Moreover, as we said before, what would these mechanical energies themselves be at all without some kind of inside to nourish them? Beneath the "tangential" lies the "radial." The "impetus" of the world revealed by the great thrust of consciousness can only have its ultimate source, and it can only find its explanation for the tendency of its irreversible advance toward a higher psyche, in the existence of some kind of interior principle of movement.

How can life really operate freely from inside while entirely respecting the determinism of the outside? Perhaps someday we will understand this better.[2]

In the meantime, as soon as the reality of a fundamental impetus is accepted, the main outlines of the vital phenomenon take on a natural and possible shape. Better still, its very microstructure is clarified. For in addition to the general current of biological evolution, we now see a new way of explaining the advance and particular disposition of its different phyla.*

---

* There inevitably will be those who, in one aspect or another of the following explanation, manage to find the thought too Lamarckian (with exaggerated emphasis on the influence of the "inside" on the organic arrangement of bodies). But the fact should not be overlooked that I have left a fundamental part in the "morphogenic" action of instinct, as I understand it here, to the (Darwinian) play of external forces and chance. Life proceeds not only by strokes of luck, but strokes of luck that are recognized and grasped, that is, psychically selected (as I have shown above). Understood correctly, Neo-Lamarckian "antichance" is not merely the negation, but on the contrary, the utilization of Darwinian chance. There is a function of complementarity between the two factors—a "symbiosis," one might say.

Let me add only that as soon as we allow a place for the fundamental (although seldom observed) distinction between a biology of small and of large complexes (just

It is one thing to observe how along the same animal lineage limbs become solid-hoofed or teeth carnassial, and quite another to understand how this variation could have come about. True, it could have occurred from a mutation on the verticil at the point where the ray was attached. But after that? Later modifications along a phylum are so gradual—and the organs they affect are occasionally so stable from the time of the embryo (teeth, for example)—that in every one of these instances we definitively have to give up speaking merely of survival of the fittest or mechanical adaptation to environment and usage. But what then?

The more often I have had to confront and deal with this problem, the more firmly convinced I am that when it occurs, we are faced with an effect of psychology, not of external forces. According to our current way of speaking, an animal develops its carnivorous instincts *because* its molars become sharp and its paws develop claws. Now should we not turn this proposition around? In other words, if the tiger has lengthened its fangs and sharpened its nails, might this not be precisely because according to its lineage it has received, developed, and transmitted the "soul of a carnassial"? The same would hold for timid running-creatures, for swimmers, burrowers, and long-flight birds. True, there is some evolution of character, provided that we understand "character" to mean "temperament." At first sight this kind of explanation makes us think of the scholastic "virtues."[3] But if we take a deeper look at it, the explanation becomes increasingly more plausible. Qualities and defects of an individual develop with age. Why, rather, would they not also become *phyletically* accentuated? And at these dimensions, why, or rather how, could they not react on the organism to model it in their image? After all, the ants and the termites certainly manage to reward their warriors or workers with an exterior adapted to their instinct. Are we ourselves not familiar with men and women of prey?

(c) Once we have accepted this, unexpected horizons open out ahead of biology. In order to follow the interlinkings of living beings, for obviously practical reasons we are led to use the variation in fossilizable parts. But this practical necessity must not blind us to the limited, superficial quality of such an arrangement. All such "phenocharacters" as number

---

as we have a physics of the infinitesimal and of the immense), we notice there is reason to separate out two major zones in the unity of the organized world and to treat them in different ways: with, on the one hand, (a) the (Lamarckian) zone of very large complexes (above all, the human being), where antichance visibly predominates; and, on the other, (b) the (Darwinian) zone of small complexes (lower living things), where the only way this same antichance can still be perceived beneath the veil of chance is by reason or conjecture; that is, indirectly (see below, "Summary or Postface," pp. 217–18).

of bones, form of teeth, ornamentation of integuments are actually only the garment molding a deeper support. Fundamentally, there is but one single event in process: the great orthogenesis of everything alive toward a more immanent spontaneity. Secondarily, through the periodic dispersal of this impetus, we have the verticil of small orthogeneses, where the fundamental current divides to form the interior and true axis of each "radiation." Finally, we have the veil of tissues and architecture of limbs cast over all this like a simple sheath. That is the situation.

To express the natural history of the world as it actually is, we therefore have to be able to follow it from inside, this time not as a linked succession of structural types replacing each other; but as the rise of inner sap spreading out in a forest of consolidated instincts. In its very depths, the living world is composed of consciousness clothed in flesh and bone. From biosphere to species, everything, therefore, is but one immense ramification of psyche seeking itself through forms. This is where Ariadne's thread leads us, if we follow it to the very end.

Given our present state of knowledge, we certainly cannot contemplate expressing the mechanism of its evolution in this internal "radial" form. One thing seems clear, however. If this really is the true significance of transformism, then life, insofar as it corresponds to a *directed* process, could continue along its original line only on condition that at any given moment it undergo some profound readjustment.

It is a structural law. Nothing of magnitude can increase without ending up at some critical point, some change of state (we already referred to this as we spoke of the birth of life itself). A maximum ceiling exists for velocities and temperatures. If we continue to increase the acceleration of a body's speed until we approach the speed of light, through excess of mass it acquires an infinitely inert nature. If we heat it, it melts, then vaporizes. And the same thing applies to all known physical properties. Insofar as we saw the evolutionary movement only as a simple advance toward complexity, we could conceive that it would go on developing indefinitely, without changing, and that there was actually no upper limit to pure diversification. Now that our eyes have discovered not only the quantitative but the *qualitative* augmentation of brains (and thus of consciousness) beneath the historically increasing intricacy of forms and organs, we are alerted to the fact that inevitably in the course of geological ages an event of a new order, a *metamorphosis*, was expected to bring this long period of synthesis to a close.

We must now turn our attention to the first symptoms of this great terrestrial phenomenon ending up in the human being.

3 THE TIME APPROACHES

Let us return to the movement of the wave of life where we left it; that is, at the expansion of the mammals. Or to locate ourselves in duration concretely, let us take ourselves in thought, back to the world as we can imagine it toward the close of the Tertiary.

At that moment, a great calm seems to reign over the surface of the Earth. From southern Africa to South America and throughout Europe and Asia, there are fertile rich plains and thick forests. Then more plains and forests. And among this endless vegetation are myriads of antelopes and zebras; varieties of herds of proboscideans; of stags, with every kind of antler; of tigers, wolves, foxes, and badgers, just like those today. In short, the landscape is somewhat similar to the remnants we are trying to preserve in our national parks in Zambia, the Congo, or Arizona. Except for a few lingering archaic forms, its characteristics are so familiar to us that we must make an effort to convince ourselves that *nowhere at all* is there any smoke rising from campsite or village.

The period is one of calm profusion. The layer of the mammals has spread out. And yet the evolutionary movement could not have stopped. Surely something is accumulating somewhere, ready to spring up for another leap forward. But what? and where?

To detect what is ripening at this moment in the womb of the Universal Mother, let us make use of the index we have at hand from now on. We have just recognized that life is a rise of consciousness. If life is still in progress, this must mean that internal energy is secretly rising at certain points beneath the mantle of the Earth in bloom. Here and there psychic tension is certainly mounting in the depths of nervous systems.

Just as the physicist or doctor applies a delicate instrument to the body, so let us move our "thermometer" of consciousness over nature as it slumbers. At the Pliocene, in what region of the biosphere is the temperature rising?

Let us search, of course, among those in the lead.

Aside from the plants, which clearly do not count,* two and only two summits of main branches emerge before us into air, light, and

---

* In the sense that in the plants we are unable to follow the evolution along a nervous system of a psyche that has obviously remained diffuse. Whether or not this psyche exists, or grows in its own way, is entirely another matter. And we certainly will refrain from denying that it does. To take just one among a thousand examples, is it not true that we need only to look at the traps for insects set up by certain plants to be convinced that the plant branch, like the other two main branches, does obey the rise of consciousness, even if only remotely?

spontaneity. On the arthropod side, the *insects*; and on the vertebrate side, the *mammals*. To which side does the future belong—and the truth?

(a) *The insects.* In the higher insects a cephalic concentration of nervous ganglions is coupled with an extraordinary wealth and precision of behaviors. To see a world alive around us both so marvelously adapted and so appallingly remote makes us stop and think. Are these our competitors? Perhaps successors? Must we not say, rather, that they are a crowd pathetically trapped and struggling in a dead end?

In fact, what seems to eliminate the hypothesis that the insects represent the way out for the evolutionary movement—or even simply *one way* out—is that, although they are by far the oldest of the higher vertebrates according to the date of their unfolding, they now seem to have irremediably reached their "ceiling." Although they have grown endlessly more complicated perhaps for geological periods, like Chinese written characters, it looks as though they will not manage to change levels; as if their impetus or fundamental metamorphosis has been arrested. And when we think about it, we begin to see certain reasons for the fact that they are at a standstill.

They are too small, first of all. An external chitinous skeleton is a poor solution for the quantitative development of organs. In spite of repeated sheddings, the carapace is a prison, and it rapidly gives way under increasing interior volumes. The insect cannot grow more than a few centimeters without becoming dangerously fragile. For no matter how much we have sometimes belittled "questions of size," we cannot deny that *by the very fact that they are linked to a material synthesis*, certain qualities can be manifested only above certain quantities. Higher psyches physically require large brains.

Next, precisely because of their size perhaps, the insects show a strange psychic inferiority exactly where we would be tempted to place their superiority. Our own dexterity is put to shame before the astonishing precision of their movements and constructions. Yet be careful. Observed more closely, this perfection stems, in the end, from the extreme rapidity with which their psychology is hardened and mechanized. It has been demonstrated conclusively that the insect has an appreciable margin of uncertainty of choice at its disposal for its operations. But hardly are its actions formulated, when they seem to become weighed down by habit and soon are transcribed into organically set reflexes. One might say that as their consciousness becomes extroverted, it automatically and continually stiffens: (1) first of all in its behaviors, which grow more and more precise through immediately recorded corrections; and (2) eventually in its somatic morphology, where distinctive characteristics disappear, absorbed by their function. This results in those kinds of adjustments of organs and movements that rightfully astonished Fabre,[4] and also, in the

101

simply prodigious constructions that group the swarms of hive or termitary into a single living machine.

A paroxysm of consciousness, if you like; but one that fuses the inside with the outside, so that it becomes materialized in rigid arrangements. A movement that is the direct inverse of concentration!

(b) *The mammals.* Leaving the insects, therefore, let us now turn to the mammals.

Right away, we feel at ease here and so much so, that this sense of relief could be credited to an "anthropocentric" impression. Is the fact that we can breathe, now that we have left hive and termitary, simply because we are "at home" among the higher vertebrates? Oh how the threat of relativity still hangs over our minds!

And yet no, it is impossible for us to be mistaken. At least in this case we are not deceived by an impression, but it is our intelligence that really makes the judgment, with the power it has to appreciate certain absolute values. No, if a furry quadruped does seem so "animated," literally so alive, compared to an ant, this is not just because together with it we find ourselves in our own family zoologically. In the cat, the dog, and the dolphin's behavior, there is something so supple and unexpected, so much given to exuberance for life and to curiosity! In this case instinct is no longer channeled and paralyzed in a single function as in the spider or the bee. It remains flexible, individually and socially. It takes an interest in everything, flutters about, plays. In fact, it is an entirely different form of instinct; and knows nothing, itself, of the *boundaries imposed on a tool by the limits of precision it has attained.* Unlike the insect, the mammal is already no longer an element strictly enslaved to the phylum on which it has appeared. An "aura" of freedom and a flicker of personality begin to hover around it. And this consequently is the direction in which unknown and never-ending possibilities outline themselves ahead.

But who, then, will eventually dash toward those promised horizons?

Let us take another and more detailed look at the immense horde of Pliocene animals, at those limbs, brought to the height of simplicity and perfection; those forests of antlers, crowning the heads of stags; those lyres, spiraling up from the starred or striped foreheads of the antelopes; those tusks weighing down the muzzles of the proboscideans; those fangs and cutting hooks in the jaws of the large carnassials. Is it not precisely such luxuriance and such achievement that condemn the future of these magnificent creatures, regardless of the vitality of their psyche? Do they not mark for imminent death, forms that are pinned in a morphological dead end? Are we not watching the end of something rather than its beginning?

Yes, true. But aside from the polycladines, the strepsiceros, the elephants, the machairodons, and so many others, *there are still the primates.*[5]

(c) *The primates.* Until now I have only mentioned the primates once or twice, in passing. When I spoke of the tree of life, I did not assign any place to these forms so close to our own. The omission was deliberate. At that point in my argument their importance still had not revealed itself; the primates could not have been understood. Now, however, after what we have seen of the hidden driving force that moves zoological evolution, at this fated moment at the close of the Tertiary they can, and must, make their entrance. Their hour has come.

Morphologically, like all other animal groups, the primates form as a whole a series of fans or overlapping verticils, clearly marked out at the periphery and blurred in the region of their peduncles (FIGURE 3).[6] At the top, we have the monkeys, properly speaking, with their two large

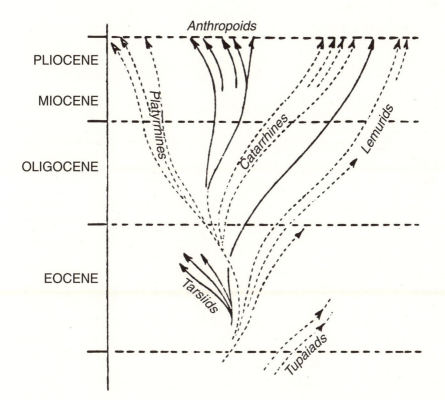

FIGURE 3   Diagram symbolizing the development of the primates.

geographical branchings: the authentic Old World catarrhine monkeys with thirty-two teeth—and the South American platyrrhine monkeys with a flat snout, all with thirty-six teeth. Below are the lemurids, which generally have an elongated snout, often with forward-slanting incisors. At the very base, at the origin of the Tertiary, these two, tiered verticils of the monkeys seem to detach from the "insectivore" fan of the tupaiads[7] and to represent a simple ray of tupaiads in a fully unfolded state. But there is something else. At the heart of each of these two verticils, we distinguish a central subverticil with forms that are particularly "cephalized." On the lemurid side, the tarsiids, tiny leaping animals with a round inflated cranium and huge eyes, whose sole survivor today, the Malaysian tarsier, strangely reminds us of a little man. On the catarrhine side, the anthropoids (gorillas, chimpanzees, orangutans, gibbons), the tailless monkeys, which are the largest and most alert monkeys, so familiar to us.

The lemurids and the tarsiers were the first to reach their apogee, toward the end of the Eocene. As for the anthropoids, they can be discerned in Africa from the Oligocene. But they evidently must not have achieved their maximum diversification and size until the close of the Pliocene, in Africa and in India, always in tropical or subtropical zones. Let us keep both this date and distribution in mind. They contain an entire lesson in themselves.

Here, therefore, is how the primates are situated from the outside, by their exterior form and in duration. Now let us penetrate the interior of things and try to understand what distinguishes these animals from the others, seen from the inside.

At first sight, what catches the anatomist's eye on observing the monkeys (and above all the higher monkeys) is the surprisingly slight degree of differentiation shown by their bones. In the monkeys, cranial capacity is relatively much more voluminous than in any other of the mammals. But what can be said about the rest? Their teeth? An isolated molar belonging to the dryopithecus[8] or to the chimpanzee can easily be mistaken for a tooth belonging to an Eocene omnivore, such as the condylarth.[9] Their limbs? With their rays wholly intact, their limbs precisely preserve the plan and proportion they had in the first tetrapods of the Paleozoic. In the course of the Tertiary, the hoofed mammals radically transformed the adjustment of their legs; the carnassials reduced and sharpened their dentition; the whales, dolphins, and porpoises retapered themselves like fishes; the proboscideans formidably complicated their incisors and molars. And all during this time, the primates were the ones who kept their ulna and fibula intact; who jealously protected their five fingers; who remained typically tritubercular. Would this mean that they are the conservatives among the mammals, the most conservative of all?

No, but they proved themselves to be the most wary.

Grasped at its optimum, differentiation of an organ is in itself immediately a factor of superiority. But because it is irreversible, differentiation also locks the animal undergoing it into a narrow path, at the end of which, under the thrust of orthogenesis, the animal risks ending up either as something monstrous or fragile. Specialization paralyzes; ultraspecialization kills. Paleontology is made up of such catastrophes. Because until the Pliocene the limbs of the primate remained the most "primitive" among the mammals, the primates remained the most *free*. Now what did they make of this freedom? They used it to lift themselves in successive bursts to the very frontiers of intelligence.

And here, simultaneously with the true definition of the primates, we have right in front of us the answer to the problem that had led us to look at the primates: "After the mammals at the close of the Tertiary, where will life be able to continue?"

First of all, we see that the interest and the biological value of the primates lie in the fact that they represent a *phylum of pure and direct cerebralization.* Certainly nervous system and instinct are gradually going to increase in other mammals as well. But in the others this internal work has been diverted, limited, and finally arrested by secondary differentiation. At the same time as their psyche was rising, the horse, the deer, and the tiger, like the insect, turned into partial prisoners of the instruments for running and catching prey *that their limbs had become.* In the primates, on the other hand, neglecting the rest and consequently allowing it to remain plastic, the evolutionary movement worked directly on the brain.

And that is why it is the primates who hold the lead in the rising advance toward greater consciousness. *In this privileged and singular case, the orthogenesis of the phylum coincides exactly with the principal orthogenesis of life itself;* according to an expression of Osborn's, which I will borrow, changing the meaning, it is "aristogenesis"—and thus limitless.

From this we draw our first conclusion, that if the mammals form a dominant branch, *the* dominant branch on the tree of life, the primates, that is the *cerebro-manuals*, are the ones who form the axis or main stem of this branch and the anthropoids the very bud in which it terminates.

And since this is the case, let us add, it is easy to decide where to fix our attention on the biosphere as we wait for what is to happen. Everywhere, as we knew before, the summits of the active phyletic lineages grow warm with consciousness. But in a clearly defined region at the center of the mammals, where the most powerful brains ever constructed by nature are being formed, they redden. And already, even, at the heart of this zone, a point of incandescence flares.

Let us not lose sight of that line crimsoned with the dawn.

After rising for thousands of years below the horizon, in a narrowly localized spot a flame is about to burst forth.

Thought is here!

Part III
Thought

Chapter I

THE BIRTH OF THOUGHT

Preliminary Observation. The Human Paradox

From a purely positivistic point of view, the human being is the most mysterious and disconcerting of subjects science has encountered. In fact, we must admit that science has not yet found a place for the human in its descriptions of the universe. Physics has succeeded provisionally in defining the world of the atom. Biology has managed to put some kind of order into the constructions of life. Based on physics and biology, anthropology in its turn in some fashion describes the structure of the human body and certain of its physiological mechanisms. But once all these traits are put together, the picture clearly does not correspond to reality. The human as reconstructed by science today is an animal like the others—whose anatomy is so little separable from the anthropoids that the most modern classifications of zoology, going back to the position of Linnaeus, include the human with them in the same superfamily of hominoids. Yet judging from the biological results of the fact of the human being's appearance, is not the human precisely something entirely different?

There is an infinitesimal morphological leap, and at the same time an incredible disturbance of the spheres of life—this is the whole human paradox. And consequently it is clear evidence that science in its present reconstructions of the world fails to grasp an essential factor, or, to be more exact, an entire dimension of the universe.

According to the general hypothesis that has guided us from the beginning of these pages toward a coherent and expressive interpretation of how the Earth looks to us at present, in this new part devoted to thought I would like to show that to give a *natural* place for the human being in the experimental world, all we need to do is to take the inside of things into account at the same time as the outside. This method has already allowed us to assess the size and direction of the vital movement. It is this same method again that, in an order harmoniously redescending on life and matter, will reconcile for our sight the insignificance and the supreme importance of the human phenomenon.

Between the last strata of the Pliocene where the human is absent and the next level where the geologist is dumbfounded to recognize the first chipped pieces of quartz, what has happened? And what is the true magnitude of the leap?

These are the questions we will somehow have to resolve and weigh, before following humanity as it advances, phase by phase, to the decisive pass it is engaged in today.

1   THE STEP OF REFLECTION

A. The Elementary Step: Hominization of the Individual

(a) Nature

Just as uncertainty still prevails among biologists about the existence of a direction, and therefore even more, a definite axis, of evolution—so for a related reason the widest divergence of opinion can still be seen among psychologists about whether or not the human psyche differs specifically (by "nature") from the psyche of the beings that came before it. In fact, the majority of "scientists" rather tend to contest the validity of such a break. How much has been said and is still being said about animal intelligence!

If we are to settle this question of the "superiority" of the human over the animal (as necessary to decide for the ethics of life as for purely intellectual reasons), I see only one way: to resolutely put aside all secondary and equivocal manifestations of internal activity in the network of human behaviors and to squarely confront the central phenomenon of *reflection*.[1]

From the experimental point of view we take here, reflection, as the world itself indicates, is the power acquired by a consciousness of turning in on itself and taking possession of itself *as an object* endowed with its own particular consistency and value: no longer only to know something—but to know *itself*; no longer only to know, but to know that it knows. Having until then been scattered and divided over a diffuse circle of perceptions and activities, by this individualization of itself in the depths of itself, the living element is formed for the first time into a punctiform *center*, where all representations and all experiences join together and consolidate into a whole that is conscious of its organization.

Now what are the consequences of such a transformation? They are immense, and as clearly visible to us in nature as any of the other facts registered by physics or astronomy. By its very turning in on itself, the reflective being suddenly becomes capable of developing within a new sphere. Actually, another world is born. A world of abstraction, logic, systematic choice and invention, of mathematics, art, calculated perception of space and duration, of anxieties and dreams of love. All these activities of *the inner life* are nothing but the effervescence of the newly formed center exploding on itself.

Having said this, now I ask, as it follows from the preceding, if what constitutes the truly "intelligent" being is the fact of being "reflective," how can we seriously doubt that intelligence is the evolutionary endowment of the human being *alone*? And consequently, how can we hesitate from some kind of false modesty to acknowledge that for the human to possess it represents a radical advance over all of life that has come before? The animal *knows*, of course, but certainly *it does not know that it knows*; or a long time before this it would have multiplied inventions and developed a system of internal constructions that could not have escaped our observation. As a result, a domain of reality remains closed to it, in which we ourselves move, but where it can never enter. A gulf—or threshold—lies between us that it can never cross. Because we are reflective, we are not only different from the animal, but something entirely other. There is not merely a change in degree, but a change in nature, as a result of a change in state.

And here we come face to face with exactly what we expected (the chapter on Demeter ended in this expectation). Because life is a rise of consciousness, it could not continue to advance indefinitely along the same line without undergoing a radical transformation. Like every increasing magnitude in the world, to remain itself, life, as we said, had to become different. More clearly definable than when we scrutinized the obscure psyche of the first cells, what is revealed to us here in the access to the power of reflection is the specific and critical form of transformation for life in which this supercreation—or rebirth—consisted. And here at the same time we see the entire curve of biogenesis reappearing, summarized and clarified in this singular point.

(b) Theoretical Mechanism

In every age, naturalists and philosophers have upheld the most contradictory theses about the nature of the animal psyche. For traditional Scholastic thinking, instinct is a kind of homogeneous and fixed subintelligence that marks one of the ontological and logical stages through which being "degrades," in a spectrum that extends from pure spirit to pure materiality. For the Cartesian, thought alone exists; and the animal is only an automaton, devoid of any inside. Finally, as I mentioned above, for most modern biologists, nothing clearly separates instinct from thought—neither being much more than a kind of luminescence enveloping the only thing essential, the play of matter's determinisms.

The truth, as well as error, in all these various opinions becomes apparent when, putting ourselves in the perspectives of these pages, we decide to recognize that: (1) far from being an epiphenomenon, instinct in its various expressions translates *the* vital phenomenon itself; and that (2) it consequently represents a *variable* magnitude.

If we look at nature from this angle, what is really happening?

First of all, our mind realizes more clearly the fact and reason for the *diversity* of animal behaviors. From the moment evolution becomes a primarily psychic transformation, we see that in nature there is not just *one* instinct, but a multitude of forms of instincts, each one corresponding to a specific solution for the problem of life. The psyche of an insect cannot (and can never) be that of a vertebrate—nor can the instinct of a squirrel be that of a cat or an elephant—and this by very virtue of the position each one has on the tree of life.

From the very fact of this variety, we begin to see some kind of configuration emerge and the outlines of a gradation. If instinct is of variable magnitude, the different instincts cannot simply be diverse: beneath their complexity they must form a growing system—as a whole they outline a kind of fan, where, on each vein, the higher terms are seen, each time, to have reached a wider range of choice based on a better defined center of coordination and consciousness. And that is precisely what we do see. Whatever else we might say, the psyche of a dog is positively higher than the psyche of a mole or fish.*

Having said as much, where all I have done is to present what the study of life has already shown us, but from another angle, the proponents of the spiritual view can rest assured when they notice, or someone forces them to see, mannerisms and reactions in the higher animals (the larger monkeys in particular) that are strangely reminiscent of those they themselves have used to define the nature and claim the presence in the human of a "rational soul." If, as we have said, the history of life is nothing but the movement of consciousness veiled in morphology, it is inevitable that toward the summit of the series, in the vicinity of the human, psyches occur and appear to be *at the full bloom of intelligence*. Which is exactly what happens.

---

* From this point of view one could say that every form of instinct tends in its own way to become "intelligence"; but it is only along human lines (for extrinsic and intrinsic reasons) that the operation has been successful to the very end. Thus, having reached the reflective state, the human being would represent just one of the innumerable modalities of consciousness life has tried in the animal world. With just as many psychic worlds that it is very difficult for us to enter into, not only because the knowledge of something is more confused there, but because it functions in a different way from our own.[2]

And this being the case, the "human paradox" itself is clarified. In spite of certain incontrovertible mental superiorities, it is disturbing for us to observe how little "anthropos" differs anatomically from the other anthropoids—so disturbing that we almost give up trying to separate them, at least toward their point of origin. But is not this extraordinary resemblance exactly what had to happen?

When water under normal pressure has reached 100 degrees Celsius, and we continue to heat it, the first event that follows—without a change in temperature—is the tumultuous expansion of freed and vaporized molecules. And when section follows section of a constantly decreasing area along the rising axis of a cone, the moment comes when, through another infinitesimal displacement, the surface vanishes, having become a *point*. It is by remote comparisons such as these that we can imagine what the mechanism of the critical step of reflection must have been like.

At the end of the Tertiary, psychic temperature in the cellular world had been rising for more than 500 million years. At the same pace, from main branch to main branch, layer to layer, as we have seen, nervous systems continued to become more and more complicated and concentrated. Finally, on the primate side, so remarkably supple and rich an instrument had been constructed that the step immediately following could only be made if the entire animal psyche were to be recast and consolidated on itself. Yet this movement did not stop, for there was nothing in the structure of the organism to prevent it from going ahead. To the anthropoid, "mentally" brought to 100 degrees, a few more calories had therefore been added. In the anthropoid, having almost reached the summit of the cone, a final effort was exerted along the axis. And nothing more was needed for the entire inner equilibrium to be turned upside down. What was still only a centered surface became a center. Through an infinitesimal "tangential" increase, the "radial" turned around and, so to speak, leaped infinitely ahead. Hardly anything had apparently changed in the organs. But a great revolution had occurred deep within: consciousness was now leaping and boiling in a space of supersentient relationships and representations; and simultaneously consciousness was capable of perceiving itself in the gathered simplicity of its faculties—and all that for the first time. *

The proponents of a spiritual view are right when they so hotly defend

---

* Need I repeat once again that I restrict myself here to the phenomenon, that is, to the experimental relationships between consciousness and complexity, without prejudging in the least what action from deeper causes might be calling the play. By virtue of the limitations imposed on our sensory knowledge by the play of the temporal-spatial series, it seems that it is only *under the appearances* of a critical point that we can experimentally grasp the hominizing (spiritualizing) step of

a certain transcendence of the human being over the rest of nature. Materialists are not wrong, either, when they maintain that the human being is only one more term in the series of animal forms. Here, as in so many other cases, two antithetical facts are resolved in a movement— provided that the essential part in this movement is given to the highly natural phenomenon of "changes of state." From the cell to the thinking animal, as from the atom to the cell, a single process (psychic heating up or concentration) goes on without interruption, and always in the same direction. But by virtue of this permanence in the operation itself, it is inevitable from the standpoint of physics that certain leaps abruptly transform the subject undergoing the operation.

(c) Realization

The birth of thought presents itself to us in the theory of its mechanism as a discontinuity in continuity, just like the first appearance of life.

And now, how did this mechanism come into play in its concrete reality? How much of the metamorphosis would have outwardly filtered through to an observer, a theoretical witness to the crisis?

As I soon will say in treating the "outward appearances of the original humans,"[3] this representation we are so eager for will probably remain as impossible for our mind as the origin of life itself—and for the same reasons. In this case, the greatest resource we have to guide us is contemplating the awakening of intelligence in the child during the course of ontogenesis. Still it is worth making two observations—one of them circumscribing for our imagination the mystery that shrouds this singular point, the other deepening it even further.

The first is that to end up in the human being at the step of reflection, it was necessary for life to prepare, long beforehand and simultaneously, a network of factors that at first glance had nothing about them to suggest any "providential" connection.

Ultimately it is true that from the organic point of view the entire hominizing metamorphosis comes down to the question of a better brain. But how did this cerebral perfecting take place—how could it have functioned—unless a whole series of other conditions had been realized together precisely at the same time? If the living being the human was born

---

reflection. But having said this, there is nothing to prevent the thinker adopting a spiritual explanation—for reasons of a higher order and at a subsequent phase of dialectic—from placing any "creative operation" or "special intervention" one might wish *under the phenomenal veil* of a revolutionary transformation (cf. "Author's Note"). Actually, is it not a universally accepted principle of Christian thought in its theological interpretation of reality that for our mind there are different and successive (yet coherent) levels of knowledge?

of had not been a biped, its hands would not have been free in time enough to relieve the jaws of their prehensile function, and as a result the thick band of maxillary muscles that imprisoned the skull would not have been relaxed. Thanks to bipedalism freeing the hands the brain could enlarge; and thanks to it at the same time the eyes, drawing near to each other on the diminished face, could begin to converge and fix their gaze on what the hands took hold of, brought near, and, in every sense of the word, presented: the very act of reflection, exteriorized! In itself there is nothing surprising in this marvelous conjunction. Is not the smallest thing formed in the word in this way always the fruit of an incredible coincidence—a knot of fibers running together forever from the four corners of space? Life works not by following an isolated thread or by starting over again. It pushes its whole net ahead at the same time. This is how the embryo is formed in the womb that bears it. We should have known. And this is precisely why we feel some satisfaction in recognizing that the human being was born under the same maternal law. We are glad to admit that the birth of intelligence corresponds to a turning back on itself, not only of the nervous system, but of the entire being. On the contrary, what frightens us at first sight is to have to see that for this step to be taken, it had to be made *all at once*.

For this must be my second observation—one that is unavoidable. In the case of human ontogenesis we can slide over the problem of knowing the exact moment when the newborn child can be said to reach intelligence and become a thinking being; in the same individual a continuous series of *states* succeed each other from ovum to adult. What does it matter where the place is, or even that a break exists? But in the case of phyletic embryogenesis, where each stage, each state, is represented by a *different being*, the situation is entirely different. Here there is no way of avoiding the problem of discontinuity (at least with our present methods of thought). If, as its physical nature seems to require, and as we have admitted, the passage to reflection is truly a critical transformation, a mutation from zero to everything, it is impossible for us to represent for ourselves an intermediary individual at this precise level. Either the being has to be still on this side—or else already on that side—of the change of state. Whatever way we choose to look at the problem, either we have to make thought unthinkable in denying its psychic transcendence over instinct, or else we have to resign ourselves to admitting that it made its appearance *between* two individuals.[4]

Certainly the terms of this proposition are disconcerting, but the proposition becomes less strange, inoffensive, even, if we notice that speaking strictly scientifically, nothing prevents us from assuming that intelligence could (or even must) have been outwardly as imperceptible at its phyletic origins, as it still is for our eyes at the ontogenic stage in each newborn child. In which case, all tangible subject for debate between observer and theorist vanishes.

And this fails to account for the fact (the second form of the "imperceptible," see below, p. 127*) that today all scientific debate has become impossible about the probable outward appearance presented by the first emergence of reflection on Earth (even supposing it to have been perceptible to a contemporary spectator): since right here, if anywhere, we are in the presence of one of those *beginnings* (those infinitely small "evolutionary quantities") automatically and irremediably removed from our sight by a sufficient thickness of the past (see above, p. 75†).

Without trying to picture for ourselves the unimaginable, let us therefore only keep in mind that the access to thought represents a threshold—a threshold that must be crossed with one step. A "transexperimental interval" about which we can say nothing scientifically, but beyond which we find ourselves transported to an entirely new biological level.

(d) Prolongation

And it is only here that the nature of the step of reflection is fully disclosed. First of all, it is a change of state. But then, from this very fact, it is the beginning of another kind of life, precisely that inner life I introduced above. A moment ago we compared the simplicity of the thinking mind to a geometrical point. But we should have spoken of it rather as a line or axis. For the intelligence, to be "posited" does not mean, to be actually "completed." No sooner is the infant born, than it must breathe, or it dies. In the same way, once gathered on itself, the reflective psychic center can subsist only through a double movement in one: centering itself further on itself by penetrating into a new space; and at the same time centering the rest of the world around it by establishing a continually more coherent and better organized perspective among the realities that surround it. Not as the immutably fixed focal point, but the vortex, deepening as it sucks up the fluid at the core of which it is born. The "I," which subsists only in becoming more and more itself, in the degree to which it makes everything else itself. *The person in and through personalization.*

Clearly the entire structure of life is modified by the effects of such a transformation. Until then the animate element was so strictly a slave to the phylum that its own individuality could have seemed secondary and sacrificed. Receiving, preserving, and if possible acquiring, reproducing, and transmitting. And so on and on, unremittingly. Caught in the chain of generations, the animal seemed to have no right to live, and it had no apparent value in itself. Except as a fleeting toehold for a race that passed over it, unaware of its existence. Life, once again, more real than lives.

After the appearance of the reflective, which is fundamentally a property of the element (at least to begin with!), everything changes, and we then begin to see that secretly beneath the more striking reality of collective transformations, a parallel advance to individuation was being carried out. The more charged with psyche each phylum became, the more it tended to "granulate," with a growing self-actualization of the animal in relation to its species. Finally, at the level of the human being, the phenomenon accelerates and takes a definitive form. Now that the "person" has been endowed by "personalization" with an indefinite power of elementary evolution, the branch ceases to bear the exclusive promises of the future in its anonymous whole. The cell has become "someone." After the grain of matter, after the grain of life, here, finally constituted, is the *grain of thought*!

But does this mean that from this moment on the phylum loses its function and volatilizes, like those animals lost in the dust of germs they give birth to as they die? Above the point of reflection, does the whole interest of evolution reverse, to pass from life into a plurality of isolated living beings?

Nothing of the kind. It only means that, without stopping in the slightest, from this crucial date, the global outpouring gains a degree, an order of complexity. No, because from now on the phylum is charged with thinking centers, it does not break like a fragile spray; it does not dissipate into its elementary psyches, on the contrary, as it is lined interiorly with another armature, it becomes reinforced. Until then it was enough for us to take into account a simple broad vibration in nature: the rise of conscious*ness*. From now on it is going to be a question of defining and harmonizing in its laws a rise of conscious*nesses* (a much more delicate phenomenon!). A progress made of other progresses as durable as itself. A movement of movements.

Let us try to lift ourselves high enough to get a perspective on the problem. And to do this, let us temporarily forget the individual destiny of the spiritual elements engaged in the general transformation. It is only by following the rise and spreading out of the whole in its main outlines, that we can arrive, by means of a long detour, at a determination of what part is reserved for the individual in the overall success of the whole.

It is through the hominization of the entire group that we shall reach the personalization of the individual!

<u>B</u>. The Phyletic Step: Hominization of the Species

So then, across the leap of intelligence, whose nature and mechanism we have just analyzed for the thinking particle, life somehow continues spreading out as though nothing had happened. Evidently, in both animal

117

and human, multiplication and ramification pursue their customary course, after, as well as before, the threshold of thought. One might say that nothing in the current had been modified. Yet the waters have already changed. Like the torrents of a river enriched by contact with a silted plain, as it crossed through the passes of reflection the vital flux has been charged with new principles; and as a result is going to manifest new activities. From now on it is not only animal grains that are being tossed and propelled along in the living stem by the evolutionary sap, but, as we said, grains of thought. What signs of this influence will show in the color or form of the leaves, the flowers, the fruit?

It is not possible to answer this question immediately in any detail or depth without jumping ahead to developments which come later. But what does seem appropriate to mention here right away is that, from the step of thought onward, three distinctive characteristics are going to manifest themselves in all operations or productions of the species, whatever they might be. The first of these characteristics has to do with the composition of the new branches—another with their general direction of growth—and finally, the last, with how as a whole they are related to or different from what had opened out before them on the tree of life.

(a) The Composition of the Human Branches

Whatever idea we may have formed about the internal mechanism of evolution, one thing is certain, that each zoological group is surrounded by some psychological envelope. This was what we said above (p. 112). Each type of insect, bird, or mammal has its own instinct. Up to now there has been no systematic attempt to connect both somatic and psychic elements of the species. Some naturalists describe and classify forms. Others specialize in behavioral studies. Below the human it actually works very well to use methods that have purely morphological criteria for the distribution of species. But from the human on there are evident difficulties. We are well aware of the extreme confusion still reigning today about the significance and distribution of the vast variety of groups into which the human mass is fragmented right before our eyes: races, nations, states, countries, cultures, and so on. Ordinarily we tend only to see these diverse and shifting categories as heterogeneous units overlapping each other irregularly at different levels, some natural (race . . .) and others artificial (nation . . .).

Yet this unpleasant and needless kind of irregularity vanishes once the slightest place is given to the inside as well as the outside of things!

From this more comprehensive viewpoint, even though it seems to be so mixed, the composition of the human group and branches can apparently still be reduced to the general laws of biology. In fact, by exaggeration of a variable that remained negligible among animals, the composition simply reveals the fundamentally double weave of these laws, if not the contrary, their fundamental unity (if soma itself is woven by psyche . . .). It is not an exception to, but a generalization of, these laws. There is no doubt about it. In the world become human it is certainly still the same zoological ramification that, in spite of all appearances and complexities, continues to prolong itself and to operate according to the same mechanism as before. Only, as a result of the quantity of internal energy freed by reflection, in this case the operation tends to emerge from material organs and to be formulated *also*, or even *above all* in the mind. Psychic spontaneity is no longer only an aura of the somatic. It becomes the appreciable, or even principal, part of the phenomenon. And because variations in intellect are much richer and have many more nuances than the often imperceptible organic alterations that accompany them, it is very evident why an inspection of bones and integuments alone can no longer manage to follow, explain, and catalogue the progress of the entire zoological differentiation. That is the situation. And the remedy for it as well. Anatomy alone is no longer enough to unravel the structure of the thinking phylum, because from now on it must be accompanied by psychology.

Granted this is a laborious kind of complication, since it is clearly only through the combined play of two partially independent variables that any satisfactory classification of the human "genus" can be established. But it is also fruitful, and for two reasons.

On the one hand, at the price of this difficulty, order and homogeneity, that is to say, truth, are reintroduced into our perspectives of life extended to the human; and because, correlatively, the organic value of all social constructions is revealed to us, we already feel more disposed to treat it as a subject for science, and therefore to respect it.

On the other hand, from the very fact that the fibers of the human phylum are shown to be surrounded by their psychic sheath, we begin to understand why they present such an extraordinary power of agglutinization and coalescence. And here, simultaneously, we find ourselves on the path of a fundamental discovery, in which our study of the human phenomenon will finally culminate: the "convergence of the personal."[5]

(b) The General Direction of Growth

As long as our perspectives on the psychic nature of zoological evolution rested only on the examination of animal lineages and their nervous systems, knowledge of the direction of this evolutionary movement was also bound to remain as vague to us as the intellect itself of these distant brothers. Consciousness rises through living beings, was all we could say. The moment, on the other hand, that life, having crossed the threshold of thought, not only gains access to the level where we ourselves are now, but also begins by its free activities to openly spill over the limits into which it has been channeled by its physiological requirements, its progress becomes easier for us to decipher. The message is more clearly written and we can also read it better because we recognize ourselves in it. Above, as we observed the tree of life, we noted the fundamental characteristic that along each zoological branch brains increase in size and become differentiated. To define the extension and equivalent of this law above the step of reflection, it will be enough from now on for us to say: "Along each anthropological lineage, the human seeks itself and grows."[6]

Just a moment ago, in passing I called to mind the image of the human group in its unparalleled complexity: those races, nations, and states whose entanglement defies the discernment of anatomists and of ethnology. The fact of so many rays in the spectrum discourages analysis. Let us rather try to perceive what this multiplicity represents when taken as a whole. We will then see that its disconcerting assemblage is nothing but a massing of sequins, sending back the same light to one another by reflection. Hundreds of thousands of facets, but each one expressing from a different angle a reality that seeks itself among a world of groping forms. We are not surprised (because it is happening to *us*) to see the spark of reflection developing in each person around us from year to year. Also, we are at least vaguely conscious that in the course of history *something* in our atmosphere is changing. But putting these two facts together and at the same time correcting certain exaggerated views on the purely "germinal" and passive nature of heredity, why is it, then, that we are not more sensitive to the presence of something on the move at the heart of us that is greater than ourselves?

Up to the level of thought we could still pose a question to the natural sciences about the value and transmission of acquired characteristics. As we know, biology tended and still proves itself to be evasive and skeptical about this question. And after all, within the fixed zones of the body to which it would like to restrict itself, perhaps it is right. But what happens if we give the psychic its legitimate place in the integrity of living organisms? Immediately the individual activity of the soma asserts its rights over the alleged independence of the phyletic "germ plasm." Underlying the play of animal spontaneities in the insects, for example, or with the beaver, we already grasp, and in a blatant way, the existence of instincts that are hereditarily formed or even fixed. From reflection onward, the reality of this mechanism becomes not only evident but preponderant. Under the free and ingenious effort of successive intelligences, in the course of the ages quite obviously *something* is irreversibly accumulating (even in the absence of any measurable variation of skull or brain) and being transmitted, at least collectively, through education. We will come back to this. Now this "something," whether a material construction or construct of beauty, system of thought or system of action, always ends up translating itself into an increase of consciousness—consciousness, in turn, as we know now, being nothing less than the substance and blood of life as it evolves.

But what does this mean except that, over and above the particular phenomenon of individual access to reflection, there is room for science to recognize another phenomenon of the reflective kind, but this time of total human extension! Here, too, as everywhere else in the universe, the whole reveals itself to be greater than the simple sum of the elements of which it is formed. No, the human individual does not exhaust in itself the vital possibilities of its race. But along each of the threads distinguished by anthropology and sociology, a hereditary and collective current of reflection is being established and propagated: the advent of humanity through the varieties of the human—the emergence of the human branch through human phylogenesis.[7]

(c) Relationships and Differences

Having seen and accepted this, under what form are we to expect this human branch to spring up? Since it is a thinking branch, is it going to break the fibers attaching it to the past—and develop, from new elements and on an entirely new plane, at the summit of the vertebrate branch like some kind of neoplasm? Once again, it would be a mistake to imagine such a break and to underestimate the organic unity of the world and the methods of evolution at the same time as our own "greatness." In a flower, the parts—the calyx, the sepals, petals, stamen, and the pistil—are not leaves. They probably never were. But they bear, recognizable in their attachments and texture, all that a leaf would have given had they not been shaped by a new influence and a new destiny. Similarly, in the human inflorescence are found, transformed and in process of transformation, all the vessels, dispositions, and even the sap of the stem on which this inflorescence is born; not only the individual structure of organs and interior ramifications of species, but even the tendencies of "soul" and its behaviors.

In humans considered as a zoological group, everything is prolonged simultaneously: sexual attraction, with the laws of reproduction; the tendency toward struggle for life, with its competitiveness; the need to be nourished, with its taste for seizing and devouring; the curiosity for seeing things, with its pleasure of investigation; the attraction for drawing closer so as to live together. Each of these fibers runs through each one of us, coming from below us and rising higher, so that for each one of them the story (no less true for this) of its entire evolution could be told: the evolution of love, the evolution of war, the evolution of research, the evolution of the social sense. But each one of them, precisely because it is evolutionary, also undergoes metamorphosis at the passage to reflection. And from there it sets out again, enriched with new possibilities, new colors, and new fruitfulness. In some sense remaining the same thing. But also becoming entirely different. The shape transforming as it changes space and dimensions. With, once again, discontinuity following on continuity. Mutation on evolution.

In this supple inflection, this harmonious recasting which transfigures the whole external and internal network of vital antecedents, how can we fail to find the priceless confirmation of everything we have already supposed? When something begins to grow through something secondary to itself, it is thrown off balance and becomes deformed. To remain symmetrical and beautiful, a body must be modified as a whole, simultaneously, following one of its principal axes. Reflection, as it reshapes them, conserves all the lines of the phylum on which it rests. And thus it does not represent the fortuitous excrescence of a parasitic energy. The human species progresses only in slowly elaborating from age to age the essence and totality of a universe deposited within us.[8]

To this great process of sublimation, it is fitting we apply the term *hominization* in its fullest sense. Hominization, which at first, we could say, is the individual instantaneous leap from instinct to thought, but which also in the wider sense is the progressive phyletic spiritualization in human civilization of all the forces contained in animality.

And here, having considered the element—having envisaged the species, we are led to look at the whole Earth.

C. The Planetary Terrestrial Step: The Noosphere

Observed in relation to all the living verticils as a whole, the human phylum is not like other phyla. Because the specific orthogenesis of the primates (driving them toward growing cerebralization) coincides with the axial orthogenesis of organized matter (driving all living beings toward a higher consciousness), the human, having appeared at the heart of the primates, unfolds on the main stem of zoological evolution. It was in this observation, as we remember, that our considerations of the state of the Pliocene world culminated.

What privileged value will this unique situation confer on the step of reflection?

It is easy to see.

The change of biological state ending up in the awakening of thought does not simply correspond to a critical point passed through by the individual, or even by the species. Vaster than that, it affects life itself in its organic totality, and consequently it marks a transformation that affects the state of the whole planet.

It is this evidence, born of all the others gradually added and linked together in the course of our inquiry, that irresistibly imposes itself on our logic and our sight.

From the time of the floating contours of the juvenile Earth, we have continued to follow the successive stages of one great event. Beneath the pulsations of geochemistry, geotechtonics, and geobiology,[9] we could always recognize one and the same fundamental process, which, after having materialized in the first cells, prolonged itself in the building up of nervous systems. Geogenesis, as we said, emigrating into biogenesis, which ultimately turned out to be nothing else but psychogenesis.

With and in the crisis of reflection, no less than the next term of the series is uncovered. Psychogenesis had led us to the human being. Now it vanishes, replaced or absorbed by a higher function: first to give birth to mind, then later to all its developments—*noogenesis*. When instinct, in a living being, saw itself in the mirror of itself for the first time, the whole world took a step.

For the choices and responsibilities of our actions, the consequences of this discovery are enormous. We will come back to this. For our understanding of the Earth, they are decisive.

The zonal composition of our planet has long been agreed on and accepted by geologists. We have already mentioned the central, metallic barysphere—surrounded by its rocky lithosphere—itself surmounted by the fluid layers of hydrosphere and atmosphere. To these four overlapping surfaces, from the time of Seuss, science habitually, and with good reason, adds the living membrane formed by the plant and animal matting of the globe: the biosphere,[10] mentioned so often in these pages; as distinctly universal an envelope as the other "spheres," and even much more distinctly individualized than they, since, instead of representing a somewhat loose grouping, it all forms a single piece—the very tissue of genetic relations, which, once deployed and set in place, makes the pattern of the tree of life.

From having recognized and isolated the new era of noogenesis in the history of evolution, we are obliged correlatively to distinguish among the majestic assemblage of telluric sheets a support proportional to the operation; another membrane: the advances of a circle of fire around the spark made by the first reflective consciousnesses. The point of ignition has expanded. The fire has spread from place to place. Finally it has covered the whole planet with incandescence. Only one interpretation and one name are on the scale of this great phenomenon. Just as extensive but even more coherent still, as we will see, than all the preceding layers, it truly is a new layer, the "thinking layer," that, after having germinated at the close of the Tertiary, since that time has been spreading out on top of the plant and animal world. Over and beyond the biosphere there is a *noosphere*.[11]

Here we can see the blatant disproportion that distorts any classification of the living world (and indirectly any construction of the physical world) in which the human logically figures only as a genus, or a new family. This error of perspective deforms and strips the universal phenomenon of its crown! To give the human its true place in nature, it is not enough just to open a supplementary division within the context of systematics—or even one more order or branch. Despite the insignificance of the anatomical leap, through hominization a new age begins. The Earth "makes a new skin." Better still, it finds its soul.

And consequently, once the historic step of reflection is put back into the true dimensions of things, it becomes something much greater than any zoological break marking the origin of the tetrapods, or even of the metazoans themselves. Among the grades successfully crossed by evolution, the birth of thought directly follows in order of magnitude, and can only be compared to, the condensation of terrestrial chemisms or the appearance of life itself.

The human paradox resolves itself by becoming immeasurable!

Despite the depth and harmony this perspective brings to things, at first sight we find it unsettling because it runs counter to the illusion and habits that tend to make us measure events by their material aspect. It seems so immeasurable to us because, drowned in the human as we are, like fish in the sea, it is difficult for us to emerge from it mentally to appreciate its specificity and sheer size. But let us look around us more carefully at such a sudden deluge of cerebration, such a biological invasion by a new animal type gradually eliminating or subjugating every form of life that is not human; such an irresistible tide of fields and factories; such an immense and growing edifice of material and ideas. Do not all these signs we see all day long without trying to understand them, cry out to us that something on the Earth has changed "planetarily"?

Actually, for an imaginary geologist who might come in the distant future to inspect our fossilized globe, the most astounding of revolutions experienced by the Earth would unequivocally be put at the beginning of what has been so aptly called the *Psychozoic Era*. And at that very moment, for some Martian capable of analyzing sidereal radiations psychically as much as physically, the primary characteristic of our planet certainly would not seem to be how blue it is with seas or green with forests—but how phosphorescent with thought.

What might be most revealing of all for our modern science is to perceive how everything precious, everything active and progressive originally contained in the cosmic fragment from which our world has come, is now concentrated in the "corona" of a noosphere.

And what is supremely instructive at the origin of this noosphere (if we know how to see!) is to notice how *imperceptibly* the event its birth represents took place, having been so universally and so long prepared.

The human came into the world silently . . .

2   THE ORIGINAL FORMS

The human being came silently . . .

After almost a century in which the scientific problem of human origins has been posed—a century in which an ever-swelling team of researchers has been passionately at work excavating the past at its initial point of hominization—I fail to find any more expressive formula than this to summarize the discoveries of prehistory. However unique it might be at the entitive level to which reflection has brought it, through the continual multiplication of human fossil finds and the increasing clarity of their anatomical characteristics and geological succession, from the continual convergence of all signs and proofs, the more evident it has become that the human species disturbed nothing in nature at the moment of its appearance. In fact, if we look at it in light of its surrounding forms—or consider it in the morphology of its stem—or inspect it in terms of the global structure of its group, in our eyes it emerges phyletically *like any other* species.

In its surrounding forms, first of all. As we know from paleontology, no animal form ever appears in isolation, but is outlined at the heart of a verticil of neighboring forms, among whom it takes shape gradually as if by trial and error. The human is the same. Considered zoologically the human cuts an almost solitary figure in nature today, yet was much more closely surrounded in the cradle. It is now well established that, over a clearly-defined but immense zone extending from southern Africa to South China and Malaya, at the end of the Tertiary the anthropoids were far more numerous in the rocky terrains and forests than they are still at present. Alongside the gorilla, the chimpanzee, and the orangutan, which have now retreated into their last places of refuge, as have today's Australian aborigines and the African pygmies, at that time there existed another population of large primates. And among these forms there seem to have been certain types such as the australopithecines of Africa, for example, that were much more hominoid than any known to exist today.

In the morphology of its stem, next. Besides the multiplication of "sister-forms," another sign for the naturalist of the origin of a living branch is a certain convergence of that branch's axis with the axis of neighboring branches. As leaves approach a node, they draw close to each other. Grasped in its nascent state, not only does a species form a bouquet with others, but it still shows visible signs of its zoological kinship with them much more clearly than in adulthood. The further we follow an animal lineage back into the past, the more numerous and clear in it are the "primitive" traits. Here again, the human on the whole rigorously obeys the habitual mechanism of the phyletic. We only need to see what happens when we try to put *Pithecanthropus* and *Sinanthropus*, in descending order, after the Neanderthaloids, below the human existing today. Paleontology does not often manage to trace such a satisfactory lineage.

In the structure of its group, finally. However clearly delineated a phylum is in its characteristics, we never come upon one in a wholly simple state, as a pure radiation. But as far down as we have been able to follow it, it continues to show an internal tendency toward cleavage and dispersion. From the moment it is born—even right as it is being born—the species already fragments into varieties or subspecies. This is a well-known fact to any naturalist. Keeping this clearly in mind, let us turn one last time toward the human being—whose most ancient prehistory, even, does nothing but analyze, and thus prove, the human's congenital aptitude for ramifying. Can there be any doubt that we humans ourselves are isolated as a fan within the fan of the anthropoids, subject in this to the laws of all animate matter?

Therefore I am not exaggerating in the least. The more science plumbs the past of our humanity, the more it conforms, *insofar as it is a species*, to the rules and rhythm that have marked each new burgeoning before it on the tree of life. But in this case we need to follow our logic to the end— and take one last step. Since the birth of the human species is so similar to that of all the other phyla, let us stop being surprised that, just as with the rest of the living assemblages, the fragile secrets and very first origins of the human being elude our techniques; and from now on let us refrain from trying to force and falsify this natural condition with inappropriate questions.

The human came silently, as I said. In fact, the human tread so softly that when we begin to catch sight of human traces, betrayed by the indelible stone tools that multiply the human presence, the Old World from the Cape of Good Hope to Peking is already covered by humans. It is certain that the human already speaks and lives in groups, and already makes fire. But after all, is this not precisely what we should have expected? Surely we know that every time a new living form arises before our eyes from the depths of history, it springs up in its finished state and is already legion?

In the eyes of science, therefore, which from so far away can only see things as a whole, the "first human" is, and can only be, *a crowd*; whose youth is made up of thousands and thousands of years.*

It is inevitable that this situation is disappointing for us, leaving our curiosity unsatisfied. Are we not precisely the most concerned about what could have happened in the course of those first thousands of years? And even more about what might have marked that first moment? How we long to know what our first parents looked like outwardly on the very edge of the gulf of reflection, just after it had been crossed. The leap, as I said, had to be made in a single stride. Just imagine what the past would have looked like photographed section by section: at that critical moment of first hominization, what would we see unfolding on our film as we develop it?

If we have any comprehension of the limits of enlargement imposed by nature on the instrument helping us search the skies of the past, we would let go of these fruitless desires—and we will see why. No photograph can ever record on the human phylum that passage to reflection which so rightfully intrigues us, for the simple reason that the phenomenon took place at the interior of what is *always* missing in a reconstructed phylum: the peduncle of its original forms.[13]

If it is true that the tangible forms of this peduncle elude us, can we at least make an indirect guess at its complexity and initial structure? Paleontology still has no fixed opinion on these points. But it is possible to try to form an opinion for ourselves.†

Some of the best anthropologists hold that the peduncle of our race must have been composed of several related but distinct groupings. Just as the same idea can spring to light simultaneously throughout the human intellectual milieu when it has reached a certain degree of preparation and tension, so they estimate humans must have begun simultaneously in different regions throughout the Pliocene anthropoid stratum, and this would in fact be the mechanism for every living thing.

---

* This is why the problem of *monogenism* in the strict sense (I do not say, "of *monophyletism*"—see what follows below) seems to elude science by its very nature. For in the depths of time where hominization takes place, the presence and movements of a unique couple are positively imperceptible and indecipherable for our direct sight at any degree of magnification. So that we might say that in *this interval* there is room for everything that a transexperimental source of knowledge might require.[12]
† The case of the Australopithecines mentioned above may offer the suggestion of an idea of how the passage to the human being was made zoologically. In this family of South African Pliocene anthropomorphs (a group evidently in an active state of mutation), where a whole series of hominoid characteristics appeared dispersed over a still clearly simian background, we perhaps grasp an image or the faint echo, even, of what was happening at about the same epoch, and even not far from there, in another group of anthropoids, who ended up in true hominization.

Not "polyphyletism," strictly speaking, since the various germination points would be localized on the same zoological sheet; but an extensive mutation of the entire sheet. "Hologenesis" and therefore polycentricity. With a whole series of hominization points widely disseminated along a subtropical zone of the Earth; and consequently with various human lineages genetically fusing somewhere *beneath* reflection. Not a focal point, but a "front" of evolutionary movement.

Without disputing the scientific value and probability of this perspective, I personally feel drawn to a hypothesis with a slightly different emphasis. Several times already I have stressed the distinctive feature that zoological branches show of bearing certain traits attached to them as if they were fundamental characteristics, but whose origin is clearly particular and accidental: the tritubercular teeth and seven cervical vertebrae of the higher mammals; the tetrapodism of walking vertebrates; the unilateral rotary power of organized substances. Precisely because these are secondary and accidental traits, their universal occurrence, sometimes in immense groups, can, as I said, be adequately explained only if these groups have unfolded from a main bud that was highly individualized and therefore extremely localized. With perhaps nothing more at the origin than a simple ray with a verticil to support a layer, or a main branch, even, or even the whole of life. Or, if some convergence has come into play, this only could be a factor between fibers extremely close to each other.

Influenced by these kinds of considerations, and above all, given a group as homogeneous and specialized as the group we are concerned with here, I would be inclined to minimize as much as possible the effects of parallelism on the initial formation of the human branch. In my opinion the human branch has not gleaned its fibers here and there, thread by thread, from all the rays on the verticil of the higher primates. But it more nearly than any other species represents, at most, the thickening and success of a single stem among all others—this stem, moreover, being the most central of the spray because it is the most vigorous and the least specialized, except for its brain. All human lineages, in this case, would join genetically toward their base at the point of reflection itself.*

Beyond this, if we accept the existence of such a strictly unique peduncle for human origins, can anything more be said (still remaining on the purely phenomenal plane) about its length and probable thickness? Should we agree with Osborn, who pictures it as separating very low down, at the Eocene or Oligocene epochs, in a fan of preanthropoid

---

* And this amounts to saying that although the science of the human being can affirm nothing directly for or against monogenism (a single initial couple, see above, p. 127*), it, on the other hand, seems to speak out decisively in favor of *monophyletism* (a single phylum).

forms? Or on the other hand, is it better to see it, with W. K. Gregory, as a radiation issued only at the Pliocene from the anthropoid verticil?

And there is still another question, ever the same one! As we continue to look at it from the same strictly "phenomenal" viewpoint, what *minimum* diameter of biological possibility must we attribute to it (regardless of its depth) if we consider it in relation to its initial point of hominization? What is the smallest number of individuals (in order of magnitude) that must have simultaneously undergone the metamorphosis of reflection for the ray to have been able to "mutate," resist, and live? Regardless of how monophyletic it is, does not a species always take shape like a diffuse current at the heart of a river—through mass effects? Or does it rather perhaps propagate like crystallization, from a few grains—through unit effects? I mentioned this earlier as I outlined the general theory of phyla. The advantages and attractions of each of these two symbols vie in our minds (each perhaps partly true). We must content ourselves with waiting until their synthesis is established.

We must learn to wait. And in the meantime, let us remember the following two things.

The first is that however solitary the human species might appear to have been, in all probability it emerged from a general experimentation of the Earth. The human was born in a direct line with a total effort of life. And that is what gives our species its supereminent dignity and axial value. To satisfy our understanding and what is required for action, this is fundamentally all we need to know.

And the second is that no matter how fascinating it is to solve the problem of origins, to solve it even in detail will not solve the human problem. We have every reason to consider the discovery of human fossils to be one of the most illuminating and critical lines of modern research. Yet we ought not to have any illusions about the limits, in all domains, of embryogenesis as a form of analysis. If the structure of the embryo of each thing is fragile and fleeting and as a result for all practical purposes imperceptible in the past, how much more ambiguous and indecipherable must its traits be! Things are not manifested in their germ, but in their unfolding. The greatest rivers, taken at their source, are only narrow streams.

In order to grasp the truly cosmic scope of the human phenomenon, we have had to follow its roots back through life to the first of the Earth's envelopments of itself. But if we want to comprehend the specific nature of the human and divine the human secret, the only method we have is to observe what reflection has already provided and what it announces *ahead*.

Chapter II

THE DEPLOYMENT OF THE NOOSPHERE

To multiply the contacts necessary for its experimentations and to be able to store up the polymorphous variety of its riches, life can only advance by deep masses. And therefore when its course leaves the gorges where it seemed as though a new mutation had choked it, the more tightly drawn the net it emerges from and the vaster the surface it must cover with its flow, the more necessary it is also for life to regenerate itself in multitude.

The whole of prehistory and human history, from the beginning to our own time, is summed up and expressed in this effort of multiplication and expansion—for those who know how to see. With humanity, impelled by some obscure instinct, working to overflow its narrow point of emergence until it submerges the Earth, with thought making up the numbers to conquer all habitable space over every other form of life, with mind, in other words, weaving and deploying the layers of the noosphere.[1]

In a few broad strokes, let us try to sketch the phases, or successive waves, of this invasion (FIGURE 4).[2]

1   THE RAMIFIED PHASE OF THE PREHOMINIDS

Toward the very end of the Pliocene epoch,* a vast movement, a positive spasm of uplifting, seems to have affected the continental masses of the Old World from the Atlantic to the Pacific. Almost everywhere at that time, basins emptied, gorges hollowed out, and thick alluvial masses

---

* More precisely, at the end of the Villafranchian. Already many geologists place this stage outside and above the Pliocene, making it the true Lower Quarternary. This is simply a matter of how it is bracketed.

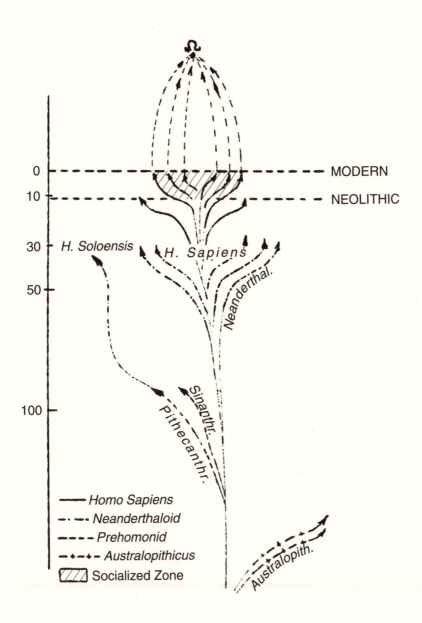

FIGURE 4   Schematic diagram symbolizing the development of the human layer. The numbers at the left refer to *thousands* of years. They represent a minimum duration and should probably be at least doubled. The hypothetical zone of convergence on Omega (in dots) obviously is not drawn according to scale. In analogy to the other living layers, its duration would be on the order of millions of years.

spread into the plains. Before this great transformation, no definite human traces had been identified anywhere. Yet hardly had it ended, when chipped stones are encountered mixed in with the gravels of almost all the terraces of Africa, western Europe, and southern Asia.

There are still only two known fossil specimens of the Lower Quarternary human, the contemporary and author of the first tools, but they are well known to us: *Pithecanthropus* of Java, represented for a long time by only a simple skull-cap, but recently found again in much more satisfactory samples;[3] and *Sinanthropus* of China, numerous examples of whom have been found over the past ten years.[4] Two beings so closely related that the nature of each of them would have remained obscure had we not had the good fortune of being able to compare them with each other.*

What do these very ancient remains, which are at least one or two hundred thousand years old, have to teach us?

A first point anthropologists now agree on is that here in *Pithecanthropus*, and in *Sinanthropus* as well, we have forms that are clearly hominid *in their anatomy*. If we arrange their skulls in a series between the skulls of the great apes and recent human types, there appears to be an obvious morphological break, a blank, between these hominid types and the anthropoids, whereas they naturally form a unit with the different human groups. Certain signs taken together make it clearly evident that we are on the human side. The relatively short face. A relatively spacious cranial box: with the cerebral capacity in the Trinal type hardly going below 800 cubic centimeters, and in the large Peking males, reaching 1100.† Their lower jaw is constructed essentially according to the anthropic type, forward toward the symphysis.[5] Above all, finally, they have free forelimbs and bipedal posture.

And yet, however hominid they might have been, judging from their physiognomy *Pithecanthropus* and *Sinanthropus* were still strange creatures. The skull is elongated and markedly pinched behind enormous orbital ridges. It is flattened, and instead of being ovoid or pentagonal, as in ourselves, its transverse section generally forms an open arc at ear level. It is a powerfully ossified skull, with a braincase that instead of forming a prominent hump at the back is encircled posteriorly by a thick occipital fold. And finally, the skull is prognathous, where the dental arcs project strongly forward beyond its upper part, over a symphysis, which is not only lacking a chin, but recedes. And then, to finish it all, there is an

---

* For simplicity's sake I will say nothing of the Mauer human type. However ancient and remarkable a jaw it has, we still do not know enough about it to establish its real place anthropologically.

† In the large anthropoids today, the cerebral capacity does not exceed 600 cm³.

extremely pronounced sexual dimorphism: the females being small, gener-ally with gracile teeth and jaws; but the males robust, with powerful molars and canines. From these various characteristics, which are not malformations and monstrosities but expressive of a solidly established, well-balanced architecture, how can we fail to recognize an anatomical convergence below, toward the "simian" world?

Taking all these factors into account, thanks to the discovery of both the Trinal and Peking human types, from now on we can scientifically affirm that we have knowledge of one more morphological notch—evol-utionary stage—and zoological verticil inside humanity.

A morphological notch: since the shape of the skull, for example, places them almost midway along the line separating a Caucasian from a chimpanzee.

An evolutionary stage, also: since whether or not any of their direct descendants have been left behind anywhere at present, they most likely represent a type which the modern human must have passed through at some moment in the course of phylogenesis.

A zoological verticil, finally: since however narrowly localized their group might seem to have been on the extreme border of eastern Asia, this group obviously formed part of a much wider grouping, whose nature and structure I will return to a little further along.

In short, *Pithecanthropus* and *Sinanthropus* are much more than just two interesting anthropological types. Through them we catch a glimpse of a whole wave of humanity.

Paleontologists thus have once again shown their sense of the natural perspectives of life in setting this very ancient and primitive human layer apart as a distinct natural unit. They even have created for it the name "prehominid."[6] The term is expressive and correct if we are considering the anatomical progression of forms. But it risks masking or inappropri-ately placing that psychic discontinuity in which I hold the vital core of hominization must lie. To identify *Pithecanthropus* and *Sinanthropus* as prehominids could imply that they were not yet absolutely human types—which means, to my way of speaking, that they have not yet crossed the threshold of reflection. But what seems much more likely to me, on the contrary, is that without yet having reached our level of intelligence, and far from it, both of them already were intelligent beings in the full sense of the word.

The general mechanism of phylogenesis, first of all, seems to require that they were so. Such a fundamental mutation as thought, one that gives its specific impetus to the whole human group, could not, in my opinion, have appeared midway along the stem. It dominates the whole edifice. Its place, therefore, belongs *below* every recognizable verticil, in the un-attainable depths of the peduncle—and, therefore, even below any beings, however prehominid in cranial structure they may be, who are already clearly located *above* the point of origin and unfolding of our humanity.

But there is still something else!

We do not yet know of any traces of industry directly associated with the remains of *Pithecanthropus*. This is explained by the conditions of deposit. The state of the bones of the fossils around Trinil shows they have been carried by rivers into a lake. Near Peking, on the other hand, where we come upon *Sinanthropus* in the deposit of a filled-in cave, we find an abundance of implements of stone mixed in with charred bones. Are we to interpret this industry (occasionally displaying a surprising quality, I admit), as Professor Boule suggested, to be the vestiges left by another unknown human for whom *Sinanthropus*, not a toolmaker, must have served as game? Insofar as no bones of this hypothetical human have been found, the idea seems to me gratuitous, and all else taken into account, less scientific. *Sinanthropus* already cut stones, and already made fire. Until proven to the contrary, these two attributes make up an integral part of the "peduncle" for the same reasons as reflection. Bound inseparably together in a single cluster, these three elements arise universally at the same time as humanity. Objectively, that is the situation.

If this really is the case, then we see that despite having osteological characteristics so reminiscent of the anthropoids, the prehominids were psychologically much closer to us—and as a result were phyletically not so young and primitive as we might have thought. For after all, it took a long time to discover fire and the art of making a cutting tool. So long, that there would have been ample room behind them for at least one other human verticil, which we will perhaps ultimately find in the Villafranchian.

At the same time as *Pithecanthropus* and *Sinanthropus*, as we said above, other hominids certainly existed which had reached the same stage of development. Unfortunately the remains we have of them are still inadequate: the famous Mauer jaw in Germany, perhaps; and in East Africa, the partially conserved skull of *Africanthropus*.[7] That is not enough to determine the general physiognomy of the group. One observation, however, may indirectly serve to cast light on what we would like to know.[8]

We now know two species of *Pithecanthropus*: a relatively small one, and another, much more robust and "brutish." Added to these are two positively giant forms: one in Java, represented by a jaw fragment; one in South China, by an isolated tooth. This, along with *Sinanthropus*, gives us in all (for the same period and on the same continental border) five different types that are certainly related.

Does not such a multiplicity of adjacent forms squeezed together in a narrow band as well as such a curious tendency to gigantism suggest the idea of a "radiation" or marginal foliation, mutating on itself in a quasi-autonomous manner? And does not what was occurring in China and Malaya have its equivalent elsewhere at the same moment in radiations more to the West?

If this is true, we have to say that, zoologically speaking, the human zoological group at the Lower Quarternary still formed only a relatively incoherent group in which the divergent structure common to other animal verticils continued to dominate.

But also we must say that in the most central regions of the continents,* the elements of a new, more compact, human wave were probably already grouping themselves together, readying themselves to take over this archaic world.

2   THE FASCICLE OF THE NEANDERTHALOIDS

After the Lower Quarternary, geologically the curtain falls. During the intermission, the Trinal deposits are folded, the red soils of China gullied out, ready to receive their thick mantle of yellow loess. Africa grows somewhat more fissured. Elsewhere glaciers advance and recede. When the curtain rises again some 60,000 years ago and we can see the scene, the prehominids have vanished. And the Earth in its new setting[10] is occupied by the Neanderthaloids.

The fossils known to us of this new and more compact humanity are already much more numerous than those in the preceding period. This is probably an effect of being closer together, but it is also an effect of multiplication. The thinking network is gradually expanding and tightening.

There is progress in number, and simultaneously progress in hominization.

When first confronted with *Pithecanthropus* and *Sinanthropus*, science well might have been disconcerted and wondered what kind of creature it had encountered. But except for a brief moment of hesitation when faced with the skull of Spy or the skull of the Neanderthal, there never was any serious question about the fact that at the Lower Quarternary we were in the presence of vestiges left by some representatives of our own race. Such a vast development of the brain, the presence of a cave industry, and for the first time, undeniable instances of burial all define and point to true man.

---

* Perhaps among populations (of a still unknown anatomical type!) whose "bifacial" industry can be followed at the early Pleistocene, from the Cape to the River Thames[9] and from Spain to Java.

135

Truly human, therefore; and yet a human still not exactly like ourselves.

The Neanderthal generally had an elongated skull, low forehead, massive and prominent orbital ridges; a still perceptible prognathism of jaw beyond the upper face; an absence ordinarily of canine fossa; and an absence of chin. The Neanderthal had massive teeth, lacking a distinct neck between crown and root. From these various characteristics, no anthropologist could have failed to identify at first sight the fossil remains of a European Neanderthaloid. Actually, even among the Australian aborigine and the Ainu, nothing still exists on Earth that can be confused with these characteristics today. As I said, there is a clear advance in relation to Trinil and Peking human types. Yet the break ahead in relation to modern humans is almost equally great. Thus there is a new morphological notch to be marked, a new evolutionary stage to distinguish; and inevitably also, by virtue of the laws of phylogenesis, a new zoological verticil to be supposed—whose reality has become increasingly evident in prehistory during recent years.

When the first "Mousterian" skulls were discovered in western Europe and it was clearly recognized that they did not belong to mentally defective or degenerate types, it was entirely natural for anatomists to imagine that the Earth of the Middle Paleolithic was populated with human types that exactly corresponded to the "Neanderthal." This perhaps accounts for a certain disappointment when it began to become evident that as the number of finds multiplied they did not confirm such a simple hypothesis. Actually, it is precisely this ever increasing diversity among the Neanderthaloids that we should have expected. And we now see that diversity is what ultimately gives their grouping its true interest and physiognomy.

At our present state of knowledge we can identify two distinct groups among the so-called Neanderthaloid forms, each one indicating a different stage of phyletic evolution: a group of terminal forms and a juvenile group.

(a) There is the terminal group, first of all, where the diverse, more-or-less autonomous radiations composing the prehominid verticils survived, then became extinct. In Java, the Solo human type, the direct, generally unchanged, descendant of Trinil types.* In Africa, the extraordinarily brutish Rhodesian human type. And finally, in Europe, unless I am

---

* Found in numbers in the horizontal terraces flattening the folded beds of Trinal, *Homo soloensis* seems to be nothing but a large *Pithecanthropus* with a more rounded skull. It is the almost unique case in paleontology of the same phylum grasped at the same place, across a geological discordance, at two different stages of development.

mistaken, the Neanderthal type itself, which despite its remarkable extension over all of western Europe, seems to represent nothing but the final foliage of a dying branch.

(b) But also at the same time, there is the still nebulous and hardly distinguishable juvenile group of Pseudo-Neanderthaloids, who continue to have traits that are very primitive but distinctly modernized or capable of being modernized: with the more rounded head, less salient orbital ridges, more clearly marked canine fossa and sometimes nascent jaw. Human types such as those of Steinheim, Palestine, and even perhaps *Eoanthropus* of England (if the chimpanzee-like jaw found with him does not belong with him).[11] These are indisputably Neanderthaloids, but already so much closer to us! A progressive and dormant branch, one might say, waiting for an imminent awakening.

Let us put this triple cluster back into its proper light geographically and morphologically.[12] Far from forming a disturbing complex, its pattern reveals a familiar plan. With leaves almost all fallen, leaves still open but beginning to yellow, and leaves still folded but vigorous at the heart of a bouquet of palms, it shows three complete, almost ideal sections of a zoological fan.

3   THE *HOMO SAPIENS* COMPLEX

One of botany's great sources of astonishment at the beginning of the Cretaceous is to see the world of cycads and conifers abruptly displaced and submerged by a forest of angiosperms: by plane trees, oaks . . . , by most of what is essentially modern, unfurling in their finished state over the flora of the Jurassic from some unknown region of the globe. It is equally baffling for the anthropologist to discover "Mousterian"[13] Man and Cro-Magnon[14] or Aurignacian[15] human types superposed on one another, barely separated in the grottos by a floor of stalagmites. In this instance, there is practically no geological break. Yet there is a fundamental rejuvenation of humanity. Driven by climate, or impelled by the restlessness of soul, we see the abrupt invasion of *Homo sapiens* on top of the Neanderthaloids.

Where did this new type of human being come from? Some anthropologists like to see *Homo sapiens* as the end of certain lineages already established in earlier ages—as the direct descendant of *Sinanthropus*, for example. For specifically technical reasons and, even more, in analogy to the whole, it seems better to picture things in another way.[16] There is no doubt that somewhere and *in its own manner* the upper Paleolithic human type must have passed through a prehominid and then a Neanderthaloid phase. But like the mammals, the trituberculates and all the other phyla,

Homo sapiens seems to elude our sight in the perhaps accelerated course of this embryogenesis. There is overlapping and replacement rather than continuity and prolongation, and the *law of relay* is still dominant in history here. Thus I tend to picture the newcomer as having been born from an autonomous line of evolution, one that was long-hidden although secretly active and that triumphantly emerged one day from among all the others at the heart of the Pseudo-Neanderthaloids, whose living and probably very ancient grouping we pointed out above. Hypothetically speaking, one fact is certain and accepted by all. The human type we see everywhere at the close of the Quarternary is truly already modern—and in every respect.

Anatomically, first of all, there can be no possible doubt. All those traits so clearly marked on the last cave dwellers are definitively our own: the raised forehead with reduced orbital ridges; the amply bulging parietal bones; the faint occipital crest pushed well back under the rounded brain; the unbound jaw, with prominent chin. So clearly are they ours, that from this moment on, the paleontologist, accustomed to working with pronounced morphological differences, finds it difficult to distinguish the remains of fossil humans from those of humans living today. The paleontologist's methods and their own trained eye are no longer adequate for such subtle work; from now on paleontology must give way to the most delicate (and bold) techniques of anthropology. It is no longer a matter of reconstructing the rising horizons of life in broad outline. It is a matter of analyzing the tangle of nuances that weave our foreground over a thickness of duration of less than 30,000 years. Thirty thousand years is a long period of time on our life scale, but merely a second for an evolutionary movement. In this interval, from the osteological viewpoint there is no appreciable break along the length of the human phylum— and up to a point, even no *major* change in the progress of its somatic ramification.

For this is what takes us completely by surprise. In itself it is only very natural that studied at its point of issue, the stem of *Homo sapiens fossilis*, far from being simple, should show in the composition and divergence of its fibers the complex structure of a fan. This is the initial condition of every phylum on the tree of life, as we know. The most we would have counted on finding at these depths would be a bouquet of relatively primitive and generalized forms; something anterior in form to our present races. Now what we encounter is rather the opposite. At the "Age of the Reindeer,"[17] who were the representatives of the new human verticil just freshly opened—who were they really (insofar as bones can be trusted to give us some idea of flesh and skin)? Actually they were already just what we still see living today and at approximately the same places on the Earth. What we catch sight of all over the Old World from Europe to China at the end of the last glacier are blacks, whites, yellows (or at the very most, preblacks, prewhites, preyellows)—with these various groups already encamped for the most part from south to north, west to east, in their present geographical zones. In the upper Paleolithic humans, therefore, not only by noting their fundamental traits of anatomy, but by following the main lines of their ethnography, it is truly ourselves, our own child-hood, that we discover. Not only is there already the skeleton of the modern human—but the principal components of modern humanity. The same general body shape. The same fundamental distribution of races. The same tendency (at least the outlines of it) for ethnic groups to join together, over and above all divergencies, in a coherent system. And fundamentally the same deep aspirations of soul (and why would this not follow naturally).[18]

Among the Neanderthaloids we saw evidence of a psychic step, marked, along with other signs, by the appearance of the first burial places in the caves. Everyone is prepared to grant the flame of true intelligence even to the most confirmed of Neanderthals. But this intellectual activity seems largely to have been absorbed by the cares of survival and propagation. We do not know, or are unaware, if there was anything left over. What could these distant cousins of ours really have thought? We have no idea. But on the contrary, at the Age of the Reindeer, with *Homo sapiens*, a definitively liberated thought exploded and is still warm on the walls of the caves. The newcomers brought art with them—an incredibly consummate art, although naturalistic. And thanks to the language of this art, for the first time we can enter right into the consciousness of those vanished beings whose bones we reassemble. Spiritually they are so strangely close to us, even down to the smallest detail! Are not those rites expressed in red and black on the walls of the caverns in Spain, the Pyrénées, and Périgord, still practiced today before our very eyes in Africa, Oceania, and even in America? As it has been observed, what difference is there, if any, between the Sorcerer of "Trois Frères"[19] rigged in his deer skin and an Oceanic god? But this is still not what is most important. We can be mistaken when we give a modern interpretation to the imprint of hands, to the spell-bound bisons, to the symbols of fertility that express the preoccupations and religion of an Aurignacian or Magdalenian. Where, on the contrary, we can never be mistaken is when we perceive in the artists of this distant age—whether from the perfection of move-ment and silhouette or the unexpected play of ornamental chiselings—the sense of observation, the taste for fantasy, and the joy of creating that are the flowering of a consciousness which is not only self-reflective but over-flowing with exuberance.[20] And thus we have not been misled by our inspection of skeletons and skulls. It really is the human being of the present, in the fullest sense of the word, who appears to us at the Upper

Quaternary; the human still not fully adult, but having reached the "age of reason." From that moment the human brain has been finished in relation to ourselves—so well finished, even, that since that period no measurable variation has seemed to further perfect the organic instrument of our thought.

Has evolution therefore stopped in the human being at the end of the Quaternary?

Not at all. But without compromising what could be continuing to develop imperceptibly in the depths of nervous systems, since that date evolution has freely overflowed its anatomical modalities, to spread, or even perhaps emigrate, by what is most vital in itself, into the individual and collective zones of psychic spontaneity.

And this is the form in which we will have to recognize and follow it almost exclusively from now on.

4   THE NEOLITHIC METAMORPHOSIS

Along the living phyla, socialization represents a relatively late stage of progress, at least among the higher animals, where we can follow things more easily. It comes as an achievement of maturity. In the human being, for reasons that are strongly linked to the power of reflection, the transformation is accelerated. As far back as we catch sight of our great ancestors, they appear *in groups* and around a fire.

As clear as the signs of association are each time at these very ancient periods, the phenomenon is not fully outlined. Even the tribes we are able to distinguish at the Upper Paleolithic seem not to have consisted in much more than somewhat loose groups of wandering hunters. It is only at the Neolithic that the great fusion begins to happen between human elements, a fusion that is never to end. Although the Neolithic is too young an age for prehistorians to take seriously and neglected by historians because its phases cannot be precisely dated, still it is a critical age, and the most solemnly important of all the ages of the past: the age of the birth of civilization.

How did this birth come about? Once again and always in conformity with the laws that regulate our vision of time behind us, we do not know. A few years ago we simply referred to "a great gap" between the latest levels of chipped stone and the first beds of polished stones and pottery. Since then a series of more clearly identified and intercalated horizons has gradually drawn the lips of the fissure closer together. But the fundamental crevice remains. Was it due to the interplay of migrations, or to an effect of contagion? To the sudden arrival of some ethnic wave, which had silently been gathering somewhere else in the most fertile regions of the globe—or to the irresistible propagation of fruitful innovations? Was it primarily a movement of peoples—or a cultural movement? We still cannot say very much. What is certain is that after a lacuna of no geological significance, but in which all the same we must put the time required for the selection and domestication of all the animals and plants that we still live on today, instead and in place of hunters of horses and reindeer we find ourselves faced with a humanity that is sedentary and organized. In ten or twenty thousand years, the human being has divided up the Earth and become rooted there.

In this decisive period of socialization, as at the moment of reflection, there seems to have been a mysterious confluence of a network of partially independent factors to sustain and force the advance of hominization. Let us try to sort these factors out.

Above all, there is the incessant progress of multiplication. With the rapidly growing number of individuals, free terrain shrank. Groups collided with one another. As a result, their range of movement diminished and it became a question of how to get the most out of land that is becoming more and more limited. It is easy to imagine that, under the pressure of this necessity, the idea must have sprung up of preserving and reproducing on the spot what until then had been sought and pursued at a distance. With breeding and cultivation replacing hunting and gathering, we find shepherd and farmer.

And everything else follows from this fundamental change. First of all, from the swelling agglomerations, the complexity of rights and obligations made their appearance, forcing the imagination of all kinds of communal structures and jurisprudences, whose remaining vestiges are still visible to us today in the shadow of the great civilizations among the least progressive populations of the Earth. One could really say that socially everything had been tried in regard to property, morality, and marriage.

Simultaneously, in the more stable and denser environments created by the first agricultural settlements, the need and enthusiasm for research became more regulated and more heated. What a marvelous period of investigation and invention it must have been, when the "perpetual trial and error of life" burst forth in its reflective form, in the unparalleled freshness of a new beginning! Everything possible seems to have been tried at this extraordinary period. The selection and empirical improvement of fruits, grains, and herds. The technique of pottery. Weaving. Very soon, the first elements of picture writing—and very quickly, the first beginnings of a metallurgy.

And then accordingly, more consolidated in itself and better equipped for conquest, humanity could finally launch its last waves of assault on positions that had still escaped it. From then on it was in full expansion.

In fact it is at the dawn of the Neolithic that through Alaska, freed of its glaciers, and perhaps by still other routes, the human penetrated America, to begin there again, with new material and at new cost, the patient work of settling down and domestication. Still there were many hunters and fishermen in whom the paleolithic way of life was prolonged despite the use of pottery and polished stone. But alongside these there were equally true farmers—the maize eaters. And probably at the same time, marked by a long, still visible trail of banana, mango, and coconut trees, another layer began to expand across the Pacific in a fabulous adventure.

Emerging from this metamorphosis, whose existence we once again hardly know of except through its accomplishments, the world is virtually covered by a population whose remains of polished tools, millwheels, and fragments of vases are found strewn everywhere the soil of the continents has been exposed below the humus or recent deposits of sand.

Certainly humanity would have been very fragmented. To picture it we need to think of what America or Africa must have been like when white people arrived there for the first time: a mosaic of groups fundamentally diverse ethnically and socially.

But it is a humanity already completely sketched in and connected. From the Age of the Reindeer, peoples have gradually found their definitive place, even in detail. Through commerce and the transmission of ideas conductivity from one to another has been increased. Traditions have been organized. A collective memory has developed. However thin and granular this first membrane must have been, from now on the noosphere has begun to close on itself, encircling the Earth.

5   THE PROLONGATIONS OF THE NEOLITHIC AND THE RISE OF THE WEST

From the time when nothing was known about human paleontology, we have retained the habit of isolating the few six thousand years for which we possess written or dated documents as a special period, a period of history as opposed to prehistory. Actually no such break exists. The more clearly we reestablish the perspectives of the past, the more we observe that so-called "historical time" (up to and *including* the beginning of "modern time") is nothing but a direct prolongation of the Neolithic. There is obviously a growing complexity and differentiation, which we will speak of, but it is essentially along the same lines and on the *same level*.

From the viewpoint of biology, which is our perspective here, how are we to define and to depict the progress of hominization in the course of such a brief and enormously fertile period?

Essentially what history records through the shifting multiplicity of institutions, peoples, and empires is the normal unfolding of *Homo sapiens* in the midst of the social atmosphere created by the Neolithic transformation. It shows the gradual falling of the oldest scales,[21] some of which, like the Australian aborigines, still cling to the outermost surfaces of our civilization and of continents. And counter to this, the domination by the more central and vigorous stems that seek to monopolize soil and light. On the one hand, disappearances leaving blank spaces, and on the other, eclosion of buds thickening the branching structure. Branches drying out, dormant branches, and branches thrusting forth to invade everything. An endless criss-crossing of fans, with none of them clearly showing its peduncle, even those two thousand years behind us. We see the whole series of cases, situations, and outward appearances normally encountered in any phylum in the process of active proliferation.

But is this really all?

One might think that the proximity of the facts, which allows us to follow the biological mechanism of species' ramification as if with the naked eye, is what creates the great difficulty as well as the exceptional interest of human phylogenesis. But, in fact, something more is happening there.

So long as science only had to deal with "prehistoric" human groups that were more or less isolated and also more or less in the process of anthropological formation, the general rules of animal phylogenesis could still apply approximately. But from the Neolithic on, the influence of psychic factors clearly begins to predominate over the increasingly diminishing variations in somatic factors. And from then on, the same two series of effects emerge into the foreground that we called attention to above as we described in its main outlines the behavior of hominization: (1) first of all, the appearance of political and cultural units on top of the genealogical verticils; a complex gamut of groupings, which after having submerged "race," show themselves capable at every proportion of interfering[22] with one another on the multiple levels of geographical distribution, economic connections, religious beliefs, and social institutions; (2) and simultaneously the manifestation among these new kinds of branches of the forces of coalescence (anastamoses and confluences) freed in each one of them by the individualization of psychological sheath—or axis, more precisely. In short, an entire conjugated interplay of divergences and convergence.

There is no need for me to insist on the reality, diversity, and continual germination of the at least virtually divergent human collective units—of the birth, multiplication, and evolution of nations, states, and civilizations. The spectacle is before our eyes everywhere, and its episodes fill the annals of peoples. But if we wish to comprehend its secret and to appreciate its drama, there is one thing we must not forget. No matter how hominized the events have become, in this rationalized form human history truly prolongs in its own way and to its own degree the organic movements of life. Through the phenomena of social ramification that it relates, it is *still* natural history.

The phenomena of confluence are much subtler and more charged with biological possibilities. Let us try to follow them in their mechanism and consequences.

Among animal branches or phyla that have a weak psyche, reactions are restricted to competition and eventual elimination. The stronger one displaces the weaker, and in the end stifles it. Among lower organisms there is hardly an exception to this brutal, almost mechanical law of substitution save for the associations (functional ones, above all) made through "symbiosis" or, in the most socialized of insects, the enslavement of one group by the other.

In the human (at least Post-Neolithic human types), pure and simple elimination tends to be the exception or (at least) secondary. In the most brutal conquest, suppression is always accompanied by some kind of assimilation. Even after being partially absorbed, the conquered peoples still react upon their conquerors to transform them. As it is said in geology, they endomorphose[23] their conquerors. This is all the more true in the case of a peaceful, cultural invasion. And even more so if it is a question of equally resistant and active populations that slowly inter-penetrate under prolonged tension. Mutual permeability of psyche combines with a remarkable and significant interfertilization. Under this double influence veritable biological combinations are formed and fixed, mixing and associating ethnic traditions together at the same time as cere-bral genes. In the past on the tree of life, there was a simple intertwining of stems. Now throughout the entire domain of *Homo sapiens*, there is synthesis.

But naturally, not equally everywhere.

As a result of the fortuitous configuration of continents, certain regions exist on the Earth that are more favorable than others for the gathering and mixing of races: extended archipelagoes, narrow crossroads—above all, vast arable plains irrigated by some larger river. Here, on these privi-leged spots, the human mass has tended to concentrate, fuse together and to overheat. This brought about the probably "congenital" appearance of certain poles of attraction and organization throughout the Neolithic layer that are the sign and prelude of some higher, newer state for the noosphere. Five of these centers are recognizable in the more or less recent past: Central America, with the Mayan civilization; the South Seas, with the Polynesian; the Yellow River basin, with the Chinese; the Ganges and Indus Valleys, with the civilizations of India; and, finally, the Nile and Mesopotamia, with Egypt and Sumeria. Although these centers probably appeared at approximately the same period (except for the much later Mayan and Polynesian centers), they were largely independent of each other, each one working blindly to expand and radiate, as if it alone must absorb and transform the Earth.

Fundamentally, does not the bulk of history consist in the encounter, conflict, and ultimately the gradual harmonization of these great somato-psychic currents?

In fact, this struggle for influence quickly became localized. With the Mayan center becoming too isolated in the New World—and the Polynesian too dispersed over the monotonous dust of its distant islands—the former quickly tended to become completely extinct, the latter to radiate in a void. The contest for the future of the world, therefore, was played out in Asia and North Africa, among the farmers of the great plains.

One or two thousand years before our era, the chances between players seemed to be equal. And yet, instructed by the events that followed, we recognize today that there were already seeds of weakness in the two easternmost contestants.[24]

First of all, whether by innate character or as a result of its immensity, China (by this obviously I mean *old* China) lacked the appetite and impetus for any fundamental renewal. What a unique spectacle that gigantic country was, which only yesterday before our very eyes was the living embodiment of an almost totally unchanged fragment of what things must have been like ten thousand years ago. With its population not only based on agriculture, but fundamentally organized according to a hierarchy of territorial possessions, and its emperors nothing but the largest landowners. A population that was ultraspecialized in brick, pottery, and bronze, that carried its study of pictograms and knowledge of constellations to the verge of superstition. A civilization that was certainly incredibly refined, but just like the writing in which it so ingenuously reveals itself, one that had never changed its methods from the beginning. It was Neolithic, right in the midst of the nineteenth century, not a rejuvenated Neolithic as elsewhere, but only endlessly and increasingly complicated in itself—and not merely along the same lines, but on the same level—as though it had never been able to wrest itself free from the soil in which it had been formed.[25]

In the meantime, while China was already becoming encrusted with clay as it multiplied its experiments and discoveries without bothering to construct a physics, India, the region par excellence of philosophy and religious high pressure, let itself be drawn until it was lost in metaphysics.

We can never give enough credit to the mystical influences of the past that have come down to us from this anticyclone,[26] but even though its currents might have been efficacious in ventilating and enlightening the human atmosphere, we are forced to recognize that an excessive passivity and detachment made them incapable of building the Earth. Rising up in its own time like a great breath—like a great breath also, in its own time, the primitive soul of India passed away. And how could it have been otherwise? With phenomena seen as illusion (Maya) and their interconnections as a chain (Karma), what remained in these doctrines to stimulate and guide human evolution? A simple error was made in the definition of spirit and the appreciation of the bonds attaching it to the sublimation of matter, yet that made all the difference!

And so, gradually, we find ourselves falling back toward more western zones of the planet—those on the banks of the Euphrates, the Nile, and the Mediterranean, where in several thousand years an exceptional encounter of places and people would produce the favorable mixture to make it possible for reason to apprentice itself to facts and religion to action, so that, on the contrary, nothing was lost of their rising force. Mesopotamia, Egypt, Hellas—soon Rome—and above all of this, giving its spiritual form to Europe, the Judeo-Christian ferment (which I will return to as I conclude).

It is easy for the pessimist to discount this period of extraordinary civilizations that collapsed one after the other. Is it not far more scientific to recognize once again, beneath these successive oscillations, the great spiral of life irreversibly rising in relays as it follows the main line of its evolution? Susa, Memphis, and Athens may die. Yet an ever more organized consciousness of the universe is passed from hand to hand, and it grows more and more brilliant.

Further ahead, when I speak of the planetization of the noosphere now in progress, I will endeavor to restore the great and fundamental part reserved for the other fragments of humanity in the long-awaited fullness of the Earth. At this point in our investigation we would allow our feelings to falsify the facts if we did not recognize that during historical times the principal axis of anthropogenesis has passed through the West. In this glowing zone of growth and universal recasting, everything that makes the human being today has been found, or at least *must have been redis-covered*. For even what had long been known elsewhere has taken on its definitive human value only by becoming incorporated into the system of European ideas and occupations. It is not simple naivete to celebrate Columbus's discovery of America as a great event.

In fact, a neohumanity has been germinating around the Mediterranean for six thousand years, and just at this moment finishes absorbing the last vestiges of the Neolithic mosaic; another layer is burgeoning on the noosphere, the most tightly woven of all.

Proof of this is that in order to remain human or to become more fully human, all peoples, from one end of the world to the other, have inexorably been led to put the hopes and problems of the modern Earth in the very terms in which the West has succeeded in formulating them.

Chapter III

THE MODERN EARTH

A Change of Age

In every age human beings have believed themselves to be at a "turning point of history." And as part of a rising spiral, to some extent they have been right. But at certain moments this impression of transformation is felt much more strongly—and is particularly justified. And it is not exaggerating the importance of our contemporary existences in the least for us to say that there is a fundamental change of course for the world under way in us, and it threatens to crush us.

When do we see this shift beginning? Obviously it is impossible for us to say exactly. Like a great ship, the human mass is changing course only gradually, so gradually that the first tremors signaling a change of direction can be traced a long way back—certainly as far as the Renaissance. One thing is clear at least: that at the end of the eighteenth century, the course had been altered in the West. And no matter how stubbornly we sometimes insist that we are still the same, we have entered into a new world.

We see this, first, from economic changes. Only two hundred years ago, in spite of how much our civilization had evolved, it was still fundamentally modeled on the land and division of land. The kind of property, the nucleus of the family, and the prototype of the state (even of the universe) was still, as in the beginning of society, the cultivated field and territorial base. Now in recent times, as a result of the "dynamization" of money, property has gradually vanished into something fluid and impersonal—it has become so fluid that the fortunes of nations themselves no longer bear any relation to their frontiers.

We see it, next, from industrial changes. Until the eighteenth century, in spite of how much things had improved, fire was still the single known chemical energy—and the muscle of humans and animals, multiplied by the machine, was still the only mechanical energy used. But since that time!

And we see it, finally, from social changes and from the awakening of the masses.

These external signs alone are enough to make us see that the great upheaval we have experienced in the West since the storm of the French Revolution is caused by something much deeper and much nobler than the difficulties of a world seeking for some lost, ancient equilibrium. Just coming around the cape that sheltered us, it is no shipwreck we are heading into, but the great swell of an unknown sea.[1] What troubles us intellectually, politically, and even spiritually at this moment is quite simple, as Abbé Breuil[2] once said to me with his customary sudden intuition: "We have only just cast off the last moorings that kept us still tied to the Neolithic." Paradoxical though his words are, they are illuminating. And the more I have thought about them since then, the more I have come to see that Breuil was right.

At this very moment we are passing through a *change of age*.

The future will decide on the best name for this new era we are entering—the age of industries, the age of oil, electricity, and the atom. The age of the machine. The age of huge collectives, and of science. What we call it does not matter. What does count, on the other hand, is the fact that we can say that at the cost of what we endure, another step, a decisive step of life, is being made in and around us. There were the first humans to see our origins. There will be others to witness the great scenes of the end. The chance, and the honor, of our own brief existence is to coincide with a mutation of the noosphere.

Here in these confused zones, so full of tension, where the present merges with the future in a world in turmoil, we stand face to face with all the grandeur of the human phenomenon, a grandeur never attained before. Here and nowhere else, now or never, we can hope, more than any minds that have come before us, to measure the importance and perceive the meaning of hominization. Let us look at it carefully and make an effort to understand. And to do this, leaving the surface of things, let us try to make out what particular form of mind is being born within the modern Earth.

This Earth, billowing with factories, throbbing with enterprise, vibrating with hundreds of new radiations—this great organism ultimately only lives because of and for the sake of a new soul. Beneath the change of age there must lie a change of thought.[3]

Yet where are we to look for and locate this kind of renewing and subtle alteration, which without appreciably modifying our body has made new beings of us? Nowhere else but in a new intuition that totally alters the physiognomy of the universe in which we move—in other words, in an *awakening*.

Whatever people say, what in the space of one or two generations has made us so different from our ancestors—so ambitious—so anxious also, is not only the fact of definitively having discovered and controlled other forces of nature. At the root of it all, if I am right, is that we have become aware of the movement sweeping us along—and this has made us aware of the formidable problems posed by the reflective exercise of human effort.

1   THE DISCOVERY OF EVOLUTION

<u>A</u>. The Perception of Space–time

We each have forgotten that moment when, just having opened our eyes for the first time, we saw light and objects suddenly rushing in at us from all sides and all on the same plane. It takes a great effort for us to picture a time when we did not know how to read, or to go back again to that period when our world extended no farther than the walls of home and our family circle.

In the same way, it is impossible for us to believe that there ever was a time when men and women lived without suspecting that the stars swinging above us actually are light-centuries away, or that the contours of life stretch silhouetted millions of years behind us as far as our horizon goes.

Yet we only need to open one of the barely yellowing tomes in which sixteenth- or even eighteenth-century authors used to discourse on the structure of worlds and we find to our utter amazement that our great-great-great grandparents had the impression of being perfectly adjusted in a cubic space where the stars had been rotating around the Earth for less than six thousand years. They breathed without the slightest difficulty, even if not at full capacity, in a cosmic atmosphere which would have suffocated us instantly and in perspectives which are physically impossible for us to reenter.

What has happened between their time and ours?

I know of no scene more moving, or which so clearly reveals the biological reality of a noogenesis, than that of intelligence bent from the beginning on overcoming step by step the encircling illusion of proximity. In this process of struggling to master the dimensions and depth of the universe, it was space that yielded first, which was natural, since space had been the most tangible. In fact, the first round of the battle was won a long time ago, when someone (probably a Greek, before Aristotle), bending the apparent flatness of things back on itself, intuited that there were antipodes. From that time on the firmament itself coiled up around the round Earth. But the center of the spheres was incorrectly placed.[4] This irremediably paralyzed the elasticity of the system. It was actually only through the break with ancient geocentrism (in Galileo's time) that the heavens were freed for the boundless expansion we now have come to see in them. The Earth has become a simple grain of sidereal dust. Immensity has become a possibility and, symmetrically, as a result, the infinitesimal has sprung up.

Since the depth of centuries lacked any visible parameters, it proved to be perceived much more slowly. For it seemed then that the contours of all of matter—the motions of stars, the shapes of mountains, and the chemical nature of bodies—were expressive of an eternal present. In the seventeenth century, it was impossible for physics to give Pascal any sense of the abyss of the past. To first discover the actual age of the Earth and then its elements, the human being had to take a chance interest in an object of moderate mobility, such as life, or even volcanos. Thus from the eighteenth century on, it was through the thin fissure of "natural history," which had just been born, that light began to filter down into the vast depths under our feet. The depth estimated to be necessary for the formation of the world was still very modest. But at least the impetus had been given, and the way out opened up. After the walls of space had been shaken by the Renaissance, from Buffon on it was the floor of time that started to shift (and the ceiling as a result!). And since then, under the relentless pressure of facts, the process has only accelerated. And although the easing up has been in process for nearly two hundred years, it still has not managed to release the spirals of the world. There is always more distance between turns—and other turns that appear down below.

Now during these first phases of human awakening to cosmic immensity, space and time were so large that they remained homogeneous in themselves and independent of each other. Although they clearly became vaster and vaster, they continued to be two separate containers, where things seemed to pile up and float without any definite physical order.

Both compartments had become immeasurably enlarged. Yet the objects inside each of them seemed to be just as freely transposable as before. What difference did it make whether they were put here or there, moved forward or back, or even eliminated at will? Even if one did not formally venture into this mental game, there was still no clear idea at what point, or why, it was impossible. And no one ever posed the question.

It was not until well into the nineteenth century, again under biology's influence, that the light finally began to dawn, revealing the *irreversible coherence* of everything that exists. Showing the interlinking of life—and soon after, of matter. Showing that the smallest molecule of carbon is a function of the total sidereal process, and that the smallest protozoan is structurally so interwoven with the web of life that its existence hypothetically cannot be extinguished without, from this very fact, the entire network of the biosphere unraveling. Showing that the *distribution, succession, and mutual interdependence of beings are born from their concrescence in a common genesis*. That time and space are organically joined together so as to weave together the stuff of the universe. This is the point we have reached—and as much as we perceive today.

What psychology lies behind this initiation?

If the whole of history were not there to guarantee for us that once a truth has been seen, even if only by a single mind, it always ends up by impressing itself on the totality of human consciousness, there would be good reason to lose courage or patience when we see how many of even the best minds today still remain closed to the idea of evolutionary movement. For many, evolution still means only transformism, and transformism itself is an old Darwinian hypothesis as localized and obsolete as the Laplacean concept of the solar system or the Wegnerean theory of continental drift. They truly are blind who do not see the scope of a movement whose orbit, infinitely transcending that of the natural sciences, has successively overtaken and invaded the surrounding fields of chemistry, physics, sociology, and even mathematics and history of religions. Drawn along together by a single fundamental current, one after the other all the domains of human knowledge have set off toward the study of some kind of *development*. Does this mean evolution is a theory, a system, or a hypothesis? Not at all; yet something far more. Evolution is a general condition, which all theories, all hypotheses, all systems must submit to and satisfy from now on in order to be conceivable and true. Evolution is a light illuminating all facts, a curve that every line must follow.

For the last century and a half, perhaps the most prodigious event ever recorded by history since the step of reflection has been taking place within our minds: the entry of consciousness, forever, into a framework of *new dimensions*; and, consequently, the birth of an entirely renewed universe, simply by the transformation of its most intimate stuff, without a change of line or fold.

Until that time the world seemed to rest on the three axes of its geometry and remained static and able to be fragmented. Now the world seems to be nothing but a single flow.

What makes and classifies someone as "modern" (and scores of our contemporaries are still not modern in this sense) is to have become capable of seeing not only in space or in time, but in duration—or, what amounts to the same thing, of seeing in biological space–time—and moreover, to have become incapable of seeing anything in any other way—anything—*starting with oneself.*

Taking this last step we enter into the heart of the metamorphosis.

<u>B</u>. *The Envelopment in Duration*

Obviously humans could not become aware of evolution around them without feeling themselves borne up by it to some extent. And Darwin has clearly shown this. As we observe the progress of the transformist view from the last century, it is always surprising to note how naturalists and physicists at first could have so naively imagined that they themselves escaped the universal current they had just detected. Subject and object seem to tend almost irremediably to separate from each other in the act of knowing. We are continually inclined to isolate ourselves from the things and events surrounding us as though we were looking at them from outside, safely sheltered in an observatory where they could never reach us, as spectators rather than elements of what is happening. This explains why once the question of human origins was posed by the interlinking of life, it was restricted for such a long time to its somatic and bodily aspect. A long animal heredity could perfectly well have constructed our limbs. But our mind itself always emerged from the games whose moves it calculated. Even though the first evolutionists were such materialists, the idea never occurred to them that their own scholarly intelligence itself had anything to do with evolution.

For at this stage they had only come halfway to the truth.

From the very beginning of these pages, all I have tried to do is to show how, for invincible reasons of homogeneity and coherence, the fibers of cosmogenesis require to be prolonged in ourselves far more deeply than flesh and bone. We are not being tossed about and drawn along in the vital current merely by the material surface of our being. But like a subtle fluid, space–time, having drowned our bodies, penetrates our soul. It fills it and impregnates it. It mingles with its powers, until the soul soon no longer knows how to distinguish space–time from its own thoughts. Nothing can escape this flux any longer, for those who know how to see, even though it were the summit of our being, because it can only be defined in terms of increases of consciousness.[5] For is not the very act by which the fine point of our mind penetrates the absolute a phenomenon of *emergence*? In short, recognized at first in a single point of things, then inevitably having spread to the whole of the inorganic and organic volume of matter, whether we like it or not evolution is now starting to invade the psychic zones of the world, and this is transferring to the spiritual constructions of life not only the cosmic stuff, but the "primacy" of the cosmic, reserved by science until now for the swirling tangles of ancient "ether."

For actually how are we to incorporate thought into the organic flux of space–time without being forced to grant it the primary place in the process, and how are we to imagine a cosmogenesis extending to mind without simultaneously being faced with a noogenesis?

Thought is not part of evolution merely as an anomaly or epiphenomenon, but evolution is so clearly reducible and identifiable with the advance toward thought that the movement of our soul expresses and measures the very progress of evolution. The human discovers that, in the striking words of Julian Huxley, we are *nothing else than evolution become conscious of itself*. It seems to me that until it is established in this perspective, the modern mind (because and insofar as it is modern) will always be restless. For it is on this summit and this summit alone that a resting place and illumination await us.

C. The Illumination

Reflecting in the consciousness of each one of us, evolution is becoming aware of itself.

From such a simple perspective, which I imagine is to become as instinctive and familiar to our descendants as the perception of the third dimension of space is to a baby, a new, inexhaustibly harmonious light reflects back on the world—and it is radiating from us.

Step by step as we *climbed back up* again from the "juvenile Earth," we have followed the successive advances of consciousness in matter in the process of organization. Now having reached the summit, we can turn around and, taking a look behind us, try in a *descending glance* to encompass the order of the whole. This second check proves to be decisive; everything harmonizes. From any other perspective something clashes, it "jars," for there is no natural—genetic—place for human thought in the landscape. Here, from top to bottom, starting with and *including* our soul, the lines go on ahead or recede behind us without torsion or break. From top to bottom a triple unity is carried out and develops: unity of structure, mechanism, and movement.

(a) Unity of Structure

"Verticil" and "fan."

On every scale, this is the pattern that had emerged for us on the tree of life. It had become apparent again at the origins of humanity and the principal human waves. It had even been carried out right before our eyes in the complex kind of ramifications of the mingling of nations and races today. Now, with our eyes more sensitized and adjusted, they manage to discern still this same motif in forms that are becoming more and more immaterial and close.

We habitually compartmentalize our human world into categories of different kinds of "reality": into natural and artificial; physical and moral; organic and juridical.

In space–time that is legitimately and necessarily extended to the movements of our thought within us, the boundaries between the opposite term of each pair tend to vanish. What difference is there, really, from the perspective of life's expansion, between the vertebrate spreading or feathering its limbs and the pilot gliding on wings he has added through his own ingenuity. And is the tremendous and ineluctable play of the energies of the heart any less physically real than the forces of attraction of the universe? And ultimately, however conventional and changeable they may be on the surface, what do the intricacies of our social structures actually represent but the effort to gradually derive what someday will become the structural laws of the noosphere? In essence, and provided they maintain their vital connections with the current that rises from the depths of the past, are not the artificial, moral, and juridical quite simply the natural, physical, and organic, *hominized*?

From this perspective, which is the perspective of the future natural history of the world, the distinctions we still habitually maintain, at the risk of incorrectly compartmentalizing the world, lose their value. And immediately the evolutionary fan becomes visible again, as it continues to affect us in the thousand social phenomena we never would have guessed to be so closely linked to biology: in the formation and dissemination of languages; the development and differentiation of new industries; the formation and propagation of philosophical and religious doctrines. A superficial glance will see in all these flowerings of human activity nothing but the faint and accidental replicas of steps taken by life. It will note the strange parallelism without comment—or verbally credit it to some kind of abstract necessity.

For the mind awakened to the meaning of evolution in its fullest sense, the inexplicable similarity resolves itself in identity: the identity of a structure that is prolonged in different forms from bottom to top, threshold to threshold, from roots to flower, by an organic continuity of movement or, what amounts to the same, an organic unity of milieu.

The social phenomenon is not the attenuation, but the culmination of the biological phenomenon.

(b) Unity of Mechanism

"Trial and error" and "invention."

These were the terms we instinctively turned to when, in describing the successive appearance of zoological groups, we came up against the fact of "mutation."

But can these expressions really be of any help to us, loaded as they possibly are with anthropomorphism?

There is no question that mutation appears again at the origins of the fans of institutions and ideas that intersect to form human society. It springs up constantly everywhere around us—and precisely in the two forms biology supposes and hesitates between: mutations, on the one hand, that are narrowly limited around a single center; and "mass mutations," on the other, that suddenly like a current carry along whole blocks of humankind. But here, because the phenomenon is happening within ourselves, and we see it fully functioning, the light is decisive. And we can note that we have not been mistaken to interpret the progressive leaps of life in an active and finalist manner. For, ultimately, if our "artificial" constructions are nothing but the legitimate sequel to our phylogenesis, then *invention* also, that revolutionary act from which the creations of our thoughts emerge one after the other, can legitimately be seen to prolong in reflective form the obscure mechanism by which every new form has always germinated on the trunk of life.

This is no metaphor, but an analogy founded in nature. It is the same thing here as there, but simply more clearly definable in the hominized state.

And accordingly, here again reflected on itself, the light starts out, and in a single flash descends back to the lower reaches of the past. But this time what its beam illuminates from ourselves to what is farthest below is no longer an endless play of entangled verticils but a long trail of discoveries. On the same trajectory of fire the instinctive experimentations of the first cell join with the scientific experimentations of our laboratories. Let us therefore bow with respect under the inspiration swelling our hearts for the anxieties and joys of "trying everything and finding everything."[6] The wave we feel passing was not formed in ourselves. It comes to us from very far—having started out at the same time as the light of the first stars. It reaches us after having created everything on the way. The spirit of research and conquest is the permanent soul of evolution.

(c) And as a result, throughout the ages there is unity of movement.

"The rise and expansion of consciousness."

The human is not the center of the universe, as we once naively believed, but something much finer, the rising arrow of the great biological synthesis. The human alone constitutes the last-born, freshest, most complicated and subtly varied of the successive layers of life.

This is nothing else than the fundamental vision—and I shall leave it at that.

But keep in mind that this vision only acquires its full value, or even can only be defended, by simultaneously illuminating the laws and conditions of heredity within ourselves.

Heredity.

As I have already had occasion to say, we are still not aware of how characters are formed, accumulated, and transmitted deep inside the organic germ. Or rather, in the genesis of phyla insofar as it has to do with plants and animals, biology still has not succeeded in combining the spontaneous activity of individuals with the blind determinism of genes. As a result of its inability to reconcile these two terms, it tends to make the living being the passive and powerless witness to the transformations it undergoes, with no responsibility for them or ability to influence them.

But then, in human phylogenesis, and this is the place to settle the question once and for all, what becomes of the part played by the obviously important forces of invention?

What evolution sees of itself in the human, as it is reflected there, is enough to dispel, or at least correct, what seems to be so paradoxical.

Certainly we all feel in our inmost being the weight or reserve of obscure powers, good or bad, a kind of definite unalterable "quantum" that we have received once and for all from the past. But what we see also and just as clearly is that any further advance of the vital wave ahead of us depends on how industriously we use these energies. How could we have any question about this, when right before our eyes we see these energies being stored up irreversibly in the highest forms of life accessible to our experience through all the channels of "tradition," I mean in the collective memory and intelligence of the human biota? Still influenced by our underestimation of what is "artificial," we instinctively consider such social functions as tradition, instruction, and education to be the pale images, the parodies even, of what happens in the natural formation of species. If the noosphere is not an illusion, is it not much truer to recognize that these communications and exchanges of ideas are the higher form in which the less supple modes of biological enrichments manage to establish themselves in us by *additivity*?

In short, the more the living being emerges from the anonymous masses by its own radiation of consciousness, the larger becomes the share of its activity that can be transmitted and preserved through education and imitation. From this perspective, the human represents only an extreme case of transformation. Carried by the human into the thinking zone of the Earth, heredity, without ceasing to be germinal (or chromosomatic) in an individual, has emigrated by the heart of itself into a reflective organism that is collective and permanent, where phylogenesis merges with ontogenesis. From the chain of cells it passes into the circum-terrestrial layers of the noosphere. It is not surprising that from this moment on, and thanks to the characteristics of this new milieu, that the flowering of heredity is reduced to the pure and simple transmission of acquired *spiritual* treasures.

From being passive, as it probably was before reflection, in becoming hominized heredity springs up to become supremely active in its "noospheric" form.

It was therefore not enough for us to say that all evolution has to do in becoming conscious of itself deep within us is to look into the mirror to see into its very depths and to fathom itself. It moreover becomes free to dispose of itself—to give or to refuse itself. Not only do we read the secret of its movements in our slightest acts, but to a fundamental extent *we hold it in our own hands*: responsible for its past to its future.

Is this greatness, or bondage?

This is the whole problem of action.

2   The Problem of Action

A. Modern Disquiet

It is impossible to gain access into a fundamentally new milieu without experiencing the inner throes of a metamorphosis. Even the infant is terrified opening its eyes for the first time. In order to adjust to immeasurably expanded outlines and horizons, we are forced to give up the comfort of our familiar narrow-mindedness. Our mind must recreate the equilibrium of everything so carefully stored away at the bottom of its tiny interior. Leaving some dark prison, we are blinded by light; emerging abruptly onto a high tower, we are oeverwhelmed by a flood of emotions. We experience the dizziness, the disorientation—the whole psychology of modern uneasiness related to its abrupt confrontation with space–time.

It is obvious that human anxiety, in some primordial form, is linked to the very appearance of reflection and thus is as old as humanity itself. But I also believe that from the effects of a reflection that is becoming socialized we are now unquestionably experiencing a far greater disquiet than at any other moment in history. Consciously or unconsciously, despite our smiles, when all conversation has ceased, an anguish, a fundamental anguish of being, pierces us to the core. Yet this does not mean that we have the slightest recognition of the root of our anxiety. Something is threatening us, something is lacking more than ever, and we have no clear idea of what it is.

Let us try, then, to pinpoint the source of this malaise step by step, setting aside the causes of disquiet that are unfounded, until we actually uncover the painful spot where we need to apply the remedy, if there is a remedy.

In its first stages, "space–time sickness" manifests itself most often by an impression of being crushed and useless faced with cosmic immensity. Because our impression of the vastness of space is the most tangible, it is the most striking. How many of us, even once, have actually looked straight at and tried "to live in" a universe that is formed of galaxies spaced hundreds of thousands of light-years apart? Among those who have tried, who, having re-emerged, has not experienced the shattering of one or more beliefs? And even if we have tried to shut our eyes against what astronomers so implacably unveil to us, who has not felt that vague sense of a giant shadow passing over any serenity we find in our enjoyment? And then there is the vastness of duration, which sometimes has the effect of an abyss on the small few who manage to see it, but more often (on those who do not see it well) creates the effect of an appalling stability and monotony. Events follow each other in a dull routine; paths crisscross and lead nowhere. Finally, correlative to this is the enormous number of things: the alarming number of all that has been, all that is, and all that will be necessary to fill space and time. An ocean, where the more lucidly alive we are the more we are given the impression of our own irresistible dissolution. Try consciously putting yourself in the midst of a billion human beings—or simply in a crowd.

Sickness of multitudes and immensities.

I believe that if the modern world is to overcome this first form of disquiet, there is only one thing to do: without hesitation, to follow its intuition right to the end.

If time and space are motionless and blind (as long, I mean, as we believe we see them as motionless or blind), they are terrifying with good reason. Consequently, what would make our initiation into the true dimensions of the world dangerous is if it were left incomplete—deprived of its complement and necessary corrective: the perception that time and space are driven by an evolution. But on the contrary, what difference would it make about the dizzying number and fantastic spacing of the stars if this immensity, in symmetry with the infinitesimal, had no other function than to provide equilibrium for the layer in between; that is, the middle, where and where only life can be built up chemically. What difference would it make about the millions of years and billions of beings that have preceded us if these innumerable drops formed a current that carries us ahead. In the endless expansion of either a static or eternally mobile universe, our consciousness would evaporate, annihilated. In a flux, however incredibly vast it might be, that is not only *becoming*, but *genesis*, which is something quite different, consciousness is reinforced on itself. Actually, as soon as a definitive movement appears, giving them an expression and a face, time and space are humanized.

"Nothing under the sun has ever changed," says the person in despair.

But then oh human being, you thinking being, unless you deny your own thought, how can you explain that you yourself have emerged one day above animality? "In any case, from the beginning of history nothing has changed and nothing more will change." But then, human of the twenty first century, how can you explain that you are waking up to horizons and therefore to fears your ancestors never knew?[7]

The truth is that half our present disquiet would be transformed in elation if we would only decide, in obedience to the facts, to place the essence and measure of our modern cosmogonies in a noogenesis. Along this axis, there can be no doubt. The universe has always been moving and it continues to move at this very moment.

But will it go on moving *tomorrow*?

Tomorrow? It is only here, at this turning point where the future substitutes itself for the present that the observations of science must cede to the anticipations of faith—here legitimately is where our dilemma can and must begin. Who can truly guarantee us a tomorrow? And without the assurance that tomorrow exists, how can we possibly go on living at all, we in whom the terrible gift of foresight has awoken, perhaps for the first time in the universe?

Sickness of the dead end—anguish of feeling shut in.

This time, we have finally put our finger on the painful spot. What makes the world we live in specifically modern, as I said, is having discovered evolution in and around it. And I can now add that right at the root of what troubles the modern world is not being sure, never having any hope of being sure, that there is a way out for evolution—an acceptable way out.

What must that future be, for us to be given the strength, or even the joy, to accept its perspectives and to carry their weight?

To study the problem more closely and to see if there is any remedy, let us examine the situation as a whole.

<u>B</u>. *The Requirements of the Future*

There once was a time when life ruled only over slaves or children. To move ahead, it only needed to be nourished by obscure instincts, to respond to the lure of food and the tasks of reproduction. There was a semiconfused struggle to stay in the light by heaving over others, even if it meant suffocating them. In those days, the whole rose automatically and docile as though it were the product of an immense sum of egoisms. There was also a time, one we can almost remember, when workers or the dispossessed unthinkingly accepted their lot to be slaves of the rest of society.

Now when the first spark of thought appeared on the Earth, life brought a power into the world that was capable of criticizing and judging it. For a long time this formidable risk lay dormant, but when we first awoke to the idea of an evolutionary movement, the dangers of it exploded. Like children come of age and workers who have grown "conscious," we are in the midst of discovering that something is developing in the world by means of us—perhaps at our own expense. And even more serious, we are now aware that in the great game we are engaged in, not only are we the players, but the cards and the stakes as well. If we get up from the table, nothing will go on. And there is nothing, either, to force us to stay seated. Is the game worth it? Or are we its slaves? We humans, who for hundreds of centuries have been so used to "functioning" have hardly formulated the question in our hearts. But just the barely audible murmur of the question is the infallible sign of the rumblings to come. The last century saw systematic strikes in factories. The next certainly will not come to an end without threats of a strike in the noosphere.

The danger is that the elements of the world may refuse to serve the world through the very fact that they think; or, even more precisely, that the world may refuse itself in becoming aware of itself through reflection. What is forming and swelling beneath our modern uneasiness is nothing less than an organic crisis in evolution.

And now, at what price and on what contractual bases will order be restored? From all our evidence, this is the heart of the problem.

In the critical frame of mind we are in from now on, one point seems clear. Only on one condition will we ever apply ourselves to the task that has been placed in our hands of pushing noogenesis onward. That the effort we are asked to make has a chance of succeeding and leading us as far as possible. An animal can hurl itself headlong into a dead end or toward a precipice. A human will not take a step in a direction that is known to be blocked. And this is exactly what our trouble is now.

Having stated this, what is the most we require ahead of us to say that the way is *open*? There is one thing, but it is all or nothing. That we be guaranteed the space and chance to fulfill ourselves, I mean that as we progress we come (directly or indirectly, individually or collectively) *right to the end of ourselves*. This is our elementary request, our base salary— yet it conceals an enormous demand. To reach, in some way, the end of thought: but is this end not the still unimaginable upper limit of a convergent succession propagating itself endlessly higher and higher? Is not the end of thought precisely to have no end? Unique in this among all the energies of the universe, the magnitude of consciousness is such that it is inconceivable for us to suppose it will level off or curve back on itself. It can have any number of points along the way. But it is impossible for it to stop or revert back, for the simple reason that every increase of internal vision is essentially the germ of a new vision that includes all the others and carries even further.

This creates a remarkable situation. From the very fact that our mind is capable of discovering infinite horizons ahead of it, it can only move in the hope that something of itself will end up in a supreme consummation, without which it would justifiably feel truncated, a failure—cheated. From the nature of the work, and correlatively from what the worker demands, a total death and an insurmountable wall where consciousness would collide and disappear for good are therefore "incompossible" with the mechanism of reflective activity (they would immediately break its driving force).[8]

After this, "positive and critical" minds may well go on saying that the new generation, less easily fooled than the old, no longer believes in a future and in the improvement of the world. But have those who write or repeat such things ever understood that if what they say is true, virtually all spiritual movement on the Earth would stop? They seem to believe that although it were deprived of light, hope, and the attraction of an in-exhaustible future, the cycle of life would continue peacefully on. That is just where they are wrong. Perhaps the flowers and fruit would continue out of habit for a few years longer. But the trunk would be cut cleanly and truly from its roots. Even on stacks of material energy, even under the spur of immediate fear or desire, without *the zest for life* humankind would soon stop inventing and creating for a work it knew to be doomed in advance. And affected at the very source of the impetus that sustains it, it would disintegrate in disgust or revolt and fall into dust.

Our intelligence could no more escape the half-glimpsed perspectives of space–time than our lips, once having tasted it, could ever forget the savor of a universal and lasting progress.

If progress is just a myth; that is, if faced with our work we could say "What's the use?" our effort will collapse, dragging all evolution down with it, *because we are evolution.**

C. *The Dilemma and the Choice*

And so from the very fact that we have measured the truly cosmic gravity of the sickness we suffer from, we now possess the remedy to heal our anxiety. "After having gone as far as the human, has the world not stopped? Or if we are still moving, are not all of us just spinning our wheels?"

---

* Regardless of what they say, there is no "energy of despair." What these words really signify is a paroxysm of hope held in abeyance. All conscious energy, like love (and because it is love—see Part IV, ch. II, sec. 2), is founded on hope.[9]

Simply by formulating the dilemma that the analysis of our action has locked us into, our reply to the modern world arises spontaneously.

"Either nature is closed to what we require of the future; in which case thought, the fruit of millions of years of effort, will suffocate, still-born, aborting on itself, in an absurd universe.

"Or else an opening does exist—of supersoul above our souls; but then, for us to commit ourselves to it, this way out must open, with no restrictions, onto psychic spaces that nothing limits in a universe we can entrust ourselves to passionately."

There is no midway solution, only either absolute optimism or pessimism, because the nature of progress is to be all or nothing. There are two, and only two, directions, one that leads toward what is above, the other toward what is below, with no possibility of clinging midway between.

What's more, there is no tangible evidence for going one way or the other. Yet to give us hope there are rational invitations to an act of faith.

At this bifurcation where, driven on by life, we cannot stop to wait— forced to take a stand if we wish to continue doing anything at all—what are we freely going to decide?

To settle the choice for the human being, Pascal, in his famous wager, cast the dice baited with all to gain. Here, when one of the alternative terms is loaded by logic and somehow by the promise of a whole world, can we still speak about a simple game of chance, and do we have the right to hesitate?

Actually too much is at stake in the world for this. From the beginning it has miraculously juggled with too many improbabilities to bring us to birth for us to be risking anything at all by committing ourselves further to follow it right to the end. If it has undertaken this work, it can bring it to completion, using the same methods it began with and with the same infallibility.

Fundamentally, the best guarantee that something will happen is that it seems to us to be vitally necessary.

We just observed that, brought to its thinking stage, life cannot continue without structurally needing to rise ever higher.

This is enough to assure us of the two points required for our im- mediate action.

The first is that there be for us in the future, at least in collective form, not only survival, but *superlife*.

And the second, that all we need to do in order to imagine, discover, and attain this higher form of existence is to think and move ever further ahead in the directions where the past lines of evolution take on their maximum coherence.

Part IV
Superlife

Chapter I

THE COLLECTIVE WAY OUT

Preliminary Observation
Isolation: A Dead End to Avoid

After having recognized that the future of the world is carried within ourselves and that a boundless future lies ahead of us where we can never founder, our first human reflex has often led us to seek fulfillment in an effort to become isolated.

A first instance of this, which dangerously caters to our private egoism, is when from some natural instinct, justified by reflection, we tend to think that if we are to obtain such fullness of life for ourselves, we must separate ourselves as far as possible from the crowd of *others*. For are we not going to reach this "end of ourselves" by separating from all the rest, or at least by making everything else serve ourselves? By study of the past we are taught that in becoming reflective the element was partially freed from phyletic servitude and began to live for *itself*. So why should we not continue from now on to move forward along this ever-evolving line of emancipation, and become more by making ourselves continually more alone? In this case, humanity would culminate in a dust of active and dissociated particles like some kind of radiant substance. Probably not in a burst of sparks extinguished in the night— that hypothetical total death our fundamental option has just definitively eliminated—but, instead, in the hope that in the long run, surely some more penetrating or fortunate rays would ultimately find that path toward consummation our consciousness has always sought. Culmination in a concentration by decentration from the rest. Solitary, and by that very solitude, the elements of the noosphere that could be saved would find their salvation at the extreme limits, and by an excess, of their individualization.

Rarely do we find around us that such extreme individualism goes beyond a philosophy of instant gratification and feels any need to adapt itself to the profound requirements of action.

Another doctrine of "progress by isolation," this one less theoretical and less extreme, and also much more insidious, has whole segments of humanity under its spell at this very moment: the doctrine that there are a few select and chosen races.

Racism, since it flatters a collective egoism—something that is far more vibrant, exalted, and susceptible than any individual self-esteem—has the advantage of accepting and rigorously prolonging in its perspectives the lines of the tree of life as they are. For what in fact does the history of the animal world show us if not a succession of fans that rise up one after the other, one at the expense of the other, by the success and domination of a privileged group? And why should we exempt ourselves from this general law? The struggle for life, survival of the fittest, and confrontation still exist now, even among ourselves. Superman, like any other stem, must germinate from a single main bud of humanity.

Isolation of the individual or isolation of a group are two different forms of the same tactic—each one justifiable at first sight by a convincing extrapolation of the process life has pursued in its development as far as ourselves.

What follows will show the source of the attraction—or perversion— of these theories, which, although cynical and brutal, may still often resound with noble passion; and why we sometimes cannot keep ourselves from resonating to the core with one or the other of these calls to violence. How they are the subtle distortion of a great truth.

What is important for us right now is to see clearly how mistaken they both are and how they mislead us inasmuch as by failing to grasp the essential phenomenon of the "natural confluence of grains of thought," they distort or obscure in our eyes the true contours of the noosphere and make it biologically impossible to form a true spirit of the Earth.

1   THE CONFLUENCE OF THOUGHT

<u>A</u>. Forced Coalescence

(a) Coalescence of Elements
At all degrees of complication the elements of the world naturally have the power to influence and invade one another mutually from the inside in a way that combines their "radial energies" in beams. This psychic interpenetrability, which was only conjecturable in molecules and atoms, grows and becomes directly perceptible in organized beings. In the

human, finally, in whom the effects of consciousness reach their maximum at present in nature, it becomes extreme. It is visible everywhere in the social phenomenon and moreover is directly felt by us. But at the same time, in this case as well it only operates by virtue of the "tangential energies" of arrangement and consequently under certain conditions of spatial proximity.

And this is where a certain fact enters in, which although it appears to be very ordinary, actually reveals one of the most fundamental traits of cosmic structure: the roundness of the Earth. The geometric limitation of a heavenly body closed in on itself like a gigantic molecule. This characteristic already seemed necessary to us at the origin of the first syntheses and polymerizations on the juvenile Earth. It went without saying, that implicitly this was what has constantly subtended all the differentiations and progress of the biosphere. But can we ever say enough about its function in the noosphere!

What would have become of humanity if by some remote possibility it had been free to space and stretch out indefinitely over a boundless surface; I mean if it had been left solely to the play of its internal affinities? Something unimaginable, something most certainly very different from the modern world—and perhaps even nothing at all, judging by the extreme importance taken on by the forces of compression in its development.

At the origin, and for centuries, nothing visibly disturbed the human waves' expansion over the surface of the globe; this is probably even one of the reasons for the slowness of their social evolution. And then, as we have seen, from the Neolithic on these waves began to flow back on themselves. With all available space taken, the occupants had no choice but to squeeze closer together. And that is how, stage by stage, and simply from the effect of multiplication of generations, we have reached the present situation of constituting as a whole an almost solid mass of hominized substance.

Now the more the human elements entered into each other from the effect of this pressure, and thanks to their psychic permeability, the more their minds heated up by coming closer together (mysterious coincidence . . .). And gradually, as if dilated on themselves, each of them extended the radius of its zone of influence over the Earth, which, by this very fact, continued to shrink. What actually do we see happening in the modern paroxysm? I have already pointed it out many times. From yesterday's discovery of the railroad, automobile, and airplane, the physical influence of every human being, once restricted to several kilometers, now extends for hundreds of miles. Even better, thanks to the tremendous biological event that the discovery of electromagnetic waves represents, each individual from now on is simultaneously present (actively and passively) to the whole of the seas and continents—coextensive with the Earth.

And so it is not only by a continual augmentation of the number of its members, but also by a continual augmentation of their zone of individual activity that humanity, subjected to developing in a closed surface, is irremediably subject to an enormous pressure—a pressure that is continually accumulating by an interplay of its own: since each additional degree of tightening only has the effect of exalting the expansion of each element a little more.

This is a primary fact. If we do not take it into account, we would invalidate the projections we are to make of a future for the world.

Undeniably and beyond all hypothesis, the external play of cosmic forces combined with the exceptionally coalescible nature of our thinking souls is working toward an energetic concentration of consciousnesses; so powerful is this effort that it manages to bend under it the very constructions of phylogenesis, as we will see.

(b) Coalescence of Branches

On two occasions already, first as I presented the theory of anthropogenesis and then as I described the history of its phases, I have called attention to that strange property characteristic of human lineages of coming into contact and intermingling particularly through their sheath of psyche and of social institutions. Now the moment has come for us to observe the universal nature of the phenomenon and to discover its ultimate meaning.

What intrigues naturalists on first sight when they try to *see* hominids not merely in themselves (as so many anthropologists usually do), but in comparison to other animal forms is the extraordinary elasticity of their zoological group. In humans a primitive type of anatomical differentiation visibly pursues its course as it does everywhere in evolution. Mutations are produced from genetic effects. Varieties and races are shaped by climatic and geographical influences. Somatically speaking, the "fan" is continually in formation and perfectly recognizable. And yet the remarkable fact is that its divergent branches no longer manage to separate from each other. In conditions of spreading out, where every other initial phylum would long ago have become dissociated as a distinct species, the human verticil unfolds "intact," like a gigantic leaf, where the veins continue to remain joined in a common tissue no matter how distinct they are. There is indefinite interfertilization at all levels. Mixing of genes. Anastomoses of races in civilizations and political units. Considered zoologically, humanity offers the unique spectacle of a "species" capable of achieving something all other species before it had failed to do; not only does it become global, but it covers the Earth without a break, in a single organized membrane.

To what can we attribute this strange condition if not to the reversal, or more exactly to the radical perfecting of the ways of life by bringing into play a powerful instrument of evolution that has now finally become possible: the coalescence of an entire phylum upon itself?

Here again the event is based on the narrow confines of the Earth over which the living branches curve back and draw together by their very growth like tight stems of ivy. But this external contact had been and would always have been insufficient to arrive at a conjunction without the new binder conferred on the human biota by the birth of reflection. Until humankind, the most life had been able to accomplish as far as association is concerned was to gather the finest extremities of the same phylum together socially on themselves one by one. These were fundamentally mechanical and familial groupings materialized in a purely "functional" act of construction, defense, or propagation. The colony, the hive, the termitary, all of them organisms whose power of drawing close together was restricted to the products of a single mother. From humankind onward, thanks to the *universal* framework or support provided by thought, the forces of confluence have been given rapid expansion. Within this new atmosphere the branches themselves of a single group succeed in joining together. Or rather, they fuse together among themselves even before they manage to separate.

In this way, during the course of human phylogenesis the differentiation of groups is preserved up to a certain point—that is, to the extent that in creating new types by experimentation it becomes a biological condition of discovery and enrichment. But then (or at the same time), just as it happens on a sphere, where the meridians spring apart as they separate from one pole only to join again at the opposite, this divergence gives way and becomes subordinate to a movement of convergence, where races, peoples, and nations consolidate and complete one another by mutual fertilization (see FIGURE 4).[1]

We will understand nothing of the human being anthropologically, ethnically, socially, and morally, and, again, can never make any valid prediction regarding the future states of the human until we have seen that "ramification" (insofar as it subsists) now works with the single purpose—and in higher forms—of agglomeration and convergence. The formation of verticils, selection, and struggle for life are from now on merely secondary functions, subordinated in the human being to a work of cohesion. The enfolding in on itself of a network of virtual species around the surface of the Earth. A totally new mode of phylogenesis.*

---

* This is what I have called "human planetization."

B. Megasynthesis

The coalescence of elements and coalescence of branches. The spherical geometry of Earth and psychic curvature of mind, harmonizing in order to counterbalance the individual and collective forces of dispersion in the world and to substitute for them unification: this, finally, is the whole driving force and secret of hominization.

By why unification, what purpose does it serve?

For the answer to this ultimate question to become apparent, all we need to do is bring together the two equations that have been gradually formulated in front of us from the first moment we tried to make a place in the world for the human phenomenon.

Evolution = Rise of consciousness.

Rise of consciousness = Effect of union.

The universal coming together in which the totality of thinking powers and units are engaged at this moment through the conjugated actions of the inside and the outside of the Earth—the drawing together in a single whole, of a humanity whose fragments are fusing and interpenetrating before our eyes, despite, and in exact proportion to, the efforts they make to separate themselves—all this takes an intelligible form to its very depths once we see it as the natural culmination of a cosmic process of organization which has never varied since the distant ages of our juvenile planet.

First of all, the carbonaceous molecules, with their thousands of atoms symmetrically grouped. Next, the cell, where in a minimum of volume thousands of molecules are mounted within a system of planned parts. Next, the metazoan, where the cell is no more than an almost infinitesimal element. And beyond this still, as if in islets,[2] the multiform attempts by the metazoans to enter into symbiosis and rise to a biologically higher state.

And now, like a germ of life in the dimensions of the planet, the thinking layer is developing and intertwining its fibers over its whole expanse, not to blend and to neutralize them, but to reinforce them in the living unity of a single tissue.

I positively see no other coherent, and therefore scientific, way of grouping this immense succession of facts, except by interpreting the "superarrangement" that all thinking elements of the Earth find themselves subject to today, individually and collectively, in the sense of a gigantic psychobiological operation—as a kind of *megasynthesis*.[3]

Megasynthesis in the tangential. And therefore, by this very fact, a leap forward of radial energies, along the principal axis of evolution. Still more complexity: and therefore even more consciousness.

But if this is truly what is happening, what more do we need to recognize the vital error hidden in every doctrine of isolation?

False and contrary to nature is the egocentric ideal of a future reserved for those who have known egotistically how to reach the extremes of "everyone for himself." No element can move or grow unless with and by means of all the others as well as itself.

False and contrary to nature is the racist ideal, in which a main branch taps off all the sap of the tree for itself and rises over the death of the others. To break through to the sun, it takes nothing less than the combined growth of the whole branching structure.

The way out for the world, the gates of the future, the entry into the superhuman,[4] will not open ahead to some privileged few, or to a single people, elect among all peoples. They will yield only to the thrust of *all together** in the direction where all can rejoin and complete one another in a spiritual renewal of the Earth—it is this renewal we must deal with now, clarifying the manner of it and reflecting on its degree of physical reality.

2   THE SPIRIT OF THE EARTH

<u>A</u>. *Humanity*

The very moment modern humans awoke to the idea of progress, humanity was the first form in which they tried to reconcile their hopes for a boundless future, which they could no longer do without, with the prospect of their inevitable individual death. At first, humanity was only a vague entity, something experienced more than reasoned, where an obscure sense of permanent growth combined with a need for universal brotherhood. It was often the object of a naive faith. Yet at present its magic, stronger than any vicissitude or criticism, is still active with equally seductive force both in the soul of the masses and the minds of the "intelligentsia." Can anyone today, whether we belong to its cult or ridicule it, escape that obsessive fear or hold, even, that the idea of humanity has over us?

In reality, in the eyes of the "prophets" of the eighteenth century, the world appeared to be a confused and loosely bound whole. It truly took the determination of a believer to sense the heartbeat of such an embryo. Now here we are after less than two hundred years, almost unaware of what is happening, engaged in at least the material reality of what our ancestors hoped for. In the space of several generations, all kinds of economic and cultural ties have built up around us, and they continue to

---

* Even if it were from the influence and guidance of a few (an "elite").

multiply in geometric progression. Now besides bread, which in its simplicity has symbolized the nourishment of the Neolithic human, we each require every day our ration of iron, copper, and cotton—of electricity, gasoline, and radium—of discoveries, of international films and news. A plot of land is no longer enough to feed each one of us, no matter how large it is—it takes the whole Earth. If words mean anything at all, does it not seem as though a great body is in the process of being born— with its limbs, its nervous system, its centers of perception, its memory—the very body of that great something to come which was to fulfill the aspirations that had been aroused in the reflective being by the freshly acquired consciousness of its interdependence with and responsibility for a whole in evolution?

In fact, as it eliminates individualistic and racist heresies, the very logic of our efforts to coordinate and organize the contours of the world has brought our thought back to perspectives reminiscent of the initial intuition of the first philanthropists. The human being can have no hope of an evolutionary future except in association with all the rest. The visionaries of yesterday caught sight of this fact. And in some way we, too, really do see the same thing they did. But we see it better, for "mounted on their shoulders," we are in a position to discover the cosmic roots, also the particular physical stuff, and finally the specific nature of the humanity they could only sense—and not to see it, we have to shut our eyes.

Cosmic roots. For the earliest humanitarians human beings were thought to be following a natural precept in uniting with those like themselves. They never bothered to analyze the origins of the precept and as a result, to weigh its seriousness. In those days was not nature still treated as a dramatic character or poetic metaphor? What she demanded of us at any moment, she might have just decided yesterday, or tomorrow might not even want at all. For us, more in touch with the dimensions and structural requirements of the world, the forces that rush at us from outside us or surge up from inside us, gradually pressing us into one another, are losing their apparent arbitrariness or risk of instability.

As long as it found only a limited, plural, and disjointed cosmos for its context, humanity remained a fragile, even fictive, construction, but once it has been brought back into biological space–time and its contours appear to prolong the very lines of the universe—among other realities just as vast—humanity takes on consistency and it becomes more probable.

Physical stuff. For a good number of our contemporaries, humanity still remains something unreal, if they have not absurdly materialized it. For some, humanity is only an abstract entity or conventional term. For others, it becomes a densely organic grouping, where the social is transcribed literally in terms of physiology and anatomy. It is a general idea, a juridical entity—or even a gigantic animal. Through lack or excess, on either side we find the same incapacity to think about wholes correctly. Might not the way out of this impasse be to boldly introduce into our intellectual scheme another category, a category reserved for the superindividual? Why not, after all? Geometry, built at first on rational magnitudes, would have remained at a standstill if it had not finally accepted "e," or "π," or any other "incommensurable," to be as complete and intelligible as a whole number. Calculus would never have resolved the problems posed by modern physics if it had not been constantly raised to the conception of new functions. For exactly the same reasons, biology could never have broadened its scope to take in the dimensions of the whole of life if, on the scale of magnitude it now had to consider, it had not introduced certain stages of being that had remained unknown to common experience until then—and precisely, that of the *collective*. Yes, from now on, along with and in addition to individual realities, there are the collective realities, which are irreducible to the element and yet just as objective in their own way. Is this not how I myself have been obliged to speak in order to translate life's movements into concepts?

Phyla, layers, branches, and so forth.

For the eye adjusted to the perspectives of evolution, these directed groupings necessarily become objects as clear, as physically real, as any isolated thing. And it is in this particular class of magnitude that humanity naturally takes its place. For us to be able to represent it, all we need to do is to manage by mental readjustment or restoration to think about humanity exactly as it is—and not try to reduce it to something simpler and already known.

Specific nature, finally. And here we rejoin the problem at the point where earlier we had been brought to note the fact of the confluence of the grains of human thought. As a collective reality, and therefore in a class of its own, humanity can be understood only insofar as we go beyond its body of tangible constructions and try to determine what particular type of conscious synthesis is emerging from its laborious and industrious concentration. This can ultimately be defined only in terms of spirit.

Now, from this perspective and given the present state of things, we can imagine the form it may be led to take tomorrow in two ways and in two degrees. Either—and this is simpler—as a common power or act of knowing and doing. Or—and this goes much deeper—as an organic superaggregation of souls. Science—or unanimity.

B. Science

Taken in the full modern sense of the word, science is the twin of humanity. Born together, the two ideas (or dreams . . .) grew until in the course of the last century they acquired a quasi-religious value. Together they then suffered the same fall from favor, but that did not prevent them even more, and each supported by the other, from continuing to represent the ideal forces our imagination falls back on whenever it tries to materialize in terrestrial form its reasons for believing and hoping.

What does the future of science appear to be? In a first approximation it emerges on our horizon as the establishment of a total, and totally coherent, perspective of the universe. There once was a time when it was assumed that knowledge's only role was to cast light on objects that were ready-made and fixed in place around us—purely for the joy of speculation. Thanks today to a philosophy that gives direction and dedication to our thirst for thinking everything, we have glimpsed that unconsciousness is a kind of ontological inferiority or evil—that the world will only find its completion insofar as it expresses itself in a systematic and reflective perception. Even (if not above all) in mathematics, does not to "find" make something new spring into being? From this viewpoint intellectual discovery and synthesis are not merely speculation, but creation. From now on some physical consummation of things is bound to the explicit perception we have of them. And from now on they are at least partly right* who locate the crowning achievement of evolution in a supreme act of collective vision obtained by a pan-human effort of investigation and construction.†

To know for the sake of knowing. But also, perhaps even more, *to know for the sake of power.*

From the time of its birth, science has mainly grown from the stimulus of solving some problem of life; and its most sublime theories would always have floated rootless above human thought if they had not immediately been transformed or incorporated into some way of mastering the world. Based on this fact, the advance of humanity as it prolongs the advance of all other animate forms is unquestionably developing in the direction of a conquest of matter put to the service of spirit. *To be more powerful for the sake of doing more,* but finally, and above all, *doing more for the purpose of being more.*

Long ago, the precursors of our chemists worked furiously to find the

---

* Is this not Brunschvicg's idea?[5]
† One could say that from the fact of human reflection (both individual and collective), in going beyond the physicochemical organization of bodies, evolution doubles itself as it rebounds on itself (see following note) with a new power of arrangement vastly concentric to the first: the cognitive arrangement of the universe. In fact, to think the world—as physics is just beginning to be aware—is not merely to record it, but to confer on it a form of unity it would never have had if it had not been thought.

philosopher's stone. Today our ambition has grown. It is no longer to make gold—but life! And in view of what has been happening over the past fifty years, who would dare say this is merely a mirage? With our knowledge of hormones, are we not on the verge of taking into our own hands the development of our bodies—and of the brain itself? With the study of genes, are we not soon going to control the mechanism of organic heredity? And with the imminent synthesis of albuminoids, are we not going to be capable someday of provoking what the Earth seems no longer able to bring about, if left to itself: a new wave of organisms—a neolife, artificially stimulated?* The truth is, that no matter how immense and prolonged the universal experimentation had been from the beginning, many possible combinations were able to escape the play of chance, combinations that it had been reserved for the calculated procedures of the human being to bring to light, with thought artificially perfecting the very organ of its thought, and life rebounding ahead from the collective effect of its reflection. Yes, the dream that obscurely nourishes human research has fundamentally been to succeed in mastering, beyond any atomic or molecular affinity, that fundamental energy that all other energies merely serve: united together, to seize the tiller of the world by putting our hands on the driving force of evolution itself.

To those who have the courage to admit that their hopes extend this far, I say they are the most human of all—and that there is less difference between research and adoration than one might think. But let them clearly note the following point, and as we consider it, it will gradually lead us toward a more complete form of conquest and adoration. No matter how far science pushes its discovery of the "essential fire," no matter how capable it becomes someday of remodeling and perfecting the human element, in the end it will always find itself facing the same difficult problem: in grouping elements into the unity of an organized whole, how to give each and every one of them their final value?

C. Unanimity

Above, we spoke of megasynthesis.[6] Based on our better understanding of the collective, when we apply this term to human beings as a whole, it seems to me we must mean it in the full sense of the word and without metaphor. The magnitude of the universe is necessarily homogeneous in nature and dimensions. But could this still be true if the coils of its spiral were to lose any of their degree of reality and consistency in rising higher

---

* This is what I have called the "*human rebound*" of evolution (correlative and conjugated with planetization).

and higher? To remain coherent with the rest, that still unnamed something which the gradual combination of individuals, peoples, and races is to make appear in the world can only be a *supraphysics*, not an *infra-physics*. Deeper than the common act of vision that expresses it, greater than the common power of action it emerges from by a kind of self-birth, there is, and we must envisage it, the reality itself constituted by the living reunion of reflective particles.

But is this not the same as saying (something highly possible) that in becoming thinking, the stuff of the universe has not yet completed its evolutive cycle, and consequently that we are moving toward some new critical point ahead? In spite of its organic connections, whose existence has become apparent to us everywhere, the biosphere still only forms an assemblage of divergent lines, open at their extremities. From the effect of reflection and the inward enfolding this entails, the links of the chain are locking together; and the noosphere is tending to make up a single closed system in which each element sees, feels, desires, and suffers for itself the same things at the same time as all the others.

A harmonized collectivity of consciousnesses, equivalent to a kind of superconsciousness. With the Earth not only covered by myriads of grains of thought, but wrapped in a single thinking envelope until it functionally forms but a single vast grain of thought on the sidereal scale. The plurality of individual reflections being grouped and reinforced in a single unanimous act of reflection.

This is the general form in which we are led scientifically, by analogy and symmetry with the past, to represent for ourselves in the future a humanity apart from which no terrestrial way out opens to the terrestrial requirements of our action.

To good "common sense" and to a certain philosophy of the world where all that is possible is what has already existed, perspectives like these will seem unreal. To the mind familiar with the fantastic dimensions of the universe they will, on the contrary, appear to be entirely natural, simply because they are in proportion to astral immensities.

In the direction of thought—just as in the direction of time and space—can the universe end in any other way but by being immeasurable?

One thing is certain, in any case, that as soon as we adopt a wholly realistic view of the noosphere and the hyperorganic nature of social bonds, the present situation of the world becomes clearer; for we discover a very simple meaning for the profound disturbances troubling the human layer at this moment.

The double crisis, already considerably built up in the Neolithic Age and now approaching its maximum on the modern earth, stems first of all, as we said, from humanity's being *caught up in a mass* (from "planet-ization," one might say): with peoples and civilizations having reached such a degree, of peripheral contact, or economic interdependence, or psychic communion, that the only way they can keep on growing is by interpenetrating. But it also stems from the fact that owing to the combined influence of the machine and the overheating of thought we are witnessing a formidable *outpouring of unused powers*. We humans of the modern age no longer know what to do with the time and powers our hands have unleashed. We groan under such an excess of resources. We protest about "unemployment." And for a while we attempt to force this superabundance back into the matter from which it came—never noticing the impossibility and monstrosity of such an act against nature.

A growing compression of elements at the heart of a free energy that is also ever-increasing.

How can we fail to see in this double phenomenon the two related symptoms, ever the same ones, of a leap in the "radial"; that is, of a new step in the genesis of spirit!

To avoid changing our habits, we try in vain to regulate international conflicts by adjustments of frontiers, or treat the human activities available as "leisure" for distraction. At the rate things are going, we soon will be crushed against one another and something will explode if we stubbornly insist on absorbing material and spiritual forces that are cut to the dimensions of a world in caring for our antiquated hovels.

What we lack is a new domain of psychic expansion, and it is right in front of us, if we would only raise our eyes. Beyond all conflict of empires, peace in conquest and work in joy await us in an interior totalization of the world on itself—in the unanimous building-up of a spirit of the Earth.

But then why is it that our first efforts toward this great objective seem to result only in taking us farther from it?

Chapter II

BEYOND THE COLLECTIVE: THE HYPERPERSONAL

New Preliminary Observation
Discouragement: An Impression to be Overcome

The reasons behind the display of skepticism toward humanity, so fashionable among the "luminaries" of our time, are not at all obvious. Even after the mind has overcome the intellectual difficulties of conceiving the collective and seeing in space–time, another perhaps more serious form of doubt remains, which is linked to the apparent incoherence of the human world at this present moment. The nineteenth century had lived in sight of the Promised Land. We were thought to be approaching a new Golden Age, enlightened and organized by science and warm in communal spirit. But now we see that instead we have lapsed into ever more widespread and tragic dissension. Although the idea of a spirit of the Earth is possible, even probable, in theory, it simply does not stand up to experience. No, human beings will never manage to transcend the human by uniting with themselves. This is a utopia, to be abandoned as quickly as possible. Nothing more.

In order to explain or dismiss such apparent failure, which, if true, would not only entail the end of a beautiful dream but cause us to revert again to the idea of the radical absurdity of the universe, I would first like to point out that it is certainly premature in such a matter to speak of experience and the results of experience. How can we? Has it not taken half a million, perhaps even a million, years for life to pass from the prehominids to the modern human; and shall we now despair because less than two centuries after this same modern human has glimpsed an even higher state above, humans are still in the process of struggling with themselves to be free! This again is another faulty perspective. For us to have comprehended the immensity around, behind, and ahead of us was merely a first step. But understand that if we do not add the perception of slowness to the perception of depth, the transposition of values clearly remains incomplete and the world it generates for us is seemingly impossible. Each dimension has a rhythm of its own. And therefore planetary movement has a planetary majesty. If the whole duration of prehistory were not outlined behind the history of humanity, would not humanity itself appear to be motionless? In this same way and despite an almost explosive acceleration of noogenesis at our level, we cannot hope to see the Earth transformed before our eyes in the space of a generation. Let us restrain our impatience and take heart.

In spite of all evidence to the contrary, humanity may very well be advancing around us at this moment (numerous signs give us every reason to think it is); but if so, it can only be advancing as very large things do, that is, almost imperceptibly.

This is a point of primary importance, and we must never lose sight of it. Yet the fact of establishing it does not answer our deepest fears. For it still does not matter much if the light on the horizon appears to be stationary. What does matter is that the light we have only just glimpsed appears to be going out. If only we could believe we are just at a standstill. But does it not seem at times as if we are actually being blocked by something ahead, or even sucked back—as if we are in the grip of forces of mutual repulsion and materialization beyond our control?

Repulsion. I have already spoken about the tremendous pressures on the Earth at present that are squeezing the human parcels together. How, geographically and psychologically, individuals and entire peoples are being forced on one another in the extreme. Now the strange fact is that in spite of the intensity of the energies drawing them together, the thinking units seem incapable of falling within the radius of their internal attraction. Aside from individual instances, where sexual forces or some extraordinary common passion briefly come into play, human beings continue to be hostile or at least closed to one another.[1] Like a powder whose grains refuse to enter into molecular contact no matter how compressed they are, they exclude and repel one another from the depths with all their strength. Unless, even worse, their mass sets in such a way that instead of the anticipated spirit, a new wave of determinism, that is, of materiality, arises.

Materialization. Here I am not only thinking of the laws of large numbers which, whatever their hidden ends might be, structurally enslave each newly formed multitude. Like every other form of life, the human to become fully human had to become legion. And until a multitude becomes organized, however directed it might be it inevitably remains at the mercy of the play of chance and probability—those imponderable currents, which, from fashion and rates of exchange to political and social revolutions, make each of us a slave to the obscure seethings of the human mass. However spiritualized the elements of it may be, in the degree to which as every aggregation of consciousnesses is not harmonized it is automatically enveloped at its own level by a veil of "neomatter"[2]— matter, which is the tangential face of every living mass in process of unification. We must react against such conditions, of course. But with the satisfaction of knowing that they are only the sign and price of progress. But on the other hand, what can be said about that other kind of enslavement, which continually increases in the world in very proportion to the efforts we make to organize ourselves?

At no other age in history has humanity been so well-equipped and made so many efforts to create some kind of order out of its multitudes. When we speak today of "mass movements" we are no longer referring to the hordes that streamed down from the forests of the North and the steppes of Asia, but to the "men by the millions" as they are so aptly called,[3] who are scientifically assembled. "Men by the millions" geometrically arranged in quincunxes on parade grounds, standardized in factories, motorized. . . . And with Communism and National Socialism, all this has only ended up in the most appalling linkage in chains! In the crystal instead of the cell.[4] The termitary instead of the fraternity. Instead of the expected upsurge of consciousness, what we have is the mechanization that inevitably seems to emerge from totalization.

"Eppur si muove!"[5]

Faced with such a profound perversion of the rules of noogenesis, I believe that we must not react in despair, but reexamine ourselves. When energy runs out of control, far from continuing to question the energy, does not the engineer simply begin his calculations all over again so that he can find a better way to direct it? As monstrous as it seems, must not modern totalitarianism be the distortion of something very magnificent and very close to the truth? There can be no doubt about it, the great human machine was made to work—and it *must* work: by producing a superabundance of spirit. If it does not function, or rather if all it generates is matter, this is because it is working in reverse.

Is it not possible perhaps that in our theories and our actions we have failed to make room for the person and the forces of personalization?

1 Convergence of the Personal and the Omega Point
A. *The Personal Universe*

Contrary to "primitive" peoples, who endow everything that moves with personal expression[6]—or even to the first Greeks, who deified every aspect and force of nature—modern humans are obsessed by the need to depersonalize (or impersonalize) all that they most admire. There are two reasons for this tendency. The first is analysis—that marvelous instrument of scientific research to which we owe all our advances, yet which allows the soul to escape from one undone synthesis after another, until we are left facing a pile of disassembled parts and evanescent particles. The second is the discovery of the sidereal world—which is such a vast subject that it seems to destroy all proportion between our own existence and the dimensions of the cosmos around us. A single reality appears to subsist that is capable of covering both the infinitesimal and the immense at once: energy, that universal floating entity from which everything emerges and into which everything falls back, as if into an ocean. Energy is the new spirit, the new god. The impersonal is at the Omega of the world as well as its Alpha.[7]

Influenced by these kinds of impressions, one could say that we seem to have lost the sense of the true nature of the person along with our respect for it. Ultimately we admit that to be centered in oneself, and to be able to say "I," is the privilege (or rather the defect) of the element, in the degree to which shutting itself off from the rest, it manages to set itself up at the antipodes of the whole. In the opposite direction, verging on the collective and the universal, in the sense, I mean, of what is most real and durable in the world, we think of the "ego" as diminishing and being cancelled out. Personality is seen to be a specifically corpuscular and ephemeral property—a prison from which we must try to escape.

That is more or less where we stand today intellectually.

Yet if we try to push the logic and coherence of the facts to the very end, as I attempt to do in this essay, do not the ideas of space–time and evolution legitimately lead us to exactly the opposite perspective?

Evolution is a rise toward consciousness, as we have seen and acknowledged. This is no longer contested, even by the most materialistic, or at least most agnostic, of humanitarians. Evolution must culminate ahead in some kind of supreme consciousness. But precisely if it is to be supreme, must not this consciousness bear the maximum degree of our perfection within it: that illuminative bending back of our being on itself? It is an obvious error to prolong the curve of hominization toward a state of diffusion! Thought can only be extrapolated toward a hyperreflection, that is, toward a hyperpersonalization. Or else how could it store up our conquests, which are all made in the realm of the reflective? At first we recoil at the shock of associating an ego with the whole. There seems to be such a striking, almost laughable, disproportion between these two terms. This is because we have not mediated enough on the threefold property each consciousness possesses: (1) of partially centering *everything* around itself; (2) of always being able to center *further on itself*; and (3) by this very supercentration, of being led *to join with all the other centers surrounding it.*[8] Are we not experiencing at each instant a universe whose immensity is being gathered up more and more simply within each one of us through the interplay of our senses and our reason? And with the current establishment by science and various philosophies, of a collective human "weltanschauung"[9] in which each of us cooperates and participates, are we not experiencing the first symptoms of an assembling of an even higher order, the birth of some kind of unique focal point from the converging fires of millions of elementary focal points scattered over the surface of the thinking Earth?

All our difficulties and repulsions regarding the opposition between the whole and the person would dissipate if we would only realize that structurally the noosphere and in a more general sense, the world represent an ensemble that is not merely closed, but *centered.* Because it contains and generates consciousness, space–time is necessarily *convergent by nature.* Consequently, followed in the right direction, its boundless layers must coil up somewhere ahead in a point—call it *Omega*—which fuses them and consummates them integrally in itself. For however immense the sphere of the world may be, it ultimately exists and is perceptible only in the direction where its rays meet one another (even if this is beyond time and space). Better still, the more immense this sphere is, the richer, also the deeper, and therefore the more conscious, it means that point will be where the "volume of being" it encompasses is concentrated: since, seen from our side, spirit[10] is essentially the power of synthesis and organization.

Envisaged from this point of view, the universe takes on a definite shape without losing any of its enormousness and therefore without becoming anthropomorphicized: consequently we see that it is *beyond* our souls, not in the reverse direction, that we must look in order to think, undergo, and activate the universe. In the perspectives of a noogenesis, time and space become truly humanized—or rather, superhumanized. Far from being mutually exclusive, the universal and the personal (that is, the "centered,") grow in the same direction and culminate in one another at the same time.

It is therefore an error to look for the prolongation of our being and of the noosphere in the direction of the impersonal. The future of the universe can only be hyperpersonal—in the Omega Point.[11]

B. The Personalizing Universe

Remember that it was by *personalization*, the internal deepening of consciousness on itself, that we characterized the individual destiny of the element become fully itself through the step of reflection (section (d), p. 116); and there our investigation stopped temporarily insofar as it was concerned with the fate of the human individual. Now this same process of *personalization* appears here again, but this time as it defines the collective future of the grains of thought added together. For the element and for the sum total of synthesized elements the function is the same. How should we conceive and predict the way that these two movements are going to harmonize with each other? How can the innumerable individual curves be inscribed or even prolonged inside their common envelope without being hindered or deformed?

The time has come for us to treat this problem; and with this in mind, to continue to pursue our analysis of the nature of the personal Center of convergence on whose existence, as we have just seen, the evolutionary equilibrium of the noosphere is suspended. If it is to be equal to its role, what must this higher pole of evolution be like?

By definition, the quantity of consciousness gradually freed on Earth by the noosphere is added together and gathered in its flowering and integrity, in Omega. This point has been made. But what precisely do such seemingly simple words as "addition of consciousness" mean, and what do they entail?

To listen to the disciples of Marx, it would seem that all humanity needs to do in order to grow and to justify the sacrifices it imposes on us is to gather up the successive acquisitions that each one of us relinquishes to it as we die: our ideas, our discoveries, our artistic creations, our example. Are not all these imperishable works the best part of our being?

Think about it for a moment, and we will see that if a universe hypothetically acknowledged to be the "collector and conserver of consciousnesses"[12] were limited only to gathering such spoils as these, the operation would be a terrible waste. What emanates from each one of us by means of invention, education, and diffusion of every kind and passes into the human mass does have vital importance, and I have spoken enough of its phyletic value for anyone to suspect me of minimizing it. But after having thoroughly made this point, I am also forced to recognize that, far from communicating what is most precious in this contribution to collectivity, under the best of circumstances all we have managed to transmit to others is the shadow of ourselves. Our works? But what in the very interests of life in general is the work of human works if not for each one of us to establish in ourselves an absolutely original center where the universe is reflected in a unique and inimitable way: precisely our self, our personality? Deeper than all its rays the very focal point of our consciousness is the essential thing for Omega to retrieve if it is to be truly Omega. Now clearly we cannot divest ourselves of this essential thing for others as we would give away a coat or pass on a torch, since we are the flame. To communicate itself, my self must subsist even in the abandonment of itself or else the gift vanishes. The inevitable conclusion from this is that the concentration of a conscious universe would be unthinkable if it did not assemble in itself at the same time as *all* that is conscious, *every* consciousness, with each one of them remaining conscious of itself at the end of the operation—and even, as we must clearly understand, with each one becoming more itself, and therefore more distinct from the others, the closer it comes to them in Omega.

Not only the conservation, but the exaltation[13] of the elements by convergence!

What truly could be simpler and more in keeping with everything we know?

Whatever the domain—whether it be the cells of the body, the members of society, or the elements of a spiritual synthesis—*"union differentiates."* In every organized whole the parts perfect and fulfill themselves. By failing to grasp this universal law of union, so many kinds of pantheism have led us astray in the worship of a great Whole in which individuals were supposed to become lost like a drop of water, dissolved like a grain of salt, in the sea. If we apply it to the sum total of consciousnesses, the law of union frees us from this dangerous and ever-recurring illusion. No, in confluence along the line of their centers, the grains of consciousness do not tend to lose their contours and blend together. On the contrary, they accentuate the depths and incommunicability of their *ego*. The more together, they become the other, the more they become "themselves." How could it be otherwise, since they plunge into Omega? Can a center dissolve? Or rather is not its own way of dissolving precisely to supercenter itself?

In this way, under the combined influence of two factors, the fundamental immiscibility of consciousnesses and the natural mechanism of every unification, the only form in which we are able to correctly express the final state of a world on the path of psychic concentration is in a system whose unity coincides with a paroxysm of harmonized complexity. Thus it would be false to represent Omega merely as a center born of the fusion of the elements it gathers together or nullifies in itself. By its structure, Omega in its ultimate principle *can only be a distinct Center radiating at the core of a system of centers*. The only form that emerges if, logically and to the very end, we apply the idea of collectivity to a whole made up of grains of thought is of a grouping in which the personalization of the whole and the elementary personalizations reach their maximum simultaneously, and without blending, under the influence of a supremely autonomous focal point of union.*

And here we see the apparent motives for both the fervor and the powerlessness accompanying every egotistic solution to life. Egoism, whether it be individual or racial, is justifiably intensified by the idea that in fidelity to life the element rises to the extremes of uniqueness and incommunicability it possesses within itself. It thus *feels* right. Its only mistake, but a fatal one that leads it to go astray, is *to confuse individuality with personality.* In trying to distinguish itself as much as possible from others, the element individualizes itself; but in doing so it falls back and tries to drag the rest of the world backward toward plurality and into matter. In reality, the element diminishes itself and becomes lost. To become fully ourselves, it is in the opposite direction we must advance, in the direction of convergence with all the rest, toward the "other." The end of ourselves and the culmination of our originality is not in our individuality, but in our person; and according to the evolutionary structure of the world, the only way we can find our person is by uniting with one another. From top to bottom the law is forever the same. There can be no spirit without synthesis. The true *ego* grows in inverse ratio to "egotism." In the image of Omega that attracts it, the element becomes personal only by becoming universalized.†

This is so, however, on one obvious and essential condition. As it follows from the previous analysis, for the human particles to become truly personalized under the creative influence of union, they must not be joined haphazardly. Since it is actually a question of creating a synthesis of centers, they must enter into mutual contact center to center, and *in no other way.* If we want to work effectively toward the progress of evolution in ourselves, among the various kinds of psychic interactions

* It is for this necessarily autonomous and central focal point that we will reserve the name "Omega Point" in all that follows.

† And inversely, it is only through becoming superpersonalized that it becomes truly universalized. This makes the whole difference (and misunderstanding) between true and false political or religious mysticism: false mysticism destroys the human being, whereas true mysticism completes the human being by "loss in something greater than oneself."

animating the noosphere, it is above all the "intercentric" kind of energies that we must recognize, tap, and develop.

And this very fact brings us back to the problem of loving.

2   LOVE ENERGY

Ordinarily we consider only the sentimental side of love (and with such refined analysis!), the joys and trials it causes us. Here, for purposes of defining the ultimate phases of the human phenomenon, I intend to study it in its natural dynamism and evolutionary significance.

Taken in its full biological reality, love (namely, the affinity of one being for another) is not unique to the human being. It represents a general property of all life, and as such it embraces all the varieties and degrees of every form successively taken by organized matter. In the mammals, who are so close to us, we can easily recognize love in its various modalities of sexual passion, parental instinct, social interdependence, and so on. Farther or lower down on the tree of life, the analogies are less clear. They grow fainter and fainter until they become imperceptible. But here is the place for me to repeat what I said above about the "inside of things."[14] If some internal propensity to unite did not exist, even in the molecule, in probably some incredibly rudimentary yet already nascent state, it would be physically impossible for love to appear higher up, in ourselves, in the hominized state. Since we have observed its presence with certainty in ourselves, we have every reason to suppose that, at least inchoately, it is present in everything that exists. And, in fact, we need only to observe the rising confluence of consciousnesses around us to see its presence everywhere. Plato had already sensed this and given it immortal expression in his Dialogues. Later on, with thinkers like Nicolas of Cusa, medieval philosophy technically returned to the same idea. Driven by forces of love, the fragments of the world are seeking one another so the world may come to be. This is no metaphor—and far more than poetry. Whether force or curve, the universal gravity of bodies, so striking to us, is nothing but the underside or shadow of what really moves nature. To grasp this "fontal" cosmic energy, we must, if things have an inside, descend into the internal or radial zone of spiritual attractions.

In all its nuances, love is nothing more or less than the direct or indirect trace marked in the heart of the element by the psychic convergence of the universe on itself.

And if I am not mistaken, this is just the ray of light we need to help us see around us more clearly.

It is painful and distressing for us to observe how, contrary to our theoretical predictions and expectations, modern attempts at human collectivization only result in debasing and enslaving consciousnesses. Yet what path have we taken until now to unite ourselves? The defense of some material situation, the opening up of some new industrial territory, the creation of better conditions for a social class or underprivileged nations—it is still only on such limited grounds as these that we have tried to approach one another. Why should we be surprised that, following the animal societies, we are becoming mechanized by the very interplay of our association! Even in the supremely intellectual act of constructing science (as long, at least, as it remains on the purely speculative and abstract plane) our souls' impact operates only obliquely and indirectly. The contact remains superficial—and thus threatens to become another slavery. Love alone is capable of completing our beings in themselves as it unites them, for the good reason that love alone takes them and joins them by their very depths—this is a fact of daily experience. For actually is not the moment when two lovers say they are lost in each other the moment when they come into the most complete possession of themselves? Truly, in the couple and in the team, and all around us at every moment, does love not accomplish that magic act, reputed to be so contradictory, of "personalizing" as it totalizes. And if it does this on a daily basis on a reduced scale, why could it not someday repeat it in the dimensions of the Earth?

Humanity, the spirit of the Earth, the synthesis of the individual and peoples, the paradoxical reconciliation of the element and the whole, of unity and multitude—for all these things, said to be so utopian, yet which are so biologically necessary, to actually take shape in the world, is not all we need to do, to imagine that our power of loving develops until it embraces the totality of men and women and of the Earth?[15]

"But this is just where you have put your finger on the impossible!" someone could say. "Isn't it true that all a person can do is give affection to one or a few rare human beings? The heart's radius can go only so far and no further, leaving room for nothing but cold justice and reason. The act of loving everyone and everything is contradictory and false, and ultimately leads to loving nothing at all."[16]

But then, I will reply, if it is impossible to have universal love as you claim, how are we to explain that irresistible instinct in our hearts that draws us toward unity each time our passion is heightened in any sense? Sense of the universe, sense of the whole. The nostalgia that seizes us in the midst of nature, before beauty, music—the expectation and awareness of a Great Presence. Except for the "mystics" and their commentators, why is it that psychology has so persisted in overlooking that fundamental vibration whose tone, to the trained ear, can be distinguished at the base, rather the height, of every great emotion? Resonance to the whole is the fundamental note of pure poetry and religion. Once again, what does this phenomenon, born with thought and growing with it, reveal except a profound harmony between two realities that seek each other: the separated particle trembling at the approach of the rest?

With love of spouse, love of children, love of friends, and to some degree, love of country, we often imagine that we have exhausted the various natural forms of loving. But precisely the most fundamental form of passion is missing from this list, that passion which under the pressure of a universe closing on itself precipitates the elements upon one another in the whole. The passion of cosmic affinity, and as a result the cosmic sense.

A love that embraces the entire universe is not only something psychologically possible; it is also the only complete and final way in which we can love.

And now that we have established this point, how can we explain the fact that the degree of repulsion and hatred we see around us seems to be increasing. If we are besieged from within by such a powerful virtuality for union, what prevents it from being put into effect?

Probably this, quite simply: that we overcome the "anti-personalist" complex paralyzing us and decide to accept the possibility and reality of something loving and lovable at the summit of the world overhead. Insofar as it absorbs or seems to absorb the person, collectivity kills the love trying to be born. Collectivity as such is fundamentally unlovable. And this is where philanthropy fails. Common sense is right. It is impossible to give oneself to an anonymous number. Let the universe take on ahead of us a face and a heart, become personified for us, so to speak,* and then in the atmosphere created by this focal point, the elementary attractions will unfold. And it is probably then that, under the forced pressure of an Earth closing back on itself, the tremendous energies of attraction still dormant between human molecules will burst out.

The discoveries made over the last hundred years with their unitary perspectives have brought a new and decisive impetus to our sense of the world, our sense of the Earth, and our sense of the Human. The surge of modern pantheisms is a result of this. But that impetus will only end by plunging us back into supermatter if it does not lead to Someone.

For the failure that threatens us to be transformed into success—for the conspiration[17] of human monads to be brought about—all we have to do is, prolonging our knowledge to its utmost limits, to recognize and accept that what is necessary to close and provide equilibrium to space–time is not only some vague existence to come, but also (as I now

---

* Not, of course, by becoming a person—but by becoming charged at the very heart of its development with the governing and unitive influence of a focal point of personal energies and attractions.

must stress) the *already present* reality and radiation of that mysterious Center of our centers I have just called "Omega."

3   The Attributes of the Omega Point

After having allowed itself to fall too far under the spell of analysis, modern thought is finally growing accustomed to envisioning the creative evolutionary function of synthesis. There is definitely something *more* in the molecule than in the atom, *more* in the cell than in molecules, *more* in the social than in the individual, and *more* in mathematical construction than in calculations and theorems. We now tend to admit that with each subsequent degree of combination, *something emerges* into a new order, something that cannot be reduced to the isolated elements; and from this fact consciousness, life, and thought are very close to acquiring the right to scientific existence. Yet science is still far from recognizing the particular value of independence and solidity that this "something" possesses. Born from an incredible concurrence of chances on an edifice so precariously assembled, and creating no measurable increase of energy, are not these "creatures of synthesis" the most beautiful yet also the most fragile of things experimentally, and how could they possibly anticipate or survive beyond the ephemeral joining of particles on which their souls have just alighted? When all is said and done, and in spite of being half-converted to the spiritual side, physics and biology still look to the elementary—in the direction of infinitely diluted matter—to find eternal and total stability.

According to this state of mind, the idea that some Soul of souls is in preparation at the summit of the world is not so foreign to current views of human reason as one might think. After all, how else could our thought generalize the principle of emergence?* But at the same time, since this Soul coincides with a supremely improbable encounter between the totality of elements and causes, it remains understood or implied that it could be formed only in the far distant future and in total dependence on the reversible laws of energy.[18]

Now it is precisely these two limitations (distance and fragility) that to my mind are incompatible with the nature and function of Omega, and I would like to show that we must successively rid ourselves of them for two positive reasons: love, and superlife.

Because of love, in the first place. Expressed in terms of internal energy, the cosmic function of Omega consists in initiating and maintaining the

---

* See Part I, above, the quotation from J. B. S. Haldane, p. 25*.

unanimity of the world's reflective particles under its radiation. But how could it carry out this action if it were not somehow already loving and lovable *right here and now*? Love, as I said, dies on contact with the impersonal and anonymous. It dissipates just as infallibly with distance in space—and even much more with difference in time. To love one another it is essential to coexist. Consequently, however marvelous we envision its form to be, if it did not act with equal power, that is, with stuff of the same proximity, Omega could never even merely balance the interplay of human attractions and repulsions. With love, as with every other kind of energy, the lines of force must close together at each moment in a given existence. No ideal or virtual center can ever be enough. For the noosphere to be actual and real, the center must be actual and real. To be supremely attractive, Omega must be already supremely present.

Because of superlife, moreover. To escape the threat of disappearance, which is incompatible as I said with the mechanism of reflective activity, human beings try to refer the collective principle of the results achieved by their operation to an ever-vaster and more permanent object, to civilization, humanity, the spirit of the Earth. Aggregated into these enormous entities, at their incredibly slow rhythm of evolving, humans are given the impression of having escaped the destructive action of time.*

But all this does is to put off the problem. For finally, no matter how large is the radius traced *within* time and space, does the circle ever encompass anything except what perishes? So long as our constructions rest with all their weight on the Earth, they will vanish with the Earth. The radical defect of all forms of faith in progress as expressed in the positivist creeds is that they do not definitively eliminate death. What is the use of having detected some kind of focal point at the forefront of evolution if it can and must someday come apart? To satisfy the supreme demands of our action, Omega must be independent of the collapse of the powers with which evolution is woven.

Actuality and irreversibility.

There is only one way for our mind to integrate these two essential properties of the autonomous Center of all centers into the coherent pattern of noogenesis and that is to take up the principle of emergence again and to complete it. Our experience makes it perfectly clear that, *during the course of evolution*, emergence only happens successively and in mechanical dependence on what precedes it. There is first the grouping of elements; then the manifestation of "soul," whose operation, from the standpoint of energetics, only reveals a continually more complex

---

* On this subject see, for example, H. G. Wells's strange book, *The Anatomy of Frustration*, a remarkable account of the faith and fears of modern humans.[19]

enfolding inward of the powers transmitted by the chains of elements. The radial as function of the tangential. The pyramid whose summit is supported by its base. This is how it looks along the way. And this is even how Omega itself is discovered by us at the end of the process, insofar as the movement of universal synthesis culminates in it. But notice carefully that in its evolutionary aspect Omega still only shows *half* of itself. At the same time that it is the term of the series, it is also *outside* the series. It not only crowns but closes the series. Or else—in organic contradiction to the whole operation—the sum total would come apart on itself. Going beyond the elements, as we come to speak of the conscious pole of the world, we need to do more than say that it *emerges* from the rise of consciousnesses: we must add that it has simultaneously already *emerged*. Or else it would be incapable either of subjugating in love, or firmly fixing anything in incorruptibility. If by its very nature it did not escape from the time and space it gathers together, it would not be Omega.

Autonomy, actuality, irreversibility, and finally, therefore, transcendence are the four attributes of Omega.

In this way the diagram of the sphere—left incomplete at the beginning of this work, when we attempted to enclose the complex energetics of our universe—effortlessly locks together.[20]

In the first place, Omega is the principle we needed to explain both the steady advance of things toward more consciousness and the paradoxical solidity of what is most fragile. Contrary to the way things still appear to physics, total stability does not lie in what is below—in the infra-elementary—but above, in the ultrasynthetic. It is therefore only by its tangential envelope that the world goes on dissipating haphazardly into matter. In its radial nucleus, the world finds its shape and natural consistency by gravitating against the probable, toward a divine focal point of Spirit that draws it forward.

Something in the cosmos, therefore, escapes entropy—and does so more and more.

In some way obscurely stimulated by the action of the *Prime Mover ahead*, for immense periods during the course of evolution the radial could only manage to express animal consciousness in diffuse groupings. And since at this stage the nuclei lacked the power to attach themselves to a support above them whose order of simplicity was greater than their own, hardly were they formed when they came apart. As soon, on the other hand, as, through reflection, a type of unity appeared that was no longer closed or even centered but punctiform, the sublime physics of centers came into play. Having become centers, and therefore persons, the elements could finally react directly as elements to the personalizing action of the Center of centers. For consciousness, crossing the critical surface of hominization meant in fact to pass from the divergent to the convergent—that is, to somehow change hemisphere and pole.[21] Below that critical, "equatorial" line there is the lapse back into the multiple. Beyond it lies the fall into increasing and irreversible unification. Once a reflective center is formed, it can change only by sinking deeper into itself. Certainly the human being appears to disintegrate just like the animal. But here and there the phenomenon functions in reverse. Through death, in the animal the radial is reabsorbed into the tangential. In the human, the radial escapes the tangential and is freed from it. There is an escape from entropy by a sudden reversal toward Omega. Death itself is hominized!

In this way, forming the veritable and indestructible atoms of its stuff from grains of thought, the universe—clearly defined in its resultant—is continually building itself above our heads in the opposite direction of matter that vanishes: a universe that is the collector and conserver not of mechanical energy as we thought, but of persons. One by one, like a continual exhalation, "souls" break away around us, carrying their incommunicable charge of consciousness toward what is above. One by one, yet not in isolation. Since by the very nature of Omega, there can only be one possible point of definitive emersion:[22] the point where, from the synthesizing action of union that personalizes, the noosphere, enfolding its elements on themselves while simultaneously enfolding in on itself, collectively reaches its point of convergence—at the "end of the world."

Chapter III

THE ULTIMATE EARTH

We have recognized that without matter's bending back on itself, without, that is, the closed chemistry of molecules, cells, and phyletic branches, there never would have been either a biosphere or a noosphere. In their appearance and development, life and thought are bound to the contours and fate of the terrestrial mass not just by accident, but by structure.

And, on the other hand, we have just now seen that, ahead, to maintain and provide equilibrium for the growth of consciousnesses, there is a psychic center of universal drift that transcends time and space and is therefore essentially extraplanetary. A noogenesis rising irreversibly toward Omega through the strictly limited cycle of a geogenesis.

At some given moment in the future, from some influence of one curve or the other, or both at once, it is inevitable that the two branches separate. However convergent evolution may be, it can only complete itself on Earth through a point of dissociation.

This is how that fantastic and inevitable event, which draws closer to us with each passing day, introduces itself naturally into our perspectives and tends to take shape: the end of all life on our globe—the death of the planet—and the ultimate phase of the human phenomenon.

No one who has ever had the slightest glimpse of the incredible potential for the unexpected accumulated in the spirit of the Earth would dare to portray what the final appearance of the noosphere will be. The end of the world is unimaginable. But up to a point, using the lines of approach we have previously constructed, we can foresee the significance and circumscribe the forms of something it would otherwise be senseless to describe.

What I would like to suggest dispassionately and logically, without apocalypse, is what the Earth at the end can never be in a universe of conscious stuff, what form it will take, and what it has chances of becoming. I do this not so much to affirm anything as to stimulate thought.

1   PREDICTIONS TO DISMISS

When we mention the end of the world, the idea of some kind of catastrophe always comes to mind.

Some sidereal cataclysm, most often. With such a multitude of stars circulating around us and brushing by us, with so many worlds exploding on the horizon, and given the implacable play of chance, is it not our own turn now to be struck and annihilated?

The most we can hope for in our prison is to suffer a slow death. That seems inevitable. Ever since physics has discovered that all energy dissipates, we seem even to feel the heat lowering around us in the world. Fortunately for us, another discovery has come to compensate for this effect and to delay the cooling off to which we are condemned, that of radioactivity. If everything goes well, astronomers now promise us a good several hundred million years. We can breathe again. But meanwhile, even if the decline has been pushed back, the darkness still deepens.

And then will we even still be there to see the darkness fall? To say nothing of cosmic bad luck that threatens us, between then and now what will happen within the Earth's living layer? With increasing complication and with age, internal threats are multiplying in the midst of the biosphere and noosphere. There are so many ways to come to an end! Microbial invasions. Organic counter-evolutions. Sterility. War. Revolution. But, still, perhaps any of these is preferable to prolonged senescence.

We are all too familiar with these different scenarios. We have fantasized about them. We have seen their portrayal anticipated in the novels of the Goncourts, Benson, and Wells, or in scientific works under the signature of famous names. Each of them is perfectly plausible. It is true that we can be crushed at any moment by an enormous meteor. It is true, also, that tomorrow the Earth may tremble and give way under our feet. I, too, admit that, taken in isolation, the will of any human being can refuse the task of rising higher toward union. And yet by basing myself on everything the past of evolution teaches us, I believe I can say that *to the degree in which* any of these multiple disasters imply an idea of premature accident or decline, we have nothing to fear from them. Although possible in theory, for a higher reason, we can be sure they *will not happen.*

And this is why.

The pessimistic portrayals of the final days of the Earth as cosmic catastrophe, biological disintegration, or simply arrested growth or senescence, all have in common the fact that they extend the characteristics and conditions of our individual and elementary ends to the whole of life, *without correction*: fractures, sickness, or decrepitude make up the death of each of us; this, therefore, is how humanity will die.

Now do we really have any right to make such a simple generalization?

As soon as one individual disappears, even if prematurely, there is always another ready to take its place. The loss is not irreparable for the continuation of life. But can we say this in humanity's case? Somewhere in one of his books, the great paleontologist Matthew[1] has suggested that if ever the human branch were to disappear, another thinking branch would soon replace it.[2] But he is careful not to say where this mysterious bud could appear on the tree of life as we know it, and no doubt would be hard put to do so.

It seems to me that if we consider the whole story, biologically the situation is entirely different.

In the course of its planetary existence, the Earth has been capable of covering itself with life once and once only. Similarly, once and once only life has been capable of crossing the threshold of reflection. There is a single season for thought, just as there is for life. We must not forget, from that moment the human forms the arrow of the tree of life.[3] In the human as such, to the exclusion of all the rest, the entire hopes for the future of the noosphere are concentrated from now on; that is, for the future of biogenesis, which ultimately means of cosmogenesis. That being the case, how could humankind possibly come to an end, or a stop, or decline before its time, without the universe simultaneously aborting on itself, something we already have decided to be absurd.

In its present state the world would be unintelligible, the presence of the reflective within it would be inexplicable, unless we supposed there to be a secret complicity between the immense and the infinitesimal to warm, nourish, and sustain to the very end, through the use of chances, contingencies, and freedoms, the consciousness born between them both.[4] It is this complicity we must bank on. *The human is irreplaceable.* Therefore, however unlikely the perspective may seem, *humankind has to succeed*, probably not necessarily, but infallibly.

Whatever the final form it takes, it will not be a halt, but a final progression, coming at its biological time. A maturation and paroxysm— ever higher into the improbable out of which we have come. If we want to foresee the end of the world, this is the direction in which we need to extrapolate the human being and hominization.

2   The Approaches

Without overstepping the bounds of scientific probability, we can say that life has long geological periods at its disposal for its development.

Moreover, observed in its thinking form, life still shows all the signs of an energy in full expansion. Actually, on the one hand, compared to the zoological layers that precede it, whose average life is on the order of 80 million years at the least, humanity is so young that it could be called newborn. On the other, if we observe how rapidly thought has developed over the slight interval of a few thousands of years, this youth bears in itself every indication and promise of an entirely new biological cycle. Thus it is very likely that between Earth at the end and our modern Earth there stretches an immense duration, which is not at all characterized by a slowing down, but by an acceleration and the definitive unfolding of the forces of evolution in the direction of the human arrow.

Given the hypothesis of success—the only possible one—in what form and along what lines can we imagine the development of progress over that interval of time?

In a collective and spiritual form, first of all. Since the human's appearance we have been able to note a certain slowing down of the passive and somatic transformations of the organism to the benefit of the conscious and active metamorphoses of the individual caught up in society. The artificial has taken over from the natural. Oral or written transmission has been superposed on genetic (or chromosomatic) forms of heredity. Without denying the possibility or even probability that there will be some prolongation of the past processes of orthogenesis* in our limbs, and particularly in our nervous system, I tend to think that the influence of these processes, which has been practically imperceptible in the emergence of *Homo sapiens*, is gradually destined to die out more and more. As if there were some kind of quantitative law recording the distribution of them, one might say that life's energies could not extend to a region, or take a new form, without lowering in the surrounding areas. After the human's appearance, it seems as though the evolutionary pressure has fallen in all the main branches of the tree of life except the human. And now that the field of mental and social transformations has opened to the human being as an adult, our bodies no longer appreciably change—in the human branch they are no longer going to change; or if they continue to, this will be only under our active control. It is possible that in its individual capacities and penetration our brain has reached its organic limits. Yet this still does not mean that the movement has stopped. From West to East evolution is now busy elsewhere, in a richer, more complex domain, constructing *spirit*, with all our minds and hearts put together. Beyond nation and race, the inevitable unification has already begun.

* Taken up again and prolonged—who knows whether reflectively or artificially—by biology (as it puts its hands on the laws and forces of heredity, the use of hormones, etc.—see p. 176† and p. 177*).

Having said this, if we take as our point of departure the planetary stage of psychic totalization and evolutionary rebound into which we are entering now, *along what lines* of attack, among others, does it seem we are destined to advance, judging from the present state of the noosphere?

I can distinguish three principal ones, where we see again the very lines our analysis of the ideas of science and humanity have already led us to predict: the organization of research; the concentration of research on the human object; and the conjunction of science and religion.

The three natural terms of a single progression.[5]

A. The Organization of Research

We often boast that our age is an age of science. And up to a point we are right, if we only want to think of the dawn compared to the dark that precedes it. Through our discoveries and with our methods of research something enormous has been born in the universe; something, I am convinced, that will never stop. But, although we intensify our research, although we profit from it, we still do it today with such paucity of mind and means, and without any sense of order!

Have we ever given serious thought to this miserable situation?

We could almost say that, like art and like thought, when science was born it was seen to be something superfluous, an extravagance. An exuberance of internal activity over and above the material necessities of life. A curiosity appropriate for dreamers and those with nothing else to do. Gradually its importance and its efficiency have allowed it to establish itself. Living as we do in a world that can justly be said to have been revolutionized by science, we have come to accept science's social role—its religion even. And yet we still continue to let it grow haphazardly, almost carelessly, like those wild plants whose fruit the primal peoples gather in the forest. All is spent on production. All is spent on arms. But still nothing, or almost nothing, for the scientist and the laboratory as they multiply our strength tenfold. Actually we behave as though discoveries fall periodically ready-made from heaven like sunlight or rain—and as though there is still nothing better for humankind to do on Earth than kill one another and be killed, or eat! If we make an attempt to establish what proportion of human energies are employed *here and now* in pursuit of truth, or more practically still, if we calculate the percentage of money reserved in government budgets for the investigation of problems that are clearly formulated and whose solutions are vital for the globe, we will be appalled. Less is spent annually for the consumption of research worldwide than for a battleship! It will be no mistake for our great-grandchildren to think that we were barbarians!

The truth is that situated as we are in an epoch of transition, we still have not become fully conscious or in control of the new powers that have been unleashed. Set in our old routines, we continue to see science only as a new way of making it easier for us to have the same old things: land and bread. We make a plowhorse of Pegasus. And Pegasus is perishing—unless he flies off with the plow! The moment will come, it has to come, when humans, forced by the obvious disproportion of the harness, will recognize that science for humankind is not a secondary occupation, but, in fact, an essential form of action, a natural diversion for action that is open to the overflow of energy constantly freed by the machine.

An Earth is being created, whose ever-accumulating "leisure" and ever-heightening interest will find their vital outlet in the act of deepening everything, trying everything, and prolonging everything. An Earth where giant telescopes and atom smashers will absorb more gold and arouse more spontaneous admiration than all the bombs and guns. An Earth where the problem of the day, not only for the pooled and subsidized army of scientists, but for the common person in the street, will be the conquest of another secret and another power wrested from corpuscles, stars, or organized matter. An Earth where—as has already begun to happen—we will give our lives to know and to be rather than to possess.

If we weigh the opposing forces,* this is what is inevitably in preparation around us.

Just as it occurs in lower organisms where the retina is spread over the surface of the entire body, human vision is still being exercised in a diffuse way, mingled with the works of industry and of war. Biologically it needs to become individualized in an independent function, with its own distinct organs.

It will not be long until the noosphere has found its eyes.

B. The Discovery of the Human as Object

Once humanity has realized that its first function is to penetrate, to intellectually unify, and to tap the surrounding energies in order to further understand them and bring them under control, there is no danger that it will run up against any exterior limits to its unfolding. A commercial market can reach its peak. Someday we may ultimately empty our mines and our oil wells, even though we may find substitutes to replace them. Nothing on Earth seems to satiate our desire to know or exhaust our power to invent. For it can be said of both: *crescit eundo.*[6]

---

* That is, those exterior forces of planetary compression which oblige humanity to become organically totalized on itself; and those interior (ascendant and propulsive) forces of spiritualization which are unleashed or intensified by technicosocial totalization.

Nevertheless this does not mean that science is to propagate indifferently in all directions at once like a wave in an isotropic medium. The more we look around us, the more there is to see; but the more we also see where we must look. If life has been able to advance, it has done so because, through trial and error, it has successively found the point of least resistance where reality has yielded to its efforts. Similarly if research is to make progress tomorrow, it will do so largely through locating those central, sensitive, and vital zones whose conquest will effortlessly assure the control of all the rest.

From this point of view, we can predict that if we are moving toward a human era of science, that era will stand out as an era of the human sciences: the human who knows, finally perceiving that the human as the "object of knowledge" is the key to all the natural sciences.

"The human is the unknown," as Carrel has said.[7] "And the solution to all we can know," we must add.

Until now, whether through prejudice or fear, science has constantly circled around the human as object without daring to approach it head on. Materially, our body seems so insignificant, so accidental, so transitory and fragile. Why concern ourselves with it? Psychologically our soul is so incredibly subtle and complex. How can it be connected to a world of laws and formulas?

Now the more efforts we make to avoid the human in our theories, the tighter the circles we trace become, as if we are caught up in the human vortex. At the extremes of its analysis, physics, as I recalled in my preface, is no longer sure whether it has a hold of pure energy or whether on the contrary it is left with thought in its hands. At the end of its constructions, biology, if it obeys the logic of its discoveries, is forced to recognize that the terminal form of the constructions of evolution at present is in the assemblage of thinking beings. It is the human below, the human above, and most significantly the human at the center, who lives, extends, and so appallingly struggles in and around us. Ultimately, we shall have to concern ourselves with the human.

What gives the human as object its unique value, if I am right in these pages, is the twofold fact: (1) that it represents individually and socially the most synthetic state of the stuff of the universe accessible to us; and (2) correlatively, that it is at present the most mobile point of that stuff in process of transformation.

For these two reasons, to decipher the human means, fundamentally, to seek to know how the world was made and how it must continue to be made. The science of the human is the theoretical and practical science of hominization. It is the deepening of the past and of origins; but much more, even, a constructive experimentation carried out on an object that is continually renewed.

201

The program is immense; its only end, the future.

First is the care and completion of the human body, the organism's health and vigor. For, as long as its phase of immersion in the "tangential" lasts, thought can rise only from its material base. Now in the tumult of ideas accompanying the mind's awakening are we not in the process of physical degeneration? We hear it said that we should be ashamed when we compare our humanity, so full of malformed subjects, to animal societies, where in hundreds of thousands of individuals not even one articulation is lacking in a single antenna. In itself, such geometrical perfection is not in line with our own evolution, which is wholly oriented toward suppleness and freedom. Yet properly subordinated to other values does it not have a lesson to teach us? Until now we have certainly allowed our race to grow at random and we have not sufficiently reflected on *what medical and moral factors are necessary to replace the brutal forces of natural selection* if we suppress them. It is indispensable in the course of the coming centuries that a highly human form of eugenics be discovered and developed, on the personal scale.

A eugenics of the individual—and it follows, a eugenics of society as well. We would find it more convenient and even tend to consider it safer to let the contours of this great body, made of all our bodies, determine themselves from the automatic play of individual whim and growth—as if the forces of the world must not be interfered with! The mirage of instinct and of the supposed infallibility of nature still persist. But is it not precisely the world itself that, ending up in thought, waits for us to rethink the instinctive processes of nature to perfect them? For reflective substance there are reflective arrangements. If there is a future for humanity, it can only be imagined in the direction of some harmonious reconciliation of freedom with what is planned and totalized. This would mean distribution of global resources, regulation of the push toward available space; optimum use of the powers freed by the machine; physiology of nations and races; geoeconomy, geopolitics, geodemography[8]—with the organization of research broadening into a well-thought-through organization of the Earth. Whether we like it or not, all the signs and all our needs are converging in the same direction. By means of and beyond all physics, biology, and psychology, we must build, and we are irresistibly in the process of building, a *human energetics.*

It is during the course of this construction, which has in some obscure way already begun, that our science, as a result of being brought to concentrate on the human, is going to find itself increasingly faced with religion.

C. *The Conjunction of Science and Religion*

Apparently it was an antireligious movement that gave birth to the modern Earth, humans being self-sufficient and reason substituting for faith. Our generation and the two that preceded it have heard almost nothing but talk of the conflict between faith and science, to the point where, at one moment, it decidedly seemed as though science was called on to replace faith.

Now the longer the tension between them continues, the more obvious it is that the conflict is to be resolved by some entirely different form of equilibrium—not by elimination or dualism, but synthesis. After almost two centuries of passionate struggle, neither science nor faith has managed to diminish the other; quite the contrary, it becomes clear that they cannot develop normally without each other, for the simple reason that they are both animated by the same life. In fact, science cannot reach the full limits of itself either in its impetus or in its constructions without being tinged with mysticism and charged with faith.

In its impetus, first of all. We touched on this point as we treated the problem of action. The human being will continue to work and to seek only by keeping the passionate taste for doing so. Now this taste entirely depends upon the conviction, strictly undemonstrable to science, that the universe has a direction, and that, if we are faithful, it can, or even must, attain some kind of irreversible perfection. It hangs on faith in progress.

In its constructions, next. Scientifically we can envisage an almost indefinite improvement of the human organism and of human society. But as soon as it becomes a question of materializing our dreams in a practical sense, we notice that the problem remains undecided, insoluble, even, unless, by some partially suprarational intuition, we acknowledge that the world we belong to has convergent properties. Unless we have faith in unity.

But there is something more. If under pressure of facts we decide to opt for unification, beside the necessary impetus to push us ahead and the particular objective on which to focus our advance, we will encounter the technical necessity of discovering the special binder or cement to bring our lives into vital association, without falsifying or diminishing them. Faith in a supremely attractive center of personality.

In short, once science passes beyond the lower and preliminary stage of analytic investigation, and moves into synthesis—a synthesis that naturally culminates in the achievement of some higher state for humanity[9]—it is led to anticipate and wager on the future and the whole; and at the same time, going beyond itself, it emerges in option and adoration.

Renan and the nineteenth century were not mistaken, therefore, to speak of a religion of science. Their error was not to see that their worship of humanity implied a reintegration in a new form of the same spiritual forces from which they thought they had freed themselves.

In this changing universe to which we have just awoken, when we watch the temporo-spatial series diverging and unraveling around us and toward what is behind us like the layers of a cone, perhaps we are acting purely scientifically. But when we turn from the slopes of the summit toward totality and the future, we have to make a religious act as well.

Religion and science are the two conjugated aspects or phases of the same complete act of knowledge—the only act that can embrace the past and the future of evolution in order to contemplate, measure, and fulfill them.

It is in the mutual reinforcement of these two still antagonistic powers, in the conjunction of reason and mysticism, that the human spirit is destined, by the very nature of its development, to find its ultimate penetration, with maximum intensity of dynamic force.

3   THE END

Continuing to press forward in the three dimensions we have just mentioned, and taking advantage of the enormous duration it still has to live, humanity has immense possibilities before it.

Until the human, at every leap forward life became fixed and dispersed, rapidly stopped and cut off by the specializations into which it was forced to mold itself in order to act. Since the step of reflection, we have entered into an entirely new domain of evolution. And this is thanks to the astonishing properties of the "artificial," which, by separating the instrument from the organ, makes it possible for one individual to intensify and vary the modalities of its action indefinitely, while losing none of its freedom; and this is thanks at the same time to the prodigious power of thought to draw all the human particles together and combine them in one conscious effort. In fact, in this new domain, although study of the past does allow us some appreciation of the resources possessed by organized matter in a dispersed state, *we still have no conception at all of the possible magnitude* of "noospheric" effects. Of the resonance of millions of human vibrations! Of a whole layer of consciousness simultaneously pressing on the future! Of the collective additive product of a million years of thought!* Have we ever attempted to imagine what magnitudes these represent?

* In addition to the intellectual value of isolated human units, there are grounds for considering the collective exaltation (by buttressing or resonance) of these units when properly arranged. It would be hard to say whether there still is an Aristotle, Plato,

In this direction, the most unexpected is perhaps what is most to be expected.

We might seriously wonder first of all, if someday, under the increasing tension of mind on the surface of the globe, life might use its ingenuity to force the gates of its terrestrial prison, either by discovering a way of invading other uninhabited planets or, an even more staggering event, by establishing a connection psyche to psyche with other focal points of consciousness across space. Although the supposition of the meeting and mutual fertilization of two noospheres might at first sight seem insane, all it does, really, is to extend to the psychic a scale of magnitude whose validity we no longer would think of denying to matter. Consciousness would ultimately construct itself by a synthesis of planetary units. Why not, in a universe whose astral unit is the galaxy?

Without wishing in the slightest to discourage such hypotheses, whose eventuality—we notice—would incredibly broaden the dimensions of noogenesis but in no way change its convergent form or consequently its finite duration, in my estimation their probability is too slight to make it worth the effort to consider them.

The extraordinary complication and sensitivity of the human organism is so adapted to terrestrial conditions that even if it were capable of crossing interplanetary spaces, one can hardly foresee how it could acclimatize itself to another planet.

The immensity of sidereal durations is so vast that it is difficult to see how two thoughts in two different regions of the heavens could coexist and coincide in comparable phases of development.

For these two reasons among others, I imagine that our noosphere is destined to close in on itself in isolation—and that it is not in a spatial, but a psychic direction that it will find its path of escape, without having to leave or go beyond the bounds of the Earth.

And here the idea of a change of state arises again entirely naturally.

In and through us noogenesis constantly continues to rise. We have recognized the main characteristics of that movement: the drawing together of grains of thought; the synthesis of individuals and synthesis of nations or races; the necessity of an autonomous and supreme personal Focal Point to join the elementary personalities together in an atmosphere of active sympathy, without deforming them. All this, once again, from

---

or Augustine left on Earth (How can it be proved? Yet, why not?). But it is clear that, supported by each other (arranged in a single vault or mirror), our modern minds and hearts see and feel today a world that (in its dimensions, connections, and potentialities) eluded all the great thinkers of the past. Now how can anyone dare deny that this progress in consciousness corresponds to an advance in the deep structure of being?

the combined effect of two curves: the sphericity of the Earth and the cosmic convergence of mind—in conformity with the law of complexity and consciousness.

Now when from a sufficient agglomeration of a sufficient number of elements this fundamentally convergent movement has reached such intensity and quality that in order to continue unifying itself, humanity *taken as a whole* must, in its turn, as had happened with the individual forces of instinct, reflect on itself "punctiformly"* (that is to say, in this case when it must abandon its organoplanetary support to shift its center[10] onto the transcendent Center of its increasing concentration), this then will be the end and crowning achievement for the spirit of the Earth.

The end of the world: the noosphere's internal turning back on itself as a unit, having simultaneously reached its utmost degree of complexity and concentration.

The end of the world: the reversal of equilibrium, detaching the spirit, complete at last, from its material matrix, to rest from now on with its whole weight on God-Omega.

The end of the world: the critical point, simultaneously, of emergence and emersion, of maturation and escape.

We can make two almost contradictory suppositions about the physical and psychic state of our planet as it approaches its maturation.†

According to the first hypothesis, which expresses the hopes toward which it is appropriate for us to direct our efforts, ideally speaking in any case, evil will have been reduced to a minimum on the Earth as it comes to an end. Acute forms of disease and hunger will have been conquered by science and we will have nothing left to fear from them. And conquered by the sense of the Earth and the human sense, hatred and internal struggles will have vanished under the intensifying heat of Omega's rays. Some kind of unanimity will reign over the entire mass of the noosphere—the final convergence will be brought about *in peace*.‡ Some outcome like this would of course conform most harmoniously with theory.

But obeying a law from which nothing in the past has yet escaped, it is also possible that evil, increasing at the same time as good, will reach its paroxysm in the end, and it, too, in a specifically new form.

There are no summits without abysses.

---

* Which amounts to saying that human history develops between two critical points of reflection (one lower and individual—and the other higher and collective).
† On the degree of "inevitability" of this maturation of a free mass, see below, "Summary or Postface," p. 223.
‡ And yet, at the same time, since it is a question of the approach of a critical point, it will take place in extreme tension. These perspectives have nothing in common with old millenarian dreams of a period of earthly paradise at the end of time.

The powers released in humanity from the internal play of its cohesion will be immense.[11] It is possible that tomorrow, like yesterday and today, this energy will again operate in a discordant fashion.[12] Will there be a mechanizing synergy under brute force, or synergy in sympathy? Will humanity seek its completion collectively in itself, or personally in one greater than itself? Will there be a refusal or acceptance of Omega? A conflict may be generated. In that case, once having reached its point of unification, in the course of and by very virtue of the process which draws it together, the noosphere would cleave into two zones attracted respectively toward two antagonistic poles of adoration. Thought would never be completely united on itself here below. Universal love ultimately vitalizing and detaching only a fraction of the noosphere to consummate it—that fraction which will have decided to "take the step" out of itself into the Other. *Ramification once again, and for the last time.*

In this second hypothesis, one which conforms more closely to the apocalyptic traditions, three curves would perhaps continue to rise around us simultaneously in the future: the inevitable reduction of the organic possibilities of the Earth; the internal schism of consciousness as it becomes increasingly more divided over two opposing ideals of evolutionary movement; the positive attraction of the Center of centers at the heart of those who will turn toward it. And the Earth would end at the triple point where, by a coincidence in full conformity with the ways of life, these three curves would meet and reach their maximum at exactly the same moment.

The death of the planet, materially exhausted; the tearing apart of the noosphere, divided over what form its unity should take; and simultaneously, giving the event its whole significance and value, the freeing of that percentage of the universe which has succeeded in laboriously synthesizing itself, across time, space, and evil, to the very end.

Not indefinite progress—a hypothesis counter to the convergent nature of noogenesis—but ecstasy, beyond the dimensions and frameworks of the visible universe.

Ecstasy in concord or discord; but in either case, by excess of interior tension.

The only suitable and conceivable biological way out for the human phenomenon.

* * *

Among those who have tried to read these pages right to the end, many will close the book feeling unsatisfied, not knowing what to think, wondering whether I have been leading them through facts, or metaphysics, or a dream.

But have those who hesitate this way ever truly understood the salutarily rigorous conditions that the coherence of the universe, now generally admitted by all, imposes on our reason? A spot appears on a film. An electroscope shows an excess discharge. That is all it takes for physics to be forced to accept fantastic powers in the atom. It is the same for the human phenomenon. If we try to set the human being wholly, body and soul, within the framework of the experimental, we are obliged to entirely readjust the layers of time and space to the measure of the human.

To make a place for thought in the world, I have had to interiorize matter; to imagine an energetics of spirit; to conceive a noogenesis rising counter to entropy; to provide a direction, an arrow, and critical points for evolution; and to make all things finally turn in on *Someone*.

In this reordering of values, I could have been mistaken on many points. It is up to others to try to do better. All I have wished to have given, along with the reality, difficulty, and urgency of the problem, is a feeling for the order of magnitude of the solution and the form it cannot escape.

Capable of containing the human person, the universe must be irreversibly personalizing.

EPILOGUE: THE CHRISTIAN PHENOMENON

Unless a higher pole of attraction and consistency shines above it, reflective life can never continue to function or to progress either in its elementary activities, which only the hope of something imperishable can set in motion; or in the interplay of its collective affinities, which require the action of a triumphant love to join them together. Structurally there is no other way in which the noosphere can close itself, either individually or socially, except under the influence of an Omega Center.

This is the postulate we have been led to logically by the complete application of the experimental laws of evolution to the human.

But theoretical as this conclusion may be in its first approximation, who can fail to see the possible, even probable, repercussion on our experience?

If Omega were only the remote and ideal focal point destined to emerge from the convergence of terrestrial consciences at the end of time, nothing but that convergence itself would be able to reveal it to our sight. At the moment we live in, the only other energy of a personal kind recognizable on Earth would be that represented by the sum total of human persons.

But if, on the other hand, as we have admitted, Omega already exists *and is at work right here and now* in the deepest part of the thinking mass, then it seems inevitable that there would be some observable signs of its existence here and now. It is only natural that to animate evolution during its lower stages, the conscious pole of the world, veiled by biology, could only act in an impersonal form. On the thinking being we have become through hominization, it is now possible for it to radiate from Center to centers—*personally*. Is it not likely that it would do so?

Either the entire construction of the world presented here is an empty theory. Or else somewhere around us, in one form or other, we should be able to detect some excess of personal, and extra-human energy that reveals the Great Presence, if we look carefully.

And this is where we discover the importance of the Christian phenomenon for science.

The Christian phenomenon.

I have not chosen this expression randomly, or simply for verbal symmetry at the end of a study on the human phenomenon. But it attempts to define unequivocally the spirit in which I wish to speak.

Living at the heart of Christianity, I could be suspected of wanting to introduce an apologia artificially. But here again, and insofar as any of us is capable of separating the different levels of knowledge in ourselves, it is not the convinced believer, but the naturalist who speaks and who asks to be heard.

The Christian fact is before us. It has its place among the other realities of the world.

What I would like to show is how it provides the crucial confirmation we need to the perspectives of a universe that is dominated by energies of a personal kind: by the substance of its creed, first of all; next, by the value of its existence; and finally, by its extraordinary power of growth.

1   AXES OF BELIEF

To those who only know it from the outside, Christianity seems to be hopelessly dense. Actually, considered in its main outlines, it contains an extremely simple and amazingly bold solution to the world.

At the center, so disconcertingly obvious, is the uncompromising affirmation of a personal God: God who is Providence, guiding the universe with loving and attentive care, and God who is Revealer, communicating himself to the human at the level and through the modes of intelligence. After all that I have just said, in a moment it will be easy for me to convey the sense of the cost and reality of this tenacious personalism, still recently regarded as outmoded and condemned. What is important to point out here is how much such an attitude in the hearts of the faithful leaves room for, and how it allies itself with everything in the universal that is great and sound.

Taken in its Judaic phase, Christianity could well have thought that it was the particular religion of one people. Later, subject to the general conditions of human knowledge, it could imagine the world around as being much too small. At the least, even when it was hardly constituted it always tended to incorporate the totality of the system it succeeded in representing for itself into its constructions and conquests.

Christianity is characterized by personalism and universalism.

How have these characteristics found a way to be united in its theology?

For reasons of practical convenience, as well as perhaps from intellectual timidity, in pious works the City of God is too often described in conventional and purely moral terms. God and the world governed by God are seen to be a vast and essentially juridical association, conceived of as a family or government. The fundamental perspective that nourishes the Christian sap and from which it springs is something quite the opposite. It was often thought, from a kind of false evangelism, that to reduce Christianity to some gentle philanthropy was to honor it. But unless it is seen to be the most realistic and cosmic of faiths and hopes, nothing has been understood of its "mysteries." Yes, in a sense the kingdom of God is one large family. But in another sense it is also an enormous biological operation: that of redemptive Incarnation.

We already read in Paul and John that to create, complete, and purify the world is for God to make it one by organically uniting it to himself.* How does God unify it? By partially immersing himself in things, by making himself an "element," and then, from this base found interiorly at the heart of matter, by taking on the leadership and head of what we now call evolution. Because Christ, who is the principle of universal vitality, has sprung up as man among us, he has put himself in the position of, and forever has been, actively curving beneath him, purifying, directing, and superanimating the general rise of consciousnesses into which he has inserted himself. By a perennial act of communion and sublimation, he is aggregating the entire psyche of the Earth to himself. And when he has thus gathered everything together and transformed everything, then, in a final act of rejoining the divine focal point he has never left, he will close in on himself and his conquest. And then as Saint Paul tells us, "There will only be God, who is all in all." This is truly a higher form of "pantheism,"† with no taint or trace of blending or annihilation: the expectation of perfect oneness, where, because of having been immersed in this oneness, each element will find its consummation at the same time as the universe.

The universe completing itself in a synthesis of centers, in perfect conformity with the laws of union. With God, the Center of centers. Christian dogma culminates in this final vision—exactly and so clearly the Omega Point that I probably would never have dared to consider or form the rational hypothesis of it, if I had not already found in my consciousness as a believer not only the speculative model for it, but its living reality.

---

* Already according to Greek thought—according to all thought—are not "to be" and "to be one" identically the same thing?
† "*En pâsi panta Theos.*"[1]

2   VALUE OF EXISTENCE

It is relatively easy to construct a theory of the world. But it is beyond the power of an individual to artificially force the birth of a religion. Plato, Spinoza, and Hegel were able to develop views on a scale that rivals the perspectives of the Incarnation. And yet none of these metaphysics managed to go beyond ideology. Although each in turn may have enlightened many minds, none of them has ever succeeded in generating life. What gives the Christian phenomenon its importance and makes it an enigma in the eyes of the naturalist is its value of existence and reality.

Christianity is real, in the first place, by the spontaneous breadth of the movement it has managed to create in humanity. Addressing itself to all men and women and to all classes, from the start it has taken its place among the most vigorous and fruitful currents ever recorded in the history of the noosphere until now. Whether we adhere to it or break off from it, do we not find the mark and persistent influence of it visible everywhere on the modern Earth?

There is no doubt about its quantitative value, measured by the magnitude of its radius of action. But I will add that there is above all no doubt about its qualitative value, which, as in every case of biological progress, expresses itself in the appearance of a specifically new state of consciousness.

And here I am thinking of Christian love.

Christian love is something incomprehensible for those who have never tasted it. The fact that the infinite and the intangible can be lovable, that the human heart can beat in true charity for its neighbor seems simply to be impossible to many people I know—almost unnatural. And yet, whether or not it is based on an illusion, how can there be any doubt that such a feeling exists and that it is even abnormally powerful? All we need to do to see this is make a rough record of the results it continually produces around us. Is it not positively a fact that for twenty centuries thousands of mystics have drawn such burning passion from its flame that their brilliance and purity far outstrip the impulses and devotion of any kind of human love? Is it not also a fact that for having experienced that love, other thousands of men and women daily renounce all ambition and joy except for the joy of laboriously abandoning themselves to it more and more? And finally, is it not a fact, and this I guarantee, that if the love of God were ever to be extinguished in the souls of the faithful, the enormous edifice of rites, hierarchy, and doctrines the church represents would instantly fall back into the dust from which it came?

What is truly a phenomenon of capital importance for the science of the human is that a zone of thought has appeared and grown over an appreciable region of the Earth, one in which a genuine universal love has not only been conceived and preached, but has shown itself to be psychologically possible and operational in practice—and what is more, far from dying out, the movement seems to be bent on gaining speed and intensity.

3 POWER OF GROWTH

The renewal of the cosmic perspectives that are characteristic of the "modern mind" has been a crisis for almost all ancient religions, a crisis from which it can be predicted they will never recover, if they are not already dead. Closely bound to untenable myths or involved in a mysticism of pessimism and passivity, it is impossible for them to adjust to the precise immensities or constructive demands of space–time. They no longer respond to the conditions either of our science or of our action.

Christianity, on the other hand, although it, too, could at first be thought to have been weakened by the shock that caused the rapid disappearance of its rivals, gives every sign of making a rebound forward. For from the very fact that the universe has taken on new dimensions in our eyes, Christianity is revealed to be both more vigorous in itself and more necessary to the world than ever before.

More vigorous. To live and to develop, Christian perspectives need an atmosphere of spaciousness and contact. The more vast the world becomes and the more organic its interior connections, the more the perspectives of the Incarnation will triumph. And much to their own surprise, this is exactly what its faithful are starting to discover. Although momentarily frightened by evolution, the Christian is now beginning to realize that evolution simply provides a magnificent way of belonging and giving oneself more to God. When nature's stuff was thought to be pluralistic and static, Christ's sovereignty over the universe could still conceivably be confused with a power that is extrinsic and superimposed. In a spiritually convergent world, what urgency and what intensity this Christic energy acquires! If the world is convergent and if Christ occupies the center of it, then the Christogenesis found in Saint Paul and Saint John is no more nor less than both the expected and the unhoped for prolongation of the noogenesis in which cosmogenesis culminates for our experience. Christ is organically clothed in the very majesty of his creation. And accordingly, without metaphor, it is through the whole length, thickness, and depth of the world in movement that human beings see themselves capable of experiencing and discovering their God. To be able literally to say to God that we love him, not only with our whole body, our whole heart, and our whole soul, but with the whole universe in process of unification—is a prayer that can only be made in space–time.

More necessary. But to say of Christianity that contrary to all appearances it is acclimatizing itself and growing in a world that is enormously enlarged by science means only to see half of what is happening. Evolution somehow comes to infuse new blood into Christian perspectives and aspirations. But, in return, is not Christian faith destined and is it not preparing itself to save evolution or even to relay it on?

No progress is to be hoped for on Earth, as I have tried to show, without the primacy and triumph of the personal at the summit of the spirit. Now over the entire surface of the noosphere at the present time, Christianity represents the *only* current of thought bold and progressive enough to embrace the world practically and effectively, in a complete and indefinitely perfectible act where faith and hope are consummated in charity. It *alone*, absolutely alone, on the modern Earth shows itself capable of synthesizing the whole and the person in a single vital act. It alone can make us inclined not only to serve, but to love the tremendous movement sweeping us along.

What does this mean except that Christianity fulfills all the conditions we have a right to expect from a religion of the future, and therefore that the principal axis of evolution truly passes through it from this point on, as it claims?

And now let us summarize the situation.

(1) Considered objectively as a phenomenon, through its rootedness in the past, and through its ceaseless development, the Christian movement shows the characteristics of a *phylum.*

(2) Put back into evolution interpreted as a rise of consciousness, this phylum, in its orientation toward a synthesis founded on love, progresses exactly in the presumed direction of the *arrow* of biogenesis.

(3) In the impetus that guides and sustains its forward advance, this rising arrow fundamentally implies the *consciousness of being in present relationship* with a spiritual and transcendent pole of universal convergence.

Is this not exactly the counterproof we have been waiting for to confirm the presence at the head of the world of what we have called, the Omega Point?* The ray of sun that pierces the clouds? The reflection on all that rises, of what is already on high? The rupture of our solitude? The perceptible influence in our world of *another* and supreme Someone? . . .

---

* Or at least, formulated more exactly, "To confirm the presence at the head of the world of *something still higher, in its line,* than the Omega Point." This is to respect the theological thesis of the "supernatural" according to which the unitive contact initiated *here* and *now* between God and the world attains a superintimacy and therefore a supergratuity which humankind can neither dream of nor lay claim to by virtue of the requirements of its "nature" alone.

Might not the Christian phenomenon springing up from the heart of the social phenomenon be precisely that?

Faced with such coincidence, even if I were simply a scientist, and not a Christian, I believe I would ask myself the question.

PEKING, JUNE 1938–JUNE 1940

SUMMARY OR POSTFACE: THE ESSENCE OF THE HUMAN PHENOMENON

The intuition I have tried to express here has never varied in me since this book was first composed. On the whole I continue to see the human today in exactly the same way as when these pages were written for the first time. Yet this fundamental vision has not remained fixed, and it could not have. Gradually over the past ten years—through the irresistible deepening of reflection, through the slow decantation and automatic ordering of associated ideas, through access to new facts, and also through the continual necessity of being more fully understood—certain new ways of formulating and articulating things have appeared to me that tend both to heighten and to simplify the main lines of my earlier draft.

It is this essence of the "human phenomenon," unchanged but rethought, that I believe would be useful to present here, by way of summary, in the form of the following three interlinking propositions.

1 The World's Enfolding: Or the Cosmic Law of Complexity-Consciousness

Guided by astronomers, we have recently grown accustomed to the idea of a universe that for (only!) a few million years has been in process of spreading out into galaxies from a kind of primordial atom. This perspective of a world in a state of explosion is still being debated, but it would never occur to a physicist to reject it because it is tainted with philosophy or finalism. It might be good to keep this example before our eyes in order to understand the impact as well as the limits and the complete scientific legitimacy of the views I propose here. Actually, in its pure essence, the entire substance of the long pages above boils down to this simple affirmation: if the universe appears to be sidereally in process of spatial expansion (from the infinitely small to the immense), then in the same way, and even more clearly, it appears to be physicochemically in process of organic *enfolding on itself* (from the very simple to the extremely complicated)—this particular enfolding of "complexity" being bound experimentally to a corresponding increase of interiority; that is, of psyche or consciousness.

Over the limited domain of our planet (still the only one where biology can be studied), the structural relationship noted here between complexity and consciousness has always been known and remains experimentally incontrovertible. The originality of the position I have adopted in this book lies in its assumption at the outset that this particular property terrestrial substances possess of becoming continually more vitalized as they become more complicated is just the manifestation and local expression of a larger drift. It is a drift as universal as (and probably even more revealing than) those already identified by science which lead the cosmic layers, not only to fan out explosively like a wave, but also to condense corpuscularly under the forces of electromagnetism and gravity, or again, to dematerialize through radiation. These various drifts are all probably strictly conjugated among themselves (as we shall someday recognize).

If this is so, we see that consciousness, defined experimentally as the specific effect of organized complexity, extends far beyond the ridiculously small interval over which our eyes manage to distinguish it directly.

In fact, on the one hand, where either very small or medium values of complexity make it strictly imperceptible (I mean beginning with and below the very large molecules), we are logically led to suppose that some rudimentary psyche exists in every corpuscle (in the infinitely small, that is infinitely diffuse, state), just as the physicist assumes and can calculate changes of mass occurring in the case of slow movements (those completely imperceptible to direct experience).

On the other hand, precisely there in the world where, as a result of a variety of physical circumstances (temperature, gravity, etc.), complexity does not manage to reach the values at which a radiation of consciousness might influence our eyes, we are led to think that as soon as conditions become favorable, the enfolding that has momentarily stopped will immediately resume its forward progress.

Observed along its axis of complexity, as I said, the universe, as a whole and in each of its points, is in a continual tension of organic enfolding on itself and therefore of interiorization. This amounts to saying that for science, life is always under pressure everywhere; and that where it has reached an appreciable breakthrough, nothing can ever stop it from pushing to the maximum the process from which it has come.

If we wish to make the human phenomenon stand out in full relief and to explain it in a totally coherent way, it is necessary, as I see it, to place ourselves in this actively convergent cosmic atmosphere.

2 The First Appearance of the Human: Or the Individual Step of Reflection

In order to surmount the improbability of arrangements leading to unities of an increasingly more complex kind, the universe in process of enfolding, considered in its prereflective zones,* advances step by step by billions and billions of attempts through trial and error. It is this process of trial and error, combined with the double mechanism of reproduction and heredity (allowing the storing up and additive improvement of the favorable combinations once they have been achieved—without decrease or even with increase in the number of individuals involved), that gives birth to the extraordinary assemblage of living lineages, forming what I have above called the "tree of life"—but which can just as well be compared to a spectrum of dispersion where each wavelength corresponds to a particular shade of consciousness or instinct.

Seen from a certain angle, the various rays of this psychic fan might appear to be vitally equivalent, and they still, in fact, are often thought of by science as just so many instincts, so many solutions to a single problem, with each one of them equally valid and noncomparable. Beside making life a universal function on the order of the cosmic, a second "originality" of my position in *The Human Phenomenon*, contrary to making the rays of the psychic fan equivalent and noncomparable, is to give the appearance of the power of reflection on the human lineage the value of a "threshold" or change of state. This affirmation I warn you is in no way gratuitous or based initially on any metaphysics of thought. It is an option supported experimentally by the curiously underestimated fact that from the "step of reflection" onward we truly have entered into a new form of biology,† which is characterized by the following properties, among others:

(a) The decisive emergence, in the life of the individual, of factors of

---

* Beginning with reflection, the "planned" or "invented" play of combinations comes to add itself and to, in some degree, substitute itself for the play of combinations that are fortuitously "encountered" (see below).

† Exactly as physics changes (through the appearance and dominance of certain new terms) when it passes from the middle scale to the immense or, on the other hand, to the infinitesimal. We too often forget that there *should* be and there is a special biology of the "infinitely complex."

internal arrangement (*invention*) over factors of external arrangement (use of the play of chance).

(b) The equally decisive appearance, among the elements, of true forces of mutual closeness or estrangement (sympathy and antipathy) that relay the pseudo-attractions and pseudo-repulsions of prelife, or even of lower life—both of which can be referred back respectively, it seems, to simple reactions to the curves of space–time and the biosphere.

(c) Finally (and as a result of its new and revolutionary aptitude for foreseeing the future), the awakening, in the consciousness of each individual element, of the demand for "unlimited superlife." That is, the passage, for life, from a state of relative irreversibility (the physical impossibility for the cosmic enfolding to stop, once it has begun) to the state of absolute irreversibility (the radical incompatibility of the perspective of certain and total death with the continuation of evolution that has now become reflective).

These different properties confer an indisputable superiority on the zoological group that possesses them, a superiority that is not only quantitative and numerical, but functional—and I mean "indisputable," provided, however, that we decide to apply, unflinchingly and to the very end, the experimental law of complexity-consciousness to the global evolution of the entire group.

3   The Social Phenomenon: Or the Rise toward a Collective Step of Reflection

From a strictly descriptive point of view, the human, as we have just seen, originally represents just one among the innumerable veins that form the at once anatomical and psychical fan of life. But because that vein, or ray if you prefer, alone among all the others has managed, thanks to a privileged position or structure, to emerge out of instinct into thought, it shows itself capable, in its turn, of spreading out at the interior of this still entirely free domain of the world so that it generates a spectrum of the second order: the immense variety of the anthropological types that we know. Observe this second fan. By virtue of the particular form of cosmogenesis adopted by us in these pages, our existence clearly poses the following problem for our science: "to what extent and eventually in what form does the human layer still obey (or escape) the forces of cosmic enfolding that have given it birth?"

The answer to this question, which is vital for our conduct, depends entirely on what idea we have (or, more precisely, must have) of the nature of the social phenomenon as it is so rapidly developing around us.

The continually rising self-organization of the human myriad on itself is still routinely and most often regarded intellectually (and also because it is positively difficult to master a process in which we are so deeply immersed) as a juridical and accidental process showing only a superficial and "extrinsic" analogy to the constructions of biology. It is tacitly admitted that since its appearance, humanity continues to multiply, and that this naturally forces it to find more and more complicated arrangements for its members. But this practical compromise must not be confused with true ontological progress. The human has not moved evolutively for a long time—if it has ever budged at all.

This is precisely where, as a scientist, I think I must make an act of resistance and protest.

A certain form of common sense* would hold that biological evolution has reached its ceiling in ourselves, in the human. Life, in reflecting on itself, has become immobile. But should we not say the opposite, that it is on the rebound ahead? Note, rather, how the more order that humanity puts into its multitudes technically the more at an equal rate psychic tension, the consciousness of time and space, and the taste for and the power of discovery are rising. This great event seems to have no mystery for us. And yet how can we fail to see in this revealing association of technical arrangement and psychic centration that it is forever the same great force at work (although in a proportion and depth never attained before)—the very same force that made us? How can we fail to see that after having centered each one of us, both you and me, individually on ourselves, it is forever the same cyclone (but this time on the social scale) that continues its advance overhead, drawing us all tighter together in an embrace that tends to perfect each one of us as it binds us organically to all the others at once.

By human socialization, whose specific effect is to make the whole network of reflective scales and fibers of the Earth bend back on itself, it is the very axis of the cosmic vortex of interiorization that pursues its course, relaying on and prolonging the two preliminary postulates brought out above (one on the primacy of life in the universe and the other on the primacy of reflection in life). That is the third option, the most decisive of all, and it completes the definition and clarification of my scientific position in relation to the human phenomenon.

This is not the place to show in detail how easily and coherently this interpretation of the social fact in terms of living systems[1] explains the progress of history (or even in some directions allows us to foresee it). All we need to note is that if beyond the elementary hominization culminating in each individual, another hominization is really developing above us, a

---

* Notice how it is the very same "common sense" that has been corrected beyond all question on so many points by physics.

collective one of the whole species—then it is entirely natural to note that, parallel to the socialization of humanity, the same three psychobiological properties are activated on Earth that the step of reflection originally had released (see proposition 2 above).

(a) First of all, the power of invention, so rapidly intensified in our time through being rationally buttressed by all the forces of research that it has now already become possible (as I said earlier) to speak of a human rebound of evolution.

(b) Next, the capacity for attraction (or repulsion), which although still operating in a chaotic way throughout the world, is rising so rapidly around us that (whatever is said to the contrary), confronted with ideology and passion, economics threatens to be of little account in the arrangement of the Earth tomorrow.

(c) Finally, and above all, the demand for irreversibility, arising from the still somewhat hesitant zone of individual aspirations to express itself categorically in consciousness and through the voice of the species. Categorically, I said, in the sense that if one single human being can succeed in imagining that it is physically or even morally possible to contemplate a complete suppression of him or herself—then humanity itself, faced with a total annihilation in store for the fruit of its evolutionary labors (or simply insufficient preservation), is beginning to realize that the only thing to do is to go on strike once and for all. For the effort of pushing the Earth ahead is too much to bear and threatens to go on too long for us to continue to accept it, unless we are working in what is incorruptible.

All these indications taken together, along with many others, seem to me to constitute strong scientific proof that (in conformity with the universal law of centro-complexity) the human zoological group—far from drifting biologically toward an increasingly granulated state because of unbridled individualism; or again, far from orienting itself toward an escape from death by means of sidereal expansion (by astronautical means); or far from merely declining toward catastrophe or senescence—is in reality headed toward a second, collective, and higher critical point of reflection through planetary arrangement and the convergence of all terrestrial elementary reflections. We can see nothing directly beyond this point (just because it is critical; but through it we can predict (as I have shown) the contact between thought, born from the involution of the stuff of things on itself, and a transcendent focal point "Omega," the simultaneously "irreversibilizing," motive, and collecting principle of this involution.

*   *   *

All that remains for me to do now, in concluding, is to clarify my thought on three questions which usually create a problem for my readers,

221

that is (a) what place is left for freedom (therefore for the failure of the world)? (b) What value is attached to spirit (as it relates to matter)? And (c) in the theory of cosmic enfolding, what distinction remains between God and the world?

(a) In regard to the chances for the success of cosmogenesis, it does not follow at all from the position adopted here that the final success of hominization is necessary, inevitable, and assured. Certainly the "noogenic" forces of compression, organization, and interiorization under which the biological synthesis of reflection operates will never for a moment relax their pressure on the human stuff; and this is where the possibility comes in, mentioned above, of foreseeing certain precise directions for the future*—*if all goes well*. But we have to remember that by virtue of its very nature, the arrangement of large complexes (that is, of increasingly improbable states, even though they are linked together) only operates in the universe by two conjugated methods (especially in the case of the human): (1) by trial and error through the use of favorable cases (whose appearance is provoked by the play of large numbers); and (2) in a second phase, by reflective invention. But this amounts to saying that no matter how persistent, how urgent, the cosmic energy of enfolding is in its action, in its effects, it is intrinsically modified by two uncertainties linked to the double play, below, of chance and above, of freedom. Notice, however, that in the case of very large wholes (such, precisely, as the human mass), with the multiplication of the elements involved,† the process tends to "infallibilize" itself, with the chances of success increasing on the side of luck and the chances of refusal or error diminishing on the side of freedom.

(b) As far as the value of spirit is concerned, from the point of view to which I have systematically confined myself I have observed that, seen as phenomena, matter and spirit do not appear to be "things," or "natures," but simple conjugated *variables* for which it is a question of determining not their secret essence, but their curve as a function of space and time. And we are reminded that at this level of reflection "consciousness" presents itself and requires to be treated not as a particular and subsistent kind of entity, but as an "effect," the "specific effect," of complexity.[2]

Now it seems to me that, even within these seemingly modest limits,

* Such as, for example, that nothing can ever stop the human in its advance toward social unification, toward the development of the machine and automatism (freeing the mind), and toward "trying everything" and "thinking everything" to the very end.

† It is interesting to note that for the Christian believer the final success of hominization (and thus of cosmic enfolding) is positively guaranteed by the "resuscitating virtue" of God, incarnate in his creation. But here we have already left the plane of phenomena.

something of very great importance is provided by experience in favor of the speculations of metaphysics.

Actually, on the one hand, having admitted the transposition of the idea of consciousness just indicated above, nothing, as we have seen, prevents us any longer (on the contrary) from prolonging the spectrum of the "inside of things" downward in the direction of lower complexities in an invisible form, and this means that psyche shows itself to subtend the totality of the phenomenon at various degrees of concentration.

On the other hand, if we follow this same psyche upward in the direction of very large complexes, from the moment it is perceptible in individual beings it shows an increasing tendency to mastery and autonomy in relation to its matrix of complexity. At the origins of life it seems to be the focal point of arrangement in each individual (F1) that generates and controls its conjugated focal point of consciousness (F2). But we see that higher up the equilibrium is reversed. From the "individual step of reflection" (if not already before), it is very clearly F2 that begins to take charge of the progress of F1 (by "invention"). And then, higher still, that is to say at the (conjectured) approach of collective reflection, we see F2 acting as though it is dissociating from its temporo-spatial context to conjugate with the universal and supreme focal point, Omega. Emersion, after emergence! In the perspectives of cosmic enfolding, consciousness not only becomes coextensive with the universe, but the universe, in the form of thought, falls into equilibrium and consistency on a supreme pole of interiorization.

What more beautiful experimental support could there be for the metaphysical foundation of the primacy of spirit?

(c) And finally, to end once and for all the fears of "pantheism" constantly promoted about evolution by certain upholders of the traditional spiritual view, in the case of a *convergent universe* as I have presented it, who can not see that, far from being born of the fusion and confusion of the elementary centers it assembles, the Universal Center of unification (precisely in order to fulfill its motive, collecting, and stabilizing function) must be conceived of as preexistent and transcendent.* A very real "pantheism," if you will (in the etymological sense of the word), but absolutely legitimate, since ultimately, if the reflective centers of the world are really "one with God," this state is not obtained by identification (God becoming all), but by the differentiating and communicating action of love (God all *in all*)—and this is fundamentally orthodox and Christian.

ROME, OCTOBER 18, 1948

* As I have already explained in excessive detail above, cf. p. 190 and p. 211†.

APPENDIX: SOME COMMENTS ON THE PLACE AND ROLE OF EVIL IN AN EVOLVING WORLD

Throughout the lengthy developments of the preceding exposition, the reader will perhaps have been struck or even scandalized by one feature. Nowhere, if I am not mistaken, have I mentioned physical suffering and moral wrong. From the perspective of the position I have taken, would evil and the problem of evil in the structure of the world vanish and therefore not matter at all? And if this is so, have I not given a picture of the world that is oversimplified or even contrived?

My reply (or if you prefer, my excuse) to this very often heard accusation of being naively or exaggeratedly optimistic is that since my purpose has been solely fixed on isolating the *positive essence* of the biological process of hominization, I have not thought it necessary (for reasons of clarity and simplicity) to develop the negative of the image I was projecting. What good would it serve to draw attention to the shadows of the landscape, or to insist on the depth of the abysses carved between the summits? Are they not both plain enough? I assumed, without saying so, that they could be seen. Therefore, to look for some kind of human idyll in place and instead of the cosmic drama I have attempted to portray means that nothing has been understood of the vision I have proposed here.

You object that evil as such has not been mentioned in my book—perhaps explicitly. But on the other hand, is it not precisely evil in its many forms that invincibly wells up through every pore, every joint, every articulation of the system within which I place myself?

Evil in the form of disorder and failure, first of all. We have seen how the world proceeds through trial and error by *strokes of luck* right into its reflective zones. This is why in the human domain (although chance is under the most control here) it takes so many failures to make a success— so much misery for a single joy—so many sins for a single saint. First, on the material level, there is the simple physical lack of arrangement, or disorder; but soon, suffering encrusted in sensitive flesh; and higher still, the wickedness or torture of the mind's self-analysis and choosing. Statistically, at every stage of evolution, evil is always and everywhere implacably forming and reforming itself in and around us! "*It is inevitable that scandal should occur.*"[1] This is what the play of large numbers relentlessly exacts in the midst of a multitude in process of organization.

Evil of decomposition, next, a simple form of the preceding, in the sense that sickness and corruption are invariably the result of some accidental misfortune, but it must be added that this is a worse and doubly fatal form, insofar as for the living being, dying has become the regular and indispensable condition for the replacement of one individual by another along the same phylum. Death is the essential cog in the mechanism and rise of life.

Evil in the form of solitude and anguish, also: the great anxiety (this is most especially for humans) of a consciousness awakening to reflection in a dark universe where it takes century upon century for the light to reach us—a universe we still do not really understand very well, nor do we know what it wants of us.

And finally, perhaps the least tragic (because it activates us), but still just as real, *evil in the form of growth*, by which the mysterious law is expressed in us, through the throes of childbirth, that makes all progress toward more unity translate itself in terms of work and effort, from the most simple chemistry to the highest synthesis of the mind.

Actually, if we look at the world's advance from this angle, not from the perspective of its progress, but its risks and the efforts it demands, we soon become aware that under the veil of security and harmony enveloping the human ascent when we see it from a great height, a particular kind of cosmos is revealed where evil appears in the wake of evolution in as large and serious a quantity or gravity as one could wish (not by accident—which would not be important—but by the structure of the system). It is a universe that is enfolding, as I said—a universe that is becoming more and more interiorized; but also in the same motion a universe that toils, that sins, that suffers. Arrangement and centration are a double and conjugated process that, like the scaling of a mountain peak or the conquest of the air, can only be carried out objectively if it is rigorously paid for—if we knew for what reasons, and at what toll, we would have penetrated the secret of the world around us.

Physical suffering and moral wrong, tears and blood, are just the many byproducts (often precious, moreover, and able to be reused) generated by noogenesis along the way. In the end, therefore, this is what the spectacle of the world in movement reveals to us at a first phase of observation and reflection. But is that really all? Is there nothing else to see? I mean are we really sure that for an informed eye, sensitized to a light other than the light of pure science, the quantity and malice of evil spread throughout the world *here and now* does not reveal some *excess* that has no rational explanation unless we add to the *normal effect* of evolution the *extraordinary effect* of some kind of catastrophe or primordial deviation?[2]

I do not honestly feel qualified on this terrain, and moreover, here is not the place to take a position. One thing still remains clear to me and is enough for the moment to guide our thoughts, and that is to observe how in this case (exactly as in the case of the "creation" of the human soul, see pp. 113–14*) every phenomenon not only leaves, but offers entire freedom to theology to clarify and complete in depth (if it feels obliged to) the data or suggestions furnished by experience—which are always ambiguous beyond a certain point.

In one way or another, even in the eyes of a mere biologist, it is still true that nothing resembles the way of the Cross as much as the human epic.

ROME, OCTOBER 28, 1948

EDITOR-TRANSLATOR'S APPENDIX

THE SPHERE AND THE PHYLUM: THE DYNAMIC STRUCTURE AND DEVELOPMENT OF THE HUMAN PHENOMENON IN SPACE–TIME SEEN THROUGH TEILHARD'S DIAGRAMS OF 1940–1949

List and sources of diagrams of *The Human Phenomenon* referred to in Appendix A and B, in the order of their appearance in the texts, including diagrams omitted by Teilhard during revision. French language legends have been maintained in all the figures in the Appendix.

A1 The State of the World's Energetics in Three Successive States (MS B 1940, p. 42) (Omitted).

A2 The Development of Energy in a Universe of Psychic Stuff, completing Diagram A1 (MS B 1940, p. 300) (Omitted).

B1 The Formation and Ramification of Phyla (MS B 1940, p. 110) (Omitted).

B2 The Development of the Tetrapods in Layers (MS Avant Carmaux, p. 120).

B3 The Development of the Primates (MS Avant Carmaux, p. 200).

B4 The Specific (Convergent) Development of the Human Layer (MS Avant Carmaux, p. 200).

B5 The Tree of Life According to Teilhard (composite diagram).

A   THE SPHERE:
TEILHARD'S ORIGINAL SOLUTION TO THE PROBLEM OF THE DEVELOPMENT OF THE TWO ENERGIES, INCLUDING TWO COMPLEMENTARY DIAGRAMS FROM MS B 1940 OMITTED IN REVISION

Commentary

The sphere is the fundamental and dynamic form underlying *The Human Phenomenon*. In the process of revision, two complementary diagrams based on the sphere were omitted by Teilhard: FIGURE A1 "The State of the World's Energetics in Three Successive States" and FIGURE A2 "The Development of Energy in a Universe of Psychic Stuff." The diagrams, their legends, and Teilhard's original explanation of the two energies are included here for the light they shed on Teilhard's theory of tangential and radial energy (Part I, ch. II) and because the two diagrams graphically show the critical effect that the spherical shape of the Earth has on the development of life, thought, and human energy, as a result of being imprisoned in the globe and motion of the Earth (see Part I, ch. III).

The first diagram, FIGURE A1 from Part I, shows three successive states of *preliving centers* close to the origins of matter. It visibly embodies the way radial energy "lines" tangential energy as each increase in tangential energy, with its corresponding increase in radial energy, incorporates the previous layer into the next. See Teilhard's legend below.

The second diagram, FIGURE A2 from Part IV, complements the first, showing three successive states of energy in a universe of psychic stuff. The third state, having reached the step of reflection, is the first surface of hominization, and because the elementary radial energies are personal, they are supported ahead by Omega (see Teilhard's legend). Note the cone-like figure on the upper right which depicts the pass from divergent to convergent, a change of hemisphere and pole. (In MS Avant Carmaux one can see the hominized tangential and radial energies drawn in red.)

Note in FIGURE A2 how the Greek symbol for Omega, Ω, stands above and outside the Omega Point, seeming to reflect the transcendent aspect of the personal, "emerged" Center. The hominized sphere, drawn in red, depicts the state of hominization at the present time and is left *open*, in a suggested polarity with the open Omega sign.

(Note that in the English translation of Teilhard's legend and his solution to the problem of two energies in MS B 1940, all material in brackets was added in revision by pen and ink in Teilhard's hand.)

Teilhard's Legend

"FIGURE A1   Schematic Diagram Expressing the State of the World's Energetics in Three Successive States, I, II, III. C0, C1, C2 represent increasingly synthesized centers. *e. tg* 0, *e. tg* 1, *e. tg* 2 represent their increasingly complex elementary tangential energies. *e. rd* 0, *e. rd* 1, *e.rd* 2 represent their radial energies. *E. tg* 0, *E. tg* 1, and *E. tg* 2 represent the total tangential energy spread over each successive envelope. This energy forms a reserve for the building up of the following envelope.

"Not taken into account in the diagram is the effect of *reproduction*, by virtue of which, instead of progressively diminishing their number as they become complicated, starting with life the centers of the first order remultiply to the point of saturating the medium in which they are contained. It is this phenomenon of multiplication (linked to the effort of groping and trial and error) that superficially gives the look of divergence to the 'tree of life.'

"Again for simplicity's sake, without distinction and whatever their order, radial energies are represented in the diagram by a single line for each kind of center, with its specific radial neo-energy and what possibly represents in it the specific radial neo-energy belonging to the lower centers that it incorporates and covers over. In any case, these incorporated radial energies reappear in the course of analysis and decomposition.

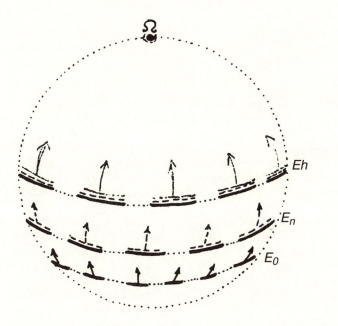

Eh

E_n

E_0

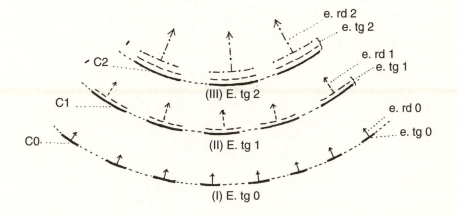

e. rd 2
e. tg 2

e. rd 1
e. tg 1

C2

(III) E. tg 2

C1

e. rd 0
e. tg 0

(II) E. tg 1

C0

(I) E. tg 0

"Roughly speaking, we can say that 'tangential' and 'radial' energy are equivalent respectively to matter and spirit [; with the restriction that the radial is only definitively spiritualized in the case of the human being (in becoming, as we will explain, irreversible).

"From this perspective *all* cosmic energy is fundamentally psychic. The 'physical' energy of science is formed by the mechanical quantum of tangential energy developed on the (outermost) *sphere-limit* of things.]

TEILHARD'S ORIGINAL SOLUTION TO THE PROBLEM OF THE TWO ENERGIES:
MS B 1940, PART I, CH. II, SECTION 3 (B)

"(b) One line of solution
"To escape an [a fundamental] impossible and antiscientific dualism—and at the same time to safeguard the natural complication of the stuff of the universe—I will therefore propose the following description, to serve as the basis of all the developments that follow.

"As close as we would like to the origins of matter, let us consider one of those preliving centers (call it C0) that are, as we have assumed, the true natural elements of the universe. And let us suppose theoretically, always in accordance with the preceding, that the *psychically* "free" internal activity of this center is the real *grain of cosmic energy*. I hold that from this infinitesimal nucleus of a *spiritual nature* we can reconstruct the physico-psychical dynamism of the world (taken simultaneously in its outside and its inside) provided that we suppose a series of linked and coherent hypotheses, which can be expressed as follows (see FIGURE A1).

"Proposition 1
"The psychically free interior energy of C0 (let us call it $e\,0$ for simplicity's sake) is composed of two different terms: one, which is fundamental (*radial energy e. rd 0*), expresses the degree of interiorization or immanence in relation to a universe with a psychically convergent curvature; the other, which is derived (*tangential energy, e. tg 0*), represents its active and passive capacity for connection with all other centers of the same order C0.*
$$e\,0 = e.\,rd\,0 + e.\,tg\,0^{1}$$

"Proposition 2
"Through statistical effects (i.e., of large numbers) the sum total of elementary tangential energies *e. tg 0* give a resultant *E. tg 0*, which is nothing but the *universal mechanical energy studied by physicists* in the most external possible envelope of things. The magnitude of this energy is obviously constant at the level of the centers C0, since at this level the number of them is fixed and invariable.

---

* This, in a proportion determined by the historical circumstances, we shall analyze further along.

"Proposition 3

"Now let us consider the total original tangential energy $E.\ tg\ 0$. It contains experimentally a certain *excess* with a capacity to produce a certain number of centers of a higher order C1 through organized grouping of C0's. Within and between these new centers:

"(a) Radial energy ($e.\ rd$ 1) is abruptly increased and transformed through the effect of synthesis (the augmentation of consciousness, see below, p. 232, pars. a, b, c)—according to a still apparently inexpressible law, although there is nothing opposed to there being a very strong augmentation, or even a veritable metamorphosis, shown in the radial energy of the element under consideration from the slightest variations in synthesis.

"(b) Elementary tangential energy ($e.\ tg$ 1), indicated in Figure A1 by the double symbol - - - -, necessarily varies and increases at the same time.* But note carefully that its specific enrichment (represented by the broken line – – – –) represents only a *superposed* term *of a new order*. It does not suppress tangential energy $e.\ tg$ 0 inherited in the process of synthesis + [nor does it *fuse with* it]. It only lines it and is supported by it [without bringing any measurable increase to it quantitatively].

"Thus for the group of C1's, a new total tangential energy $E.\ tg$ 1 appears in the universe, which is more complex than $E.tg$ 0 (even though partly identical with it), and also, in its specific zone (– – – –), partially less mechanized.*

"Proposition 4

"Total tangential energy $E.\ tg$ 1, like $E.\ tg$ 0, contains an excess of energy. By using this potential in synthesis, a new generation of centers, C2, appears from the again accumulated energy $e.\ rd$ 2 and from the still more complex tangential energy $e.\ tg$ 2 (symbolized in the diagram as •–•–•–•).

"And so a third envelope of tangential energy $E.\ tg$ 2 is formed, which in its turn is capable of a generation of C3. . . .

"And so on.

"This law of recurrence, which expresses a persistent increase of the radial energy of the world at the expense of the successive tangential energies, seems to fully satisfy the outward indications of our experience and the conditions it imposes.

"(1) On the one hand, in fact, since in their lower forms the tangential energies of a higher order are by construction always decomposable as far as you want to take them ($E.\ tg$ n), inevitably the fundamental energy $E.\ tg$ 0 reappears (in the same way as the C0's) like a constant reserve at the end of analysis: it is *conserved* in the course of successive transformations.

"(2) On the other hand, because the whole process is definitively nourished in

---

* Less mechanized for two reasons: on the one hand, because the number of C1's is smaller than the number of C0's; and on the other, because C1's are more conscious and more "free" than C0's, they are less mechanizable.

[In fact, it is only starting with life that this "complexification" of tangential energy (psychic interconnection) becomes appreciable experimentally. Below we must (but we can only) conjecture about it.]

its beginning by the excess of energy contained in *E. tg* 0, it is again conditioned and limited in its developments by the progressive reduction of this excess, in accordance with the phenomenon of entropy.

"(3) And yet, in spite of these two restrictions, the quantity of radial energy (i.e., of immanence) still keeps on increasing in the universe, in accordance with the phenomenon that further along we will call the rise of consciousness.

"[Considered as a whole, this portrayal] The schema satisfies the requirements of reality.

"However, three questions, visible on the diagram, are yet to be resolved: [However it leaves three questions to be resolved:]

"(a) First of all, what is the special energy by virtue of which the universe is propagated as it follows its principal axis in the less probable direction of higher forms of synthesis [complexity and centricity]?

"(b) Next, is there a definite limit and term to the elementary value and to the sum [total] of radial energies developed in the course of transformation?

"(c) Finally, if it exists, is this ultimate form and resultant of radial energies subject to and destined to reversibly disaggregate one day in conformity with the requirements of entropy, until, through the exhaustion and gradual leveling off of the free tangential energy contained in the successive envelopes of the universe from which it has emerged, it falls back indefinitely into the C0's and below?

"These three questions can only receive a satisfactory answer much further ahead, when the study of the human has led us to take into consideration a higher pole of the world—the 'Omega Point.'"

Teilhard's Legend

"FIGURE A2. Diagram complementing FIGURE A1 ([. . .]) to explain the developments of energy in a universe of psychic stuff.

"*Eo*, and *En* . . . are the world's energetic states at different successive stages of synthesis. *Eh* is the initial surface of hominization ("step of reflection"). From this surface on, the personalities of the elementary radial energies (reflective centers), supported ahead by Omega (because, and in as much as, they are *personal*), are indestructible, in themselves and collectively.

"Red indicates *hominized* tangential and radial energy.

"Ω indicates Omega, the *personal* and *emerged* Center of the resulting universal emergence.

"*Eh* has been depicted as 'equatorial' to express that, from hominization on, spiritual convergence prevails over biological divergence (ramification). Having crossed *Eh*, the elements radially fall into the convergent field of Omega (see text, pp. 193–4)."

B THE PHYLUM, THE MESH OF LIFE IN EVOLUTION, AND THE DIAGRAMS OF MS AVANT CARMAUX IN TEILHARD'S OWN HAND

Commentary

In *The Human Phenomenon* Teilhard traces the ramifications of life and thought in their broad outlines over the Earth along the axis of the rise in consciousness.

Biological ramification is divergent. Hominized ramification is convergent. The human forms but a single membrane over the whole of the globe, a "noosphere," soul and spirit of the Earth. In the human, the phylum continues its mental and physical development, with radial energy prevailing over tangential energy. Mental life is not artificial in relation to "natural" life, but an intensification, a higher and inward turning life. The focus of human evolution is socialization.

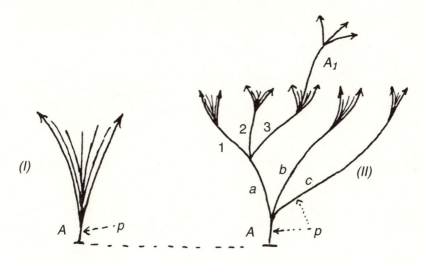

The phylum's structure in space–time is an aspect of the dynamic synthesis found in *The Human Phenomenon*. Convergent ramification has a forward and centering movement, which is shown in the construction of Teilhard's table of contents, and the larger movement from part to part, chapter to chapter, section to section. The various dimensions of the size and movement of the phylum are embodied in the structure of Teilhard's phrasing and paragraphing (see Editor-Translator's Introduction, IV).

The movement of the phylum is also visible in Teilhard's phrasing and paragraphing in the pages of his 1944–55 journal, where the phrases of an entry may branch out with elaborations and ramifications shaped like the tree of life itself and may even stretch backward and forward from one page to another.

Teilhard's Legend
"FIGURE B1. Diagram Explaining the Formation and Ramification of Phyla. I. Phylum unfolding in a simple widening. II. Phylum A unfolding in successive verticils a,b,c and 1,2,3. A1 is a new phylum reappearing by *mutation*. p stands for the peduncle of the phylum."

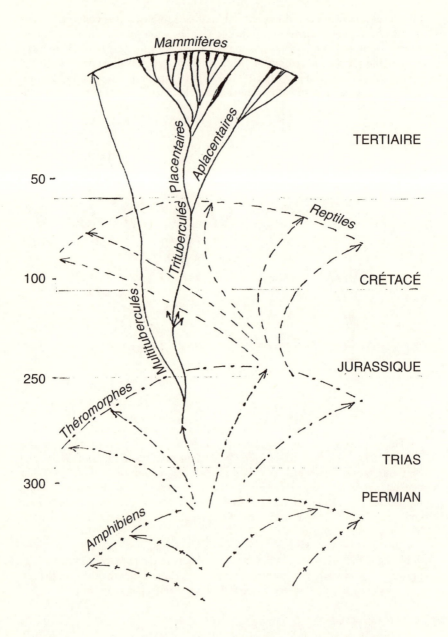

Mammifères

Placentaires

Aplacentaires

Trituberculés

Multituberculés

Reptiles

Théromorphes

Amphibiens

TERTIAIRE

50 –

CRÉTACÉ

100 –

JURASSIQUE

250 –

TRIAS

300 –

PERMIAN

Commentary

FIGURE B2. Starting with the mammals as a vantage point, Teilhard leads the reader back in space–time to follow the fanning out of the tetrapods in waves. Note that the mammals, for whom we have consecutive data, are shown as a series of fans within fans, forming a continuous phylum that descends back to the Permian. The base of each of the tetrapod fans is missing, erased by time. As we descend through the reptiles, theromorphs, and amphibians, the gaps between fans grow wider, the evidence more and more indistinct, until it disappears in the domain of the soft. (For the translation of Teilhard's legends in MS Avant Carmaux, see corresponding diagrams in the text of *The Human Phenomenon*, above.)

Commentary

FIGURE B3. The primates unfold from the heart of the placental mammals. To arrive at the primates, Teilhard takes the reader through the maze of mammals following "Ariadne's Thread" of the increasing complexity of nervous systems

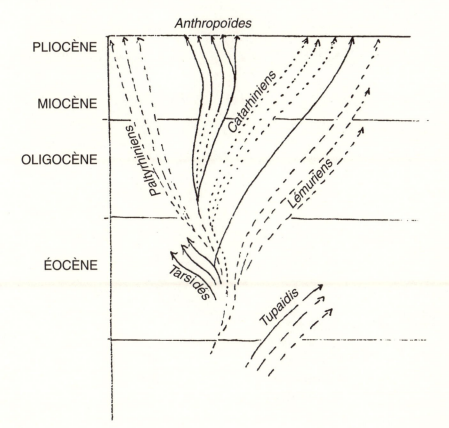

and development of the brain, revealing the rise of consciousness as the principal direction of evolution. In the contest between the main branches of life for air, light, and spontaneity, the insects yield to the mammals. Within the mammals it is in the primates, among the large monkeys or "anthropoids," where the cerebellum is most highly developed and the four limbs, five rays (fingers), and tritubercular teeth of the tetrapods have been kept intact. Having avoided the deadend of other mammals, who became overspecialized and prisoners of their tools, the primates have concentrated on developing their brain, rising up by leaps to the flowering of thought.

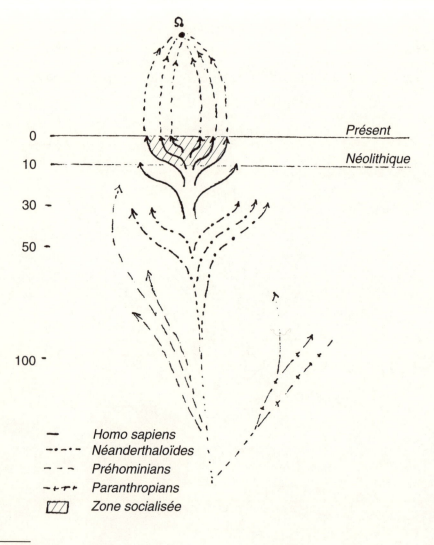

—	Homo sapiens
‒·‒·‒	Néanderthaloïdes
‒ ‒ ‒	Préhominians
‒⊢⊤⊦	Paranthropians
▨	Zone socialisée

Commentary

FIGURE B4. At the head of the primates and on the other side of the step of reflection, the specific (convergent) inflorescence of the human layer emerges from within the anthropoids and supported from ahead by Omega.

Each species in Teilhard's tree of life represents not only a morphological change, but a change of state; a new being emerges. In the human inflorescence all human types have reached the state of reflection, including the prehominids. In contrast to zoological speciation, human speciation remains virtual and a source not of separation, but enrichment. Because of its unique mode of phylogenesis through the confluence of thoughts, the human covers the whole Earth in an unbroken membrane. The importance of the step of reflection is of the magnitude of the first enfolding of the Earth and the first appearance of life on Earth. It is the focus of a separate chapter within a separate part of *The Human Phenomenon*, Part III "Thought."

Between Teilhard's three diagrams (FIGURES B2, B3 and B4), there is only a rough quantitative correspondence in time scale. (Size and length of time are not the determining factors, as in Lucien Cuénot's tree of life, but qualitative changes—see Part II, ch. II, sec. 3). FIGURE B2 "The Development of the Tetrapods in Layers" is on the scale of millions of years. The geological epochs of FIGURE B3 "The Development of the Primates" are contained within the tertiary period of the mammals. The scale of development of the human layer in FIGURE B4 is estimated by Teilhard to be perhaps 200,000 years, at the least, for the prehominids, and the pace of convergence is constantly accelerating. The hypothetical zone of convergence on Omega is not drawn to scale. In analogy to the other living layers, Teilhard estimates its duration to be in millions of years.

Commentary

If we put these three diagrams of Teilhard's together, in sequence (FIGURE B5), the thread of consciousness holds, unbroken (except across the gaps created by time and change of state) to reveal the dynamic coherence of everything that lives and has arisen within the globe and motion of the Earth to converge and concentrate on the Omega Point for the threshold and beyond.

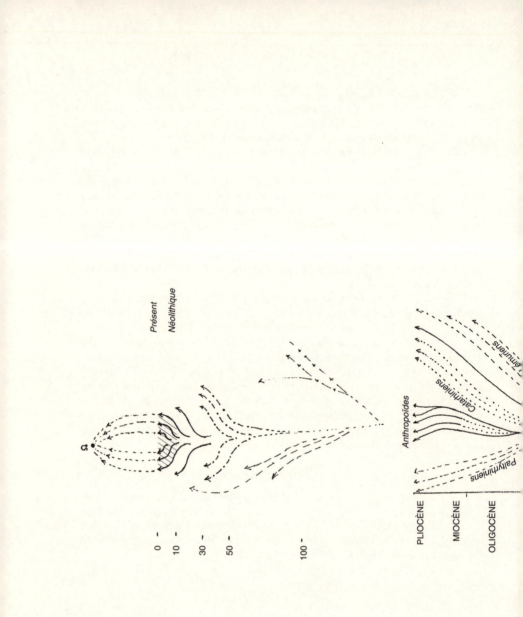

Présent
Néolithique

0 –
10 –
30 –
50 –

100 –

PLIOCÈNE
MIOCÈNE
OLIGOCÈNE

Anthropoïdes

Catarhiniens

Lémuriens

Platyrrhiniens

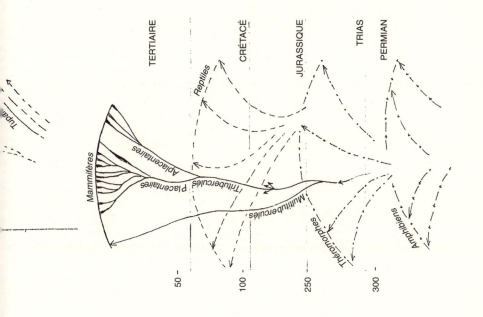

TERTIAIRE

CRÉTACÉ

JURASSIQUE

TRIAS

PERMIAN

Reptiles

Mammifères

Aplacentaires

Placentaires

Trituberculés

Multituberculés

Thériodontes

Amphibiens

Tupa

50 –

100 –

250 –

300 –

NOTES

In citing works in the notes short titles have generally been used. Works frequently cited have been identified by the following abbreviations:

HP
:   The Human Phenomenon

MS Avant Carmaux
:   MS Avant Carmaux, Paris: Fondation Teilhard de Chardin archives, "Boîte 37–39."

MS B 1940
:   MS B non-corrigé, Paris: Fondation Teilhard de Chardin, archives, "Boîte 1940."

MS Corrigé
:   MS corrigé, Paris: Foundation Teilhard de Chardin, archives, "Boîte 1940."

MS 1949
:   Pierre Teilhard de Chardin, *Le phénomène humain*, stencil from "archives P. Leroy," Washington, D.C.: Lauinger Library Special Collections, Georgetown University.

Nouveau lexique
:   Claude Cuénot, *Nouveau lexique Teilhard de Chardin*, Paris: Editions du Seuil, 1968.

Oeuvres
:   *Oeuvres de Teilhard de Chardin*, I–XIII, Paris: Editions du Seuil, 1955–76.

Oeuvre scientifique
:   *Oeuvre scientifique*, I–X, et cartes-maps, textes réunis et édités par Nicole et Karl Schmitz-Moorman, Freiburg im Breisgau: Walter-Verlag Olten, 1971.

Teilhard's Transforming Thought: Editor-Translator's Introduction

1 Paris: Editions du Seuil, 1955; now largely available only in Seuil's "Collection Points," 6, 1970.

2 London: William Collins Sons & Co, and New York: Harper Brothers, 1959, revised edition, 1970.

3 New York: Doubleday, 1977.

4 Note that Teilhard's system of capitalization, as seen in Seuil, MS 1940, and MS Corrigé, seems to be an extension of the method of scientific taxonomy to include humanity and other collective realities on the planetary scale. Also, while remaining within the domain of science, Teilhard has extended this domain inward to embrace inner as well as outer realities, spirit as well as matter. In my translation of Teilhard, to make the text more accessible for the reader I have not retained Teilhard's system of capitalization, except for the planet Earth.

5 MS B Non-corrigé, Fondation Teilhard de Chardin, archives, Boîte 1940.

6 See Editor-Translator's Appendix A.

7 See Editor-Translator's Appendix B.

8 "Corrections, addenda," Fondation Teilhard de Chardin, archives, Boîte 1947–48.

9 MS Corrigé, Fondation Teilhard de Chardin, archives, Boîte 1940.

10 MS Avant Carmaux, Fondation Teilhard de Chardin, archives, Boîte 1937–39. The copy is poorly typed on low quality paper, and does not carry out Teilhard's system of capitalization consistently. It bears many marks in Teilhard's hand in colored pencil, showing several periods of review and correction by Teilhard. It also has several comments in a hand other than Teilhard's.

11 *Lettres à Jeanne Mortier* (Paris: Editions du Seuil, 1984), p. 24.

12 This journal, Teilhard's retreat notes, reading notes, selected correspondence, and his early journals (published by Nicole and Karl Schmitz-Moorman, are now in the Jesuit Archives, 15 rue Raymond Marcheron, 92170 Vanves).

13 Rather than follow Teilhard's use of suspension points in my translation, since his use is puzzling to English-speaking readers, in most cases I have substituted a word or achieved the point of suspense through use of syntax.

14 *The Heart of Matter*, trans. by René Hague (San Diego: Harcourt Brace Jovanovich, 1978), p. 31.

15 See Lucien Cuénot and André Tetry, *L'évolution biologique: Les faits, les incertitudes* (Paris: Masson & Cie, 1951), pp. 35–6. Cuénot cites as an example Teilhard's visual representation of the development in the Shansi of three branches of mole-rats in a series of uninterrupted fossil beds from the lower pliocene to the present time. See also Teilhard's diagrams of "Le groupe zoologique humain" (entitled by the editors "La place de l'homme dans la nature," *Oeuvres*, VIII. Corrected by Mortier, *Lettres*, 48, note 3).

16 To Ida Treat, October 12, 1926 in *Letters to Two Friends* (New York: Meridian Books, 1969), pp. 43–6.

17 "Comment comprendre et utiliser l'art dans la ligne de l'énergie humaine" (my translation) *Oeuvrès*, XI, pp. 93–7.

Prologue: Seeing

1 "Metamorphism" is the transformation of rock structure by heat and pressure. In "endomorphism," molten rock, passing through dikes, transforms the sides of them and is itself chemically modified by the sides it affects. This and the following two paragraphs give the structural basis for the compelling sense of the human and the personal that permeates the whole work.

2 In geography, "node" refers to the point where two chains of mountains cross and present a characteristically higher elevation. Teilhard uses this term not only in the context of the whole passage on the human as "twice the center of the world," but to establish in the Prologue the central perspective of vision in *The Human Phenomenon* as well as the structural proportions for the whole of its narrative development.

A brief outline of the narrative may be helpful to the reader. After, in Part I, having descended with the reader to the point where the last fibers of the human merge for our eyes with the stuff of the universe, in Part II Teilhard leads the reader from the unorganized (uncentered), upward in evolution, through the organized ramifications of life and the tree of life, to, in Part III, self-reflective thought, where in the human being, the orthogenesis of a phylum coincides with the orthogenesis of life itself. In Part III, ch. III "The Modern Earth," thought is illuminated from within by the discovery of evolution. In section 1 C "Illumination," the reader sees that "reflecting in the consciousness of each one of us, evolution is becoming aware of itself." It is here that the human being (and the reader) has the experience of being the "momentary summit commanding the entire fraction of the cosmos open to our experience at present," as both center of perspective and center of construction of the universe. It is from this "node" or summit of vision that Teilhard has the reader turn back to view the coherence of the whole, before continuing forward to discover, in Part IV, by analogy and symmetry with the past, the shape that the human is to take in the future, the attracting presence of the Omega Point at the pole of convergence of the world, and the Earth in its final stages.

3 "Arrow"; that is, what points the direction.

Part I, Chapter I The Stuff of the Universe

1 "Mites" (*cirons*) is a reference to Pascal's discourse, in his *Pensées*, on the "Disproportion de l'homme." The hardest to see and most fragile of beings visible to us, these *cirons* also have their own tiny parts and their infinity of universes within, each with its firmament, planets, earth, and *cirons* (*Oeuvres complètes*, présentation et notes de Louis Lafuma [Paris: Editions du Seuil, 1963], 525–8).

2 A major omission in the Seuil text, p. 35, apparently the result of a typing error carried over from MS 1949, p. 6. MS 1949 has eliminated "But at the same time, unity of *domain* and of *collectivity*," along with the heading: "*Unity of domain.*" This omission causes the incorrect application of the definition of "domain" to "homogeneity," and eliminates the introduction of two of the three main subjects of subsection (b). The three kinds of unity,

homogeneity, domain, and *collectivity,* are fundamental components of the thought and structure of all that follows in *Le phénomène humain.* This same omission here in chapter I also causes an incorrect cross-reference to be made later in Seuil, on p. 56 (see below, ch. II, n. 2).

3 "Corpuscles" are discernible elements or particles of matter or energy.

4 Here Teilhard explains two great laws of thermodynamics, the conservation of matter; and "entropy," the "degradation" of matter. He writes within the context of these "established" laws of science throughout *Le phénomène humain* as he develops the law of complexity-consciousness and the concept of irreversibility and the attributes of the Omega Point.

5 There are many places where Teilhard's thought seems to be a response to the ideas of the astrophysicist Arthur S. Eddington as expressed in Eddington's Gifford Lectures given at the University of Edinburgh in 1927 and published in a volume called *The Nature of the Physical World* (Cambridge: Cambridge University Press, 1928). It was in these lectures that Eddington first coined the phrase "Time's Arrow," applying it to the irreversibility governing the passing of time in the physical world (see Peter Coveney and Roger Highfield, *The Arrow of Time: A Voyage Through Science to Solve Time's Greatest Mystery* [New York: Fawcett Columbine, 1990]; and Teilhard's *"Le phénomène humain"* [1930], *Oeuvres,* III, 235 ff.).

Part I, Chapter II   The Inside of Things

1 The English text, as I have presented it above, is not the precise text of Haldane, but is my translation of Teilhard's French translation of Haldane. In this way I have preserved nuances of Teilhard's thought. Teilhard modified the words of Haldane in small but significant ways, for clarity and also to integrate Haldane's thought more precisely with that of *Le phénomène humain.* For example, where Haldane says "can produce our consciousness," Teilhard says "can produce our capacity for consciousness;" and where Haldane says "what Comte called a Great Being," Teilhard says "what Comte called a Great Superhuman Being." See J. B. S. Haldane, F.R.S., "Science and Ethics," *The Inequality of Man and Other Essays* (Harmondsworth Middlesex England: Pelican Editions, A. 12, Science Ethics, 1937), p. 114. This essay was first given as the Conway Memorial Lecture April 18, 1928 and first published in 1932. The two authors share common themes. It is possible that Teilhard came upon Haldane's words while he was in England from March 24–April 1, 1939.

2 Teilhard's reference is to Part I, ch. I, sec. 1 (b) on the three aspects of the unity of matter: unity of *homogeneity,* of *domain,* and *collective* unity. In Seuil the reference is incorrect because of the omitted passage above in ch. I (see ch. I, n. 2). This error in the Seuil text obscures the correspondence Teilhard points out between the *granularity* of the outside and the inside in the case of "mechanical interaction" and "consciousness."

3 Here Seuil has omitted Teilhard's note giving a brief explanation of the indeterminacy principle. This note was written by Teilhard in October 1948 in Rome in response to his censors and included in the stenciled MS 1949,

Teilhard's final version, made for private circulation after Teilhard had received the ultimate refusal for publication from Rome. Other references to the indeterminacy (or uncertainty) principle have been omitted from the Seuil edition of *Le phénomène humain*, as will be indicated below in my notes as the omissions occur. Teilhard used these references to clarify the fact that there are several different spheres of knowledge and that *Le phénomène humain* remains solely within the sphere of science, leaving room for philosophy and theology (see above, "Author's Note," Teilhard's "Avertissement," also written in Rome in 1948). The omitted note reads as follows: "All this could be expressed in another way, starting from what physicists now call the 'indeterminacy' principle (in microphysics this means the impossibility of establishing position and movement of an isolated particle beyond a certain precision). This principle absolutely does not directly prove the existence in corpuscles of an 'elementary freedom,' but (1) it allows the supposition of one—provided that its radius ('radius of choice') remains lower than the radius of physical indeterminacy of the corpuscle, and (2) furthermore, it still permits us to understand how through multiplicative arrangements of the elementary indeterminacies, freedom ends up in very complex individuals by emerging distinctly above determinism in the field of experience," MS 1949, p. 19 (my translation).

4   "Unorganized," i.e., "uncentered."

5   In Part I, ch. II, section 3 (b) of MS B 1940, beginning at par. 2, there follow four pages of text and a schematic diagram demonstrating the "State of the Energetics of the World in Three Successive States." In the interests of simplicity, Teilhard radically reduced his original solution for the problem of the two energies and substituted the passage as found in the Seuil edition. He also omitted the schematic diagram illustrating the passage along with a diagram completing it that originally appeared in Part IV. The diagram is entitled, "The Development of Energy in a Universe of Psychic Stuff."

Before continuing, it is suggested that the reader turn to the omitted text and diagrams of MS B 1940, which are to be found in the Editor-Translator's Appendix A. In leaving out this material, Teilhard has omitted much that is basic to all that follows: his definition of radial and tangential energy in the element and in the world as a whole; the recurrent law of development underlying the interaction of the two energies and the rise of consciousness; and the critical effect that the spherical curve of the Earth has on human energy. This omission has weakened the scientific basis for Teilhard's description, in Part IV, of the megasynthesis in which humankind is now caught up, and it has concealed the power of Teilhard's prophecy of building a spirit of the Earth, the struggle in which humankind is now engaged.

6   This note on the conservation of energy appears in MS 1949, and the last sentence was added in Teilhard's hand to MS Corrigé, p. 21. The note serves to document the evolution of Teilhard's thought on tangential and radial energy from his first description of it in MS B 1940 (see Editor-Translator's Appendix A, and note 5 above).

7   "(Puisque la centréité des éléments augmente)" has been omitted on p. 63 of the Seuil edition.

Part I, Chapter III   The Juvenile Earth

1   "Juvenile" in geology refers to the molten or magmatic stage of the Earth and what is derived from sources within the Earth and coming to the surface for the first time, as opposed to fluids of surface, connate, or meteoric origin.

2   "Azote" (nitrogen) in both MS B 1940, p. 51 and MS 1949, p. 25 has been omitted in Seuil, p. 69.

3   Literally, "Man's place in nature." This subject is central to *Le phénomène humain*. Teilhard is alluding to the three essays of Thomas Huxley collected under that title and published in 1863, which defined the human being's relationship to the lower animals and set brain size as the definitive characteristic of the genus *Homo*. See John Reader, *Missing Links: The Hunt for Earliest Man*, 2nd edn (London: Penguin Books, 1988), p. 10. Teilhard took up this theme again in 1949 in *Le groupe zoologique humain*, a series of five lectures Teilhard originally planned to give at the Sorbonne, in which he again presented his work on the human phenomenon. The lectures having been interrupted by Teilhard's ill health, he later expanded them into a single volume, to be found in *Oeuvres*, VIII, entitled by his editors, after his death, as *La place de l'homme dans la nature: le groupe zoologique humain*.

Part II, Chapter I   The Appearance of Life

1   Transformism is the biological theory formulated in the nineteenth century according to which living beings are transformed in the course of geological time. See Teilhard's essay of 1920, "Note sur l'essence du transformism" (*Oeuvres*, XIII, 123–31 and others on the subject in *Oeuvres*, III).

2   For a summary of recent results of such research from 1950 to 1987, see Lynn Margulis and Dorion Sagan, *Microcosmos: Four Billion Years of Evolution from our Microbial Ancestors* (London: Allen & Unwin, 1987), ch. 2 "The Animation of Matter."

3   For the *Amphioxus*, see ch. II, note 45.

4   For the description of the verticil, see ch. II, sec. 2 "The Ramifications of the Living Mass", subsec. B.

5   Teilhard's introduction here of a supplementary interval in space and in time provides us with an example of what he calls the "retro-expansion of human consciousness" in the "discovery of the past" (*Oeuvres*, III, 265–7). The function in history of this retro-expansion of consciousness is to provide enough thickness to the present to give a solid foundation for discerning and using the living energies around us to serve in building the future (see above, Part IV, ch. III, sec. 2 "The Approaches").

6   The Cambrian is the first geological period of the Paleozoic era, and roughly 620 million years ago. New fossil, chemical, and isotopic evidence from the study of microbial evolution has now pushed the first traces of life back to between 2,500–3,900 million years ago, into the "Archaean Aeon," which is the second of three aeons stretching back as far as 4,500 million years on the Earth. See Margulis and Sagan, chs. 1–4.

7   "Eclosion" refers to birth or appearance, as in the case of insect larva hatching

from the egg, emergence of the full grown insect from the pupal case, or the unfolding of a flower from the bud.

8   This paragraph refers to the recurrent law of the rise of consciousness introduced in Part I, ch. II, sec. 3 (b) "One Line of Solution," and also in the Editor-Translator's Appendix A, fig. A1 "State of the World's Energetics," Proposition 3.

9   See ch. II, sec. 2 C "The Effects of Distance: The Suppression of the Peduncles."

10 "Un millier de millions d'années."

11 No single word in English encompasses the full range of meaning and the implications of the term *milieu*. Teilhard's use extends from its reference here to a chemical medium to the larger sense of environmental, social, and religious atmosphere as he used it for the title of his spiritual treatise, *Le milieu divin* (*Oeuvres*, IV).

12 This paragraph is broken in two by Seuil, p. 95 after "behind us." MS B 1940, p. 78 and MS 1949, p. 38 have no break.

13 "Monad" refers to a cosmic corpuscle. In contrast to Leibnitz's monadology, Teilhard transposes the nucleus of "psyche" from a static universe where the monad has no "doors or windows" to an evolutionary universe where cosmic corpuscles are mutually interdependent "at the heart of the centrogenesis where they are born" (*Oeuvres*, VII, 109). See Claude Cuénot, *Nouveau lexique Teilhard de Chardin* (Paris: Editions du Seuil, 1968), pp. 124–5.

14 The Seuil text omits "se faisant" (Seuil, 99; MS B 1940, 81; MS 1949, 40).

15 Seuil, p. 100 combines this paragraph with the next, whereas MS B 1940, p. 82 and MS 1949, p. 40 have two paragraphs.

16 Archimede Pouchet (1800–72), who was strongly criticized by Pasteur, believed he had experimentally proven his theory of spontaneous generation.

17 "The present is the key to the past." In the eighteenth century James Hutton, who defined the rock cycle, proposed that the same processes operating today could have made the ancient rocks. Later followers proposed that not only do the processes operate in the past, but they also operate at the same speed. The constant speed modification theory became "uniformitarianism." The following paragraphs are developed in this context.

18 For the background to the rise of life in the following two chapters, see Teilhard's essay of 1928, "Les mouvements de la vie," *Oeuvres*, III, pp. 201–10.

Part II, Chapter II   The Expansion of Life

1   "Scissiparity" (or "schizogenesis") is reproduction by asexual fission (cell segmentation). "Karyokinesis" is division of the cell by division of the cell nucleus.

2   "What began only as a stroke of luck or means of survival is immediately transformed and used as a tool of progress and conquest." This characteristic of life's movement is developed at the beginning of the Corollary, below, and will unfold later in Part III as the basis for "great option" given us by the world in favor of being and life; and again in Part IV as the act behind the secret

complicity of the immense and the infinitesimal to warm, nourish, and sustain the consciousness born of them both to the very end. Teilhard uses this characteristic as the evidence for the irreplaceability of the human.

3 "Anastomose" is to connect or join by union of parts or branches (as in streams, leaf veins, or blood vessels). See below, sec. 2 A "The Aggregations of Growth."

4 Bryozoa are mosslike colonies of marine animals; polyparies are colonies (structures or tissues) in which the polyps of corals and other compound forms are embedded. (Note that in MS B 1940, 97, all the various stages of association mentioned are italicized: aggregate, colony, metazoan and society. This emphasis was omitted in MS 1949, thus also in Seuil.)

5 *Metazoan* refers to any of a group comprised of all animals whose bodies are composed of cells differentiated into tissues and organs and which usually have a digestive cavity lined with specialized cells.

6 In revision, Teilhard eliminated the part of this passage where he had compared the critical transformation that resulted in the metazoan to the critical transformation lying ahead of the human collectivity, which, through an excess of compression, will lead to the appearance of a new and autonomous center, Omega (MS B 1940, 97).

7 Teilhard's revision of this passage in MS B 1940, p. 97 is not clear. Both MS 1949, p. 47 and Seuil, p. 113 omit the phrase "*présentment atteinte*" and the word "*par.*" MS B 1940 reads: "La dernière Partie de ce livre sera particulièrement consacrée à l'étude de cette forme ultime et suprême de groupement présentement atteinte, ou culmine peut-être, dans le Social réfléchi, par l'effort de la Matière pour s'organiser."

8 For the full implications of "orthogenesis" in Part II, see ch. III, subsec. 2 (b) "*The driving force of life.*"

9 It was Edouard Le Roy (1870–1954) during his close friendship with Teilhard in Paris after World War I who revealed to Teilhard the biological and psychic reality of "invention" in the rise of life and consciousness (see also above ch. II, sec. 1, Corollary, (b) "Ingenuity"). Le Roy was a mathematician and philosopher, professor at the College de France, who was influenced by Bergson and worked to reconcile in himself Christianity and science. Suspected of modernism by the Church, in 1929 two of his works were put on the Index, the list of books restricted or prohibited for Roman Catholics by church authorities. Le Roy spoke of Teilhard as his "spiritual son." During the postwar period they conversed on a weekly basis and profoundly influenced each other. Le Roy incorporated quotations and summaries from various published and unpublished works of Teilhard in his *Les origines humaines et l'évolution de l'intelligence* (Paris: Boivin, 1928), ch. 3. According to Teilhard, he himself originated the term "noosphere," while Le Roy brought it into use. The concept of "conspiration," the felt interpersonal unity of mind and soul, also originated in Teilhard's interchanges with Le Roy (see below, Part IV, ch. I, n. 6, and glossary). Their friendship can be traced through Teilhard's correspondence in *Lettres intimes de Teilhard de Chardin à Auguste Valensin, Bruno de Solages, Henri de Lubac et André Ravier 1919–1955*, introduction and notes by Henri de

Lubac (Paris: Aubier-Montaigne, 1974); and in Gérard-Henry Baudry, *Dictionnaire des correspondants de Teilhard de Chardin* (Lille: chez l'auteur, 60 boulevard Vauban, 1974).

10 At this point MS B 1940 shows a diagram facing p. 110 that illustrates the formation and ramification of phyla as it is discussed by Teilhard below in the next two paragraphs: first by a simple dilation or widening, and second by unfolding in successive verticils (see below, Editor-Translator's Appendix B). Note that for both the table of contents and the subsec. headings of ch. II, secs. A, B, and C I have used the headings as they appear in the table of contents of MS B 1940 and MS 1949 to clarify the focus and emphasis of the subsec. I have proceeded this way for Part II, ch. III's heading as well.

11 A "verticil" is a whorl or circle of similar parts about the same point on the axis, as around a stem, or sensory hairs around an antennal joint.

12 Note Teilhard has used the plural "Hommes" here (Seuil, 125) and refers to organization on the collective scale of several species of human. In the case of the human being a species may be defined not only by physical characteristics and behavior, but by political and moral differences. See Part IV, ch. I, sec. 1 "The Confluence of Thought," as well as "Les unités humaines naturelles," *Oeuvres*, III, pp. 282–7.

13 Seuil, p. 125 has substituted *utile* or "useful" for the word *ultime*, which was used in both MS B 1940, p. 112 and MS 1949, p. 54. The word "ultimate" is repeated in this translation.

14 Teilhard continues his comparison of the rise of life to the development of a wave. In this context a "node" is the point, line, or plane in a vibrating body at which there is comparatively no vibration; the "loop" or "antinode," the point or line of maximum displacement. Teilhard used this same comparison in Part I regarding the birth of planets and the juvenile Earth.

15 "Peduncle" refers to the main stalk or stem of an inflorescence in Teilhard's comparison of the development of zoological groups to the birth of phyla and the ramifications of the tree of life.

16 Although MS B 1940, p. 116 and MS 1949, p. 56 both indicate no paragraph for "inevitably, to destroy every vestige of it," Seuil, p. 129 creates a paragraph. My translation follows MS B 1940 and MS 1949.

17 Antoine-Augustin Cournot (1801–1877) was a mathematician, economist, and philosopher, whose teaching was founded on the calculation of probabilities.

18 This note of Teilhard's on the limits of our vision of the past as well as our vision of the very small, very large, or very slow was one of the "corrections, addenda" made in Rome in October 1948 in response to his censors and was included in MS 1949, p. 57. A passage from this note that referred to the indeterminacy principle was omitted from the Seuil edition after sentence 1, along with Teilhard's cross-reference to the "quantum of energy of matter," the subject of Part I, ch. II, sec. 2(c). This note complements Teilhard's note on the indeterminacy principle eliminated from the Seuil edition above (see Part I, ch. II, n. 3 and below, Part III, ch. I, n. 12). Here, the omitted passage reads: "In this organic impossibility I say that there is the mark of a 'principle' in history as universal and revealing as the indeterminacy principle recently

encountered by physics in its study of the infinitesimal" (Corrections, Addenda, p. 6. my translation).

19 The Tertiary is a geological period beginning about 70 million years ago.

20 Note that in section 3 the order and sequence of the movement of Teilhard's thought is embodied in the design of FIGURE 1, which offers the reader a clear guide to the journey downward (and backward) in time. Note also how the series of paragraphs that make up subsection A follows the series of phases depicted in FIGURE 1 of the fanning out of the vertebrates, moving downward in time from the mammals to the amphibians over five geological periods to where the roots of the tree of life are lost from sight. The kinetic power of section 3 is an aspect of the "quasi-mechanical proof" of the global evolution of the biosphere (see below, subsec. C "The Evidence").

21 Note that technically the placenta is a vascular organ (Pierre Leroy, SJ)

22 Believing that Mongolia was the staging ground for dinosaurian and mammalian evolution, and possibly for the missing link to the human, beginning in 1921 the president of the American Museum of Natural History, Henry Fairfield Osborn, sent a series of expeditions into Central Asia led by Roy Chapman Andrews, with Walter Granger as chief paleontologist. Among the most important finds of the expedition was a group of dinosaur eggs (which are still on exhibit at the museum) found in conjunction with seven skulls of rodentlike placental mammals, showing that mammals had already evolved into two distinct groups by the end of the Cretaceous (more than 70 million years ago).

　　Teilhard first met Andrews and his team in Peking in 1923. Invited by Andrews, in 1930, to be geologist for the final Central Asian Expedition, Teilhard helped to discover an ancient bog site that proved to be a graveyard for over 20 shovel-skulled mastodons. As Teilhard's Oeuvre scientifique documents, he worked intimately with the trituberculate forms named in this section, having found and classified many of their fossil parts. See Douglas J. Preston, Dinosaurs in the Attic (New York: Balantine Books, 1988), ch. 8; Roy Chapman Andrews, The New Conquest of Central Asia (New York: American Museum of Natural History, 1932), pp. 420–53; and Teilhard de Chardin, Lettres de voyage (1923–1955), ed. Claude Aragonnès (Paris: Bernard Grasset, 1956), Teilhard's letters during May and June 1930.

23 "Radiation," or "adaptive radiation," was a term coined by Osborn (see n. 22). Teilhard defines it in the context of mutation as "when new differentiations of a phylum, instead of scattering, are realized in a limited but progressive number of directions governed by the precise conditions of existence and environment." Oeuvres, III, pp. 204–5.

24 Artiodactyls and perissodactyls are even-toed and odd-toed hoofed animals.

25 Titanotheres are the form antecedent to the rhinoceroses.

26 Suids make up the family of swine.

27 Cetaceans and sirenians are whales and sea cows.

28 "Chiropterans" refers to bats.

29 "Burrowing in the steppes of Mongolia is an authentic rodent, the Myospalax, whose burrowing limbs are exactly midway between those of a rat and a mole," Teilhard, Oeuvres, III, p. 125.

30 The Secondary is a geological era of about 130 million years, comprising the Triassic, Jurassic, and Cretaceous.

31 The platyrrhines are New World broad-nosed monkeys.

32 According to Pierre Leroy, SJ, who took charge of Emile Licent's collection of fossils in Tientsin in 1939, the Tientsin museum had an example of the machairodus with exaggeratedly curved sabers (interview Nov. 11, 1989).

33 Seuil, p. 136 has "fermé" instead of "formé" due to a mistyping in MS 1949, p. 60. MS B 1940, p. 124 has "formé." This translation follows MS B 1940.

34 "Three tubercules," or *tritubercular* type. The patterns of the cusps on the teeth of the different mammalian orders can all be traced back to a common triangular form, or trigon, derived from the single cones of reptilian teeth— teeth with these triangles are called tribosphenic (three-cusped). Osborn had an important influence on the theory of dentation as an indication of morphological relationship. Teilhard used dentation as one of the bases for his classification of mammals.

35 Teilhard speaks of the *Microcleptidae*, a mammal form known only from a few tiny isolated teeth found in England and Germany. It is referred to the multituberculates. According to George Gaylord Simpson, the evidence for this form is insufficient (see *The Principles of Classification and the Classification of Mammals*, New York: Bulletin of the American Museum of Natural History, vol. 85, 1945, p. 169).

36 Musaraignes are insectivores, smaller than a mouse, which eat flowers and worms (Pierre Leroy, SJ).

37 "Ornithorhynchus" refers to the duck-billed platypus.

38 Multituberculates are mammals whose cheek teeth, in contrast to the trituberculates, carry longitudinally arranged rows of cusps.

39 Seuil, p. 138 breaks this par. into two after "dolphins," interrupting Teilhard's summary of the reptiles, the second of the four layers that comprise the tetrapods (see n. 20). MS B 1940, p. 126 and MS 1949, p. 61 have no break.

40 Theromorphs are mammallike reptiles of the Carboniferous and Permian fauna.

41 The diplodocus, an herbivorous dinosaur of the Jurassic, is the largest of all terrestrial vertebrates.

42 Convergence, in regard to phyletic developments, is where distinct lineages evolve toward morphological similarity.

43 *Crossopterygian* refers to the "living fossil" coelacanth (hollow-spined), a sub-order of Crossopterygian (lobe-fin) fishes, called *Latimeria*, that was discovered in the Indian Ocean near the Comoro Islands off Madagascar on Dec. 22, 1938, after Teilhard had begun *Le phénomène humain*. Teilhard may have heard the announcement, which was made in London on March 11, 1939, where Teilhard was visiting during his last voyage to the West before being exiled in China as a result of the outbreak of World War II.

44 Silurian is the third geological period of the Paleozoic era, characterized by the development of early invertebrate land animals and plants.

45 The *Amphioxus* (two-ended) *lanceolatus*, or the "lancelot," found around the edges of all the oceans of the world, is essentially a burrowing animal, long-

bellied and free swimming, with nearly all the features of the basic pattern of chordate organization.

46 In subsection (d) the sectors of space–time stretch below the Precambrian.

47 Annelids comprise a phylum of coelomate and usually elongated segmented invertebrates, such as earthworms, various marine worms, and leeches.

48 Echinoderms comprise a phylum including radially symmetrical coelomate marine animals, such as starfishes and sea urchins.

49 Mycelium is the mass of interwoven filaments or hyphae forming the vegetative part of a fungus.

50 "'Good' species" refers to species with little morphological and ethological variation of characteristics.

51 FIGURE 2, in this translation, is taken from the tracing upon which the diagram is based in MS 1949 and MS Corrigé.

Lucien Cuénot (1866–1951) taught this diagram of the tree of life to his students as early as 1928 (as Pierre Leroy, SJ, who studied under Cuénot, has verified). An example of a similar table can be found in Cuénot's culminating work (assisted by André Tétry), *L'évolution biologique: les faits, les incertitudes* (Paris: Masson & Cie, 1951), p. 17.

Cuénot was an influential professor of zoology and biology at the University of Nancy, a specialist in genetics and evolutionary theory, who favored the principle of "preadaptation" at the group level over the Neo-Darwinian theory of natural selection. See Cuénot's *La génèse des espèces animales*, 3rd ed., rev. (Paris: Félix Alcan, 1932). Although Teilhard and Cuénot differed in fundamental ways, they sometimes collaborated, and they shared certain concepts, which play a major role in Part II, chs. II and III: that only the fixed maxima of phyla remain (the exaggerated dispersion and also suppression of peduncles); that we can never see the first origins of anything; that a zoological phylum represents the transformation of a limb or the whole body into an instrument, and that the human, in whom the instrument becomes exterior (a tool), escapes the slavery of having to be physically transformed in order to act.

It was through his friendship with Cuénot that Teilhard began a correspondence with Cuénot's son, Claude, who wrote the pioneering and comprehensive biography of Teilhard first published in 1958. It was Claude Cuénot who assisted Jeanne Mortier in the preparation of "MS Corrigé" (1949) of *Le phénomène humain* for publication by Seuil. Among Cuénot's many publications on Teilhard, see *Pierre Teilhard de Chardin: les grandes étapes de son évolution* (Paris: Le Rocher, 1986) and *Nouveau lexique Teilhard de Chardin* (Paris: Editions du Seuil, 1968). The correspondence of Claude Cuénot with Teilhard and also with Jeanne Mortier is at the Fondation Teilhard de Chardin in Paris.

52 The following are comments by Pierre Leroy, SJ, on Lucien Cuénot's tree of life (from my interview with Leroy on Nov. 11, 1989 at Versailles). The roots of the tree are in the universe. The tree is under water up to the transverse line near the top of the diagram. The plant, animal, and insect branches rise to the same level, but because the insects are socially automatic, their outer "skeleton" does not develop, and they have reached a dead end; whereas the

mammals are free to develop socially. The whale branch has returned to the sea. For Lucien Cuénot, there is no noospheric zone, whereas for Teilhard there is a break at the step of reflection marking the individual step and the beginning of the formation of the noosphere around the Earth. Cuénot held that spirit unfolds continuously, perhaps from an "extra cosmic" source.

53 *Sequoiadendron giganteum.* Teilhard is referring to the giant sequoia found at moderately high altitudes in the Sierra Nevada range, a region he visited in August 1939, for a second time, after he attended the Pan Pacific Congress and while he was writing Part II of *Le phénomène humain.*

54 "Germ plasm" refers to the reproductive cells and "soma" to all the rest of the organism.

55 "Acquired characteristics" refers to Lamarck's theory that characteristics acquired by parents during their own lifetime can be transmitted to their offspring. This was opposed by Darwin's theory of evolution through natural selection.

56 In a crucial error, the Seuil text, p. 149, par. 3, line 14, has the term "orthogenesis" in place of what in MS B 1940, p. 138 was originally "ontogenesis." MS 1949, p. 67 was not clearly typed. "Ontogenesis" refers to the course of development of an *individual* organism. "Orthogenesis" as defined above by Teilhard in sec. 1 F, refers to the development of the phyletic *lineage.* The error undermines the logic of Teilhard's summation of the evidence for the evolution of the tree of life.

57 Seuil, p. 150 has "formée"; whereas MS B 1940, p. 139 and MS 1949, p. 67 have "forcée."

58 "Kinematics" refers to the study of motion apart from considerations of mass and force. The term is related to "cinema," the reproduction of movement by a succession of photographs. Lucien Cuénot was quick to point out the kinematic aspect of Teilhard's method of paleontology, when Teilhard visually embodied through a sequence of photographs the succession of changes in the formation of fossil mole rat skulls discovered in a series of consecutive fossil beds in China (see Lucien Cuénot, *L'évolution biologique,* 35–6). In *Le phénomène humain,* Teilhard's kinematic method has already incorporated cosmic evolutionary movements into the text, such as the enfolding of the Earth and the enfolding of the universe on itself, the lifting and sinking of the terrestrial crust, the spiral motion of galaxies, and the unfolding of the evolutionary phyletic fans (or layers) of the tetrapods. His method is suggestive of time-lapse photography; but contrary to time-lapse photography, which depicts the movement of stages in a single being or process, for Teilhard the rising movement of evolution always has breaks that express the scientifically uncrossable gap, or discontinuity due to the limits of our perception, between states and stages of being.

59 In the next two paragraphs Teilhard uses the kinematic method as a quasi-mechanical proof of the evolution of the tree of life. After having quantitatively compared the tree of life to the seemingly motionless giant sequoia, the Earth's largest living thing, Teilhard then recapitulates, in rapid succession, the unfolding of the ramifications of life in a series of fans within fans, within fans, from the smallest, to the vast assemblage of life as a whole.

By reducing the immense time frame of the growth of the tree of life, the rapid, time-lapse like motion allows the reader to experience the tree's springing to life, to *feel* its growth as a fact.

60 Seuil, p. 150 has "à l'infini"; MS B 1940, p. 139 and MS 1949, p. 67 has "à l'indéfini."

61 Seuil, p. 151 has "du plus grand au plus petit"; whereas MS B 1940, p. 140 and MS 1949, p. 67 have "du plus petit au plus grand," which recapitulates the synthesis of the preceding paragraph.

62 Seuil, p. 150 has "le cadre tracé"; whereas MS B 1940, p. 140 and MS 1949, p. 68 have "le cadre déja tracé."

63 "Phenotype" refers to the visible properties of an organism produced by the interaction of the genotype and environment, while "genotype" refers to all or part of the genetic construction of an individual or group.

64 The granitization of China was a significant conclusion drawn by Teilhard, while he was writing *Le phénomène humain*, from his visual geological survey of different regions of China (see "The Granitization of China," *Oeuvre scientifique*, VI, 3219–55).

65 Seuil, p. 152, end of footnote, has "(voir la *conclusion*, à la fin de l'ouvrage)." Teilhard first spoke of his "Summary or Postface" of *Le phénomène humain* as a form of "conclusion, resumé ou 'post-face'" written to express his most recent thinking on the human phenomenon (see, e.g., his letter from Rome, Oct. 8, 1948, to Jeanne Mortier in *Pierre Teilhard de Chardin: Lettres à Jeanne Mortier*, Paris: Editions du Seuil, 1984). To clarify Teilhard's reference, I have replaced "*conclusion*" with "Summary or Postface."

Part II, Chapter III   Mother Earth (Demeter)

1 Note that Teilhard's address to Demeter serves not only a dramatic function, but makes a transition from Part II to the content and questions of Part III, and also sets Part II in the context of the Earth. It affirms the role of the feminine in creation and, as we know from two other of Teilhard's texts, the implicit role of "Mary, Queen and Mother of all things, the true Demeter" ("Writings in Time of War," see *Oeuvres*, XII, 68). In "Les fondements et le fond de l'idée de l'évolution," "Demeter" is applied to the Earth and compared to Eve, in that we are all united in her womb (*Oeuvres*, III, 193, n. 2.). Finally, in 1950 Teilhard concluded his autobiography, "Le coeur de la matière" (*Oeuvres* XIII, 19–74), with a clausula on the feminine to clarify its role in the process of universal concentration. Wall's translation of *Le phénomène humain* omits the two lines of address to Demeter as well as Teilhard's reference to "Mother Earth" in the table of contents, entirely eliminating all direct reference to "Mother Earth" from the English text (see *The Phenomenon of Man*, trans. by Bernard Wall, rev. ed., London: Fount Paperbacks, 1977, table of contents and p. 156). I have used Teilhard's title for ch. III as it appears in the table of contents; that is, adding "Mother Earth" and putting "Demeter" in parenthesis.

2 "See above, Part I, ch. II, note 3, the outline of an explanation on the indeterminancy principle." This note of Teilhard's on the indeterminacy principle

was added in Rome in October 1948 ("Corrections, addenda," 2) and, although it appears in MS 1949, p. 74, it was also omitted by the editors of the Seuil edition along with note 3 of Part I, ch. II above.

3 In 1925 Teilhard outlined his theory of the plasmatic and formative role of the psyche in the formation of species in "Le paradox transformiste" (*Oeuvres*, III, 113–42), which is a reply to the anatomist Vialleton's critique of transformism. Teilhard proposes that a positive force, "a kind of attraction or felt capacity launched terrestrial animals into the water or the air, sharpened their claws, or diminished their hooves," which is suggestive of the "accentuation of a temperament or passion, that is, of development of a moral much more than an anatomical characteristic," so that in mutation, rather than an isolated morphological element, "it is the very center of coordination of all the organs that shifts, . . . the living being can only be transformed as a whole, harmoniously" (my translation). Teilhard is careful to distinguish his view from any return to the concept of "vital force" and also from the "virtues" of the "bad kind of scholasticism" (see pp. 135–7).

4 See Jean-Henri Fabre (1823–1915), *Souvenirs entomologiques*, 1870–89, a series of studies of the instincts and habits of insects based on Fabre's personal observation and accompanied by his diagramic drawings (see ed. of Yves Delange, Paris: Editions Robert Laffont, 1989).

5 Here, to heighten the contrast as he makes a transition from the mammals to the primates, Teilhard gathers a group of mammals that are morphologically trapped in a dead end: the polycladines, with many-tiered antlers; the strepsiceros, the African antelopes; and the elephants and the machairodons (extinct saber-toothed tigers). Teilhard himself had collected fossils of some of these animals on his expeditions in China with Emile Licent for the museum in Tientsin and with the Chinese Geological Survey based in Peking.

6 FIGURE 3 is based on a transparency of a diagram in Teilhard's hand of the development of the primates (zoological name-endings anglicized by translator). The transparency was prepared for MS Corrigé in 1949, and used as the basis for the Seuil edition of 1955. In the reproduction of the diagram as it appears in Seuil, the contrast has been lost between the static broken lines that mark the geological time scale and the more delicately broken dynamic fan lines of primate development in MS Corrigé. For a reproduction of Teilhard's diagrams in Teilhard's own hand, see Editor-Translator's Appendix B.

7 Tupaiads are ancestors of the tree shrew.

8 The *Dryopithecus* is the earliest of the high canopy apes in the Old World during the lower Miocene of Kenya and combines characteristics of cercopithecids, great apes, and the human.

9 The condylarths are an order of the oldest forms of plant-eating protungulates from the Cretaceous to the Miocene, whose joints or condyles between the lower jaw and skull are fairly loose, allowing the sideways or back and forth movement of the lower jaw.

Part III, Chapter I **The Birth of Thought**

1 The French and British spelling is "reflexion," which more clearly retains the physical sense of bending or folding back, a movement that plays a fundamental dynamic part in *The Human Phenomenon*, from the enfolding of the juvenile Earth and the double conjugated enfolding of the molecule on itself, to the cellular revolution, and the individual and the collective, or planetary, act of reflection.

2 Teilhard's original note, found in MS B 1940, p. 171, remarks on Bergson and the nature of intelligence: "Pushed to the end, *instinct* becomes *intelligence*. Thus I do not go along with the great Bergson's idea of the heterogeneity of the two functions—provided, obviously, that intelligence (that is, thought) is to be regarded as the *whole* of reflective consciousness, not purely as an instrument of retroactive analysis, but *also* as a tool of progressive synthesis. See ahead, what I will be led to speculate about the future of intuition and mysticism, in 'The Ultimate Earth'" (my translation).

3 See section 2 below, "The Original Forms."

4 The next three paragraphs, added by Teilhard in revision (see MS 1949, 86), focus on how it is scientifically impossible for us ever to have any experimental knowledge, or "perception" of the leap interval—either of what happened inwardly, or what was visible outwardly—because all traces of the "peduncle" of thought have been erased by the thickness of the past. But in MS B 1940, pp. 176–7, Teilhard speculated more fully on the problem, suggesting, on the human side of the step, a possible period of phyletic childhood for humanity which would have "absorbed" the shock.

5 Teilhard refers here to Part IV, ch. II, sec. 1 "La Convergence du Personnel et le Point Oméga." MS B 1940, p. 282 shows that this title has been revised by Teilhard and had originally read "La Convergence de l'Esprit et le Point Oméga." However, Teilhard did not carry out the revision of either the above textual reference, which uses the word "esprit," or the reference to it in the table of contents. Both MS 1949 and the Seuil text of 1955 do not carry out the revision. Seuil's "Collection Points" edition of *Le phénomène humain* (Paris: 1970) has corrected the table of contents, but not the above textual reference.

6 This passage marks the emergence of the human phenomenon. By the term "human" Teilhard refers not to the individual human being or "element," but to the biological and collective reality of humanity as a whole, evolving through human lineages as defined by both anthropology and sociology together.

7 Using the term "*rameau*" rather than "*Branche*," here, in Part III, ch. I, subsec. (b), Teilhard focuses on human phylogenesis in general as a prolongation of one of the many branches making up the main branch of vertebrates. In subsec. (c) this perspective is to be recast in light of hominization to prepare for subsection C on the effects of hominization on the whole planet.

8 Along with its sense of "to work out" or "develop" something, in biochemistry "elaborate" means to build up organic compounds from simpler ingredients; and in botany leaves are referred to as *sève élaboré*.

9 In April through June 1940, Pierre Leroy and Teilhard, for the safety of the library and major part of Émile Licent's fossil collection, moved it from the Tientsin Museum Hoangh-Ho, Pei Ho (Museum of the Yellow River and the White River) to the empty French marine barracks and rue La Brousse in Peking's Legation Quarter. There they lived, and, with Jacques Roy, SJ, founded the Institute of Geobiology, with its publication *Géobiologia*. During this time Teilhard completed Parts III and IV of *Le phénomène humain*. Restricted from work in the field by conditions of war, the three confined their work to the barracks until the arrival of American troops in Peking in 1946. See *Géobiologia* (Pékin: 1943) in *Oeuvre scientifique*, IX, pp. 3747–60; Pierre Leroy, SJ, "L'Institut de Géobiologie à Pékin, 1940–46: Les dernières années du P. Teilhard de Chardin en Chine," *L'Anthropologie*, vol. 69, Nos. 3–4 (1965), pp. 360–7.

10 The term "biosphere" was first used by Eduard Seuss in 1875. For Teilhard's reading of Seuss and discussions about the biosphere with Eduard Le Roy and Vladimir Vernadsky during 1920–23 as well as the founding of the Institute of Geobiology in Peking in 1941, see Jean Onimus, *Teilhard de Chardin et le mystère de la terre* (Paris: Editions Albin Michel, 1991), pp. 21–4. See also James Lovelock, *The Ages of Gaia: A Biography of Our Living Earth* (New York: Bantam Books, 1988), p. 11 and p. 30, on the development of Seuss's concept by Vladimir Vernadsky as *biogeochemistry*.

11 "Above the animal biosphere there is a human sphere, the sphere of reflection, conscious invention, and felt union of minds (the noosphere, so to speak), and at the origin of this new entity . . . there is a phenomenon of special transformation which affects preexistent life: hominization." (My translation. See "Hominisation" [1925], *Oeuvres*, III, 91–2.) According to a letter of Teilhard's to François Russo, SJ, on March 12, 1954, Teilhard thought that the term *noosphere* "was from me (one never knows). But it was [Edouard] Le Roy who launched it" (my translation. *Lettres intimes*, no. 31, n. 15).

12 "And here somehow the indeterminacy principle in physics reappears in history (see Part I, ch. II, n. 3)." This cross-reference to the indeterminacy principle by Teilhard was omitted from the Seuil edition (see also, Part II, ch. II, n. 18).

13 See "The suppression of the peduncles," pp. 74 ff.

Part III, Chapter II   The Deployment of the Noosphere

1 In chapter II, coordinated with the "pulsations" of geology, there is a gradual emergence of the synthesizing and convergent mode of human phylogenesis over the divergent mode of zoological evolution. The successive modes, or phases, of deployment through which the modern human must have passed in the course of phylogenesis (embodied in Teilhard's FIGURE 4) become more and more synthesized. Burgeoning at the heart of the primates as a prolongation of the main axis of the tree of life (Part II), human evolution springs up in the shape of a single inflorescence (Part III). The zoological branching structure dominated by somatic factors (still evident in the "scales" of the primitive human—see note 21—whose time span could be doubled in the diagram)

gives way to a converging confluence of thought, intensified by the coalescence of "elements" and "branches" forced by the geometrical curvature of the Earth. The "terminal" scales of the primitive human drop away and yield in the Neolithic Age to the budlike shape beginning to be formed by *Homo sapiens*, as humanity's "grouping" of virtual species coils in on itself around the curved surface of the Earth, providing the Earth with a "soul"—a complexifying center of attraction and of response to the pull of Omega. Figure 4 indicates the hypothetical zone of convergence on Omega, which, as Teilhard points out, is not drawn to size; in analogy with the other living layers its duration would be on the order of *millions* of years.

2   In MS Avant Carmaux the first three sentences of the legend read as follows (bracketed words are those omitted in MS 1949 and Seuil): "Schematic diagram symbolizing the development [of the (convergent) species] of the human layer. The numbers at the left count the years in *thousands*. They represent a minimum duration and [in the lower part of the diagram] should probably be at least doubled" (for the diagram and the rest of the legend, see Editor-Translator's Appendix B). In MS Avant Carmaux's diagram of the human layer, the socialized zone is colored in red pencil. (For a description of MS Avant Carmaux, see Editor-Translator's Introduction, sec. II.)

3   Teilhard twice visited sites of *Homo erectus* in Java, the site of *Pithecanthropus* at Sangiran and that of the Solo human near the banks of the Solo River at Ngandong. He visited, in December 1936, with Ralph von Koenigswald, and a second time, in April 1938, with Helmut de Terra and von Koenigswald, following Teilhard's excursion to Burma with de Terra. Six months before this second visit, von Koenigswald had discovered a second *Pithecanthropus* skull near Sangiran. This visit of 1938 allowed Teilhard to consolidate his understanding of the phylogeny of the prehominids. In FIGURE 4 (based on MS 1949) note that the Solo human is represented along the *Pithecanthropus* line. The corresponding diagram found in MS Avant Carmaux shows the Solo human as a distinct lineage (the actual date of this diagram is unclear). See Editor-Translator's Appendix B.

4   Teilhard played a significant role in the discovery of *Sinanthropus pekinensis* or "Peking Man," a discovery evolving over a period of many years and carried out by several teams of researchers. The search (by Westerners) for human fossils in China was begun in 1918–20 by the Swedish geologist and mining expert Johan Gunnar Andersson. In 1921 it was the Austrian Otto Zdansky, sent to assist Andersson, with W.D. Matthew from the American Museum of Natural History, who focused the search on the lime quarries of the village of Chou K'ou Tien (now "Zhoukoudian") at the foot of the Western Hills fifty kilometers southwest of Peking (Beijing). The first evidence of the Peking human, a single molar, found and literally pocketed for his own study by Zdansky, was not announced until 1926. In 1927, after long negotiations, the Canadian anatomist Davidson Black of Peking Union Medical College began a second and systematic excavation of the Chou K'ou Tien deposits, the work funded by the Rockefeller Foundation and in cooperation with the Chinese National Geological Survey. The first skull of *Sinanthropus pekinensis* was discovered on December 2, 1929, by W. C. Pei of the Chinese

survey. By then Teilhard's base of work had shifted from Tientsin to Peking. He had become a close friend of Black and associated himself with the Chinese, training some of the younger Chinese survey paleontologists in the field. He then lost the financial backing of Marcellin Boule, his mentor, for working with the Chinese and allowing fossils to remain on Chinese soil. Upon Black's death in 1934, Teilhard became temporary supervisor of the Chou K'ou Tien excavations, until the arrival in 1936 of Black's replacement, Franz Weidenreich. In collaboration with Weidenreich, in 1937, a bust was made from the skull of *Sinanthropus* by the sculptor Lucile Swan. (The first Peking human actually was a female, nicknamed in the laboratory "Nelly.") Teilhard's particular contribution to the *Sinanthropus pekinensis* discoveries was by research and publication of the fossil fauna surrounding the *Sinanthropus* site. By 1937, a total of 14 skulls had been found at Chou K'ou Tien, but because of guerilla fighting and the threat of Japanese invasion, the excavations were halted. Teilhard and his colleagues were confined to Peking, where the Institute of Geobiology was formed. A set of casts and other material safely reached America in April 1941 with Weidenreich, but during the Japanese invasion in December 1941 the original fossils of the Peking human type were lost. For full details on the Peking human, see the recent summary in John Reader, *Missing Links: The Hunt for Earliest Man*, 2nd ed (London: Penquin Books, 1988), pp. 91–111. (Reader is used as a basis for many of the definitions of terms in this chapter and other material as cited below.) The Chou K'ou Tien site was reopened by the Communist government in 1949, and excavations have resumed. The *Sinanthropus* site, which now includes a natural history museum, was revisited in May 1985 by the Association des Amis de Pierre Teilhard de Chardin and this translator.

5 A vertical ridge extending in the median line from the upper to the lower border of the jaw, indicating the fusion point of the two pieces of which the bone is composed at an early period of life.

6 This and the following paragraphs, as shown in MS B 1940, pp. 205 ff., specifically relate to the theories of Teilhard's mentor Marcellin Boule (1861–1942), Director of Human Paleontology at the French National Museum of Natural History, who supervised Teilhard's doctoral work after World War I and funded Teilhard's early research in China. From his studies of La Chapelle-aux-Saints, Boule believed that the Neanderthals were a degenerate, archaic race, diverging from the line leading to the modern human and disappearing without issue (John Reader, *Missing Links*, 21). For Teilhard, the prehominid and the Neanderthal human were, instead, primitive or "juvenile" human types who had already crossed the gap of reflection. For him the evidence lay in *Sinanthropus*'s cutting of stone and making fire; according to the idea of Lucien Cuénot, that toolmaking was a sign of the ability for abstraction and the conception of a future. Material relevant to this discussion appeared in Lucien Cuénot's lectures at the University of Nancy on March 21 and April 18, 1931, lectures illustrated by diagrams Teilhard and Cuénot had worked on together as well as by a photo of four types of reconstructed prehistoric skulls from the anthropomorph and hominid lines. The skulls are arranged in a series analogous to Teilhard's arrangement, above, of

the series between the great apes and recent types of humans.

7 *Africanthropus*. Most likely *Africanthropus* of East Africa refers to the then controversial *Australopithecus robustus*, or the Olduvai human type, in Tanzania, first discovered by Hans Beck in 1913 and ultimately verified by Louis Leakey and others, in a series of expeditions made to Olduvai Gorge during 1931–36.

8 The end of section 1 has been heavily revised by Teilhard to simplify and sharpen the focus on prehominids. He omitted his reference to examples of possible verticils below *Pithecanthropus* and *Sinanthropus*—to those hominoids or "human-like apes," among whom he had included "*Paranthropus* or *Australopithecus*" in the Transvaal, and "giant lemurians" in Madagascar. To the prehominids, Teilhard added the Mauer jaw and the East African *Africanthropus*. Note that "*Paranthropus*" or "*Australopithecus transvalis*" were terms used by Robert Broom in announcing his discovery, in 1936–38, of "A New Ancestral Link between Ape and Man" (referring to fossils of *Australopithecus* originally identified by Raymond Dart in 1925.) In this period preliminary to Teilhard's writing of *Le phénomène humain*, Teilhard would have seen casts of Broom's discovery, which Broom displayed in February 1937 in Philadelphia at the Congress of Early Man (John Reader, *Missing Links*, 118). Teilhard had attended this congress in order to plan his Burma voyage of January-April 1938 with Helmut de Terra (see above, ch. II, n. 3).

9 In this note, added to *Le phénomène humain* in an early revision in Teilhard's hand (MS B 1940, 206 verso), the "River Thames" refers to the discovery of the Swanscombe skull in gravels of a 100-foot terrace of the Thames (near the site of the Galley Hill skeleton found in 1888 to the east of London) by A. T. Marston, who, in 1937, announced his discovery as belonging to the early Pleistocene human. However, fluorocarbon dating by Kenneth Oakley in 1948 proved the skull to be Middle Pleistocene, and also showed the Galley Hill skeleton not to be Early, but Post Pleistocene. In October 1948, the month Teilhard spent in Rome making his final revisions of *Le phénomène humain* in response to two Roman censors, Oakley applied fluorocarbon dating to the Piltdown human, proving "Dawn Man" was no older than the Galley Hill skeleton (see note 11). It was after the publication of Oakley's results in 1950 that Joseph Weiner, with Le Gros Clark, proved that the Piltdown human's jaw and skull were recent and had been stained. The news of the hoax was released in 1953. (See John Reader, *Missing Links*, 54–78.)

10 "New setting": Seuil, p. 218 has omitted "*nouveau*" (compare to MS B 1940, 208; MS 1949, 102).

11 *Eoanthropus* (Dawn Man) refers to the controversial Piltdown human: "Fragments of skull and jaw bone found near Piltdown, Sussex, in 1912 . . . seemed to combine the large brain of a human with the jaw of an ape in one individual . . . exactly as some experts had proposed for the intermediate form linking the modern human with distant ancestors" (see John Reader, *Missing Links*, the caption and photos of the fragments and jaw and their reconstructions, pp. 126 and following). This phrase of Teilhard's referring to the Piltdown human, "Et tel même peut-être (si la mâchoire chimpanzoïde

trouvée avec lui ne lui appartient pas) L'*Eoanthropus* d'Angleterre," has been omitted from the Seuil edition. It exists in MS B 1940, p. 211, and MS 49, p. 103 (where the italics are omitted), and is restored to the text here at the request of M. Claude Cuénot, who assisted in the preparation of MS Corrigé.

Teilhard, during his studies at the Jesuit College at Ore Place near Hastings, first visited the Barkham Manor site of the Piltdown human on May 31, 1912, with Charles Dawson, *Eoanthropus*'s discoverer, and Arthur Smith Woodward, paleontologist and Keeper of Geology at the British Museum of Natural History. He made a second visit the weekend of August 8–10, 1913, and a third on August 30, 1913, where he picked up from the site a canine tooth attributed to the skull. Then in the summer of 1920, after his return from the front, Teilhard, with Woodward, made a final visit to Piltdown and afterward published his conclusions about the fossils in an article, "Le cas de l'homme de Piltdown" (*Oeuvre scientifique*, I, 208–14). The article shows that Teilhard remained ultimately skeptical about the jaw, remarking that it might even seem as though the missing piece that would have joined jaw to skull was missing expressly ("Comme par exprès, le condyle s'est trouvé manquer!" 213). But in the article Teilhard overtly reserved his own judgment, stating that he must cede to the collective scientific judgment of experts. When in 1953 ff. Kenneth Oakley and others pressed him to make some detailed comment on the matter, after an initial exchange of letters with Oakley (Fondation archives), in which Teilhard questioned the whole idea of a hoax and spoke for Dawson's integrity, Teilhard continued to remain silent about his opinions. For a detailed refutation of Teilhard himself having played a part in the hoax, see Winifred McCulloch, Karl Schmitz-Moorman, and Mary Lukas in *Teilhard Newsletter*, XIV, No. 1 (July 1981); Frank Spencer, *Piltdown: A Scientific Forgery, Based on the Search by Ian Langham* (1942–1984), Natural History Museum Publications (London: Oxford University Press, 1990). Most recent is Winifred McCulloch, "Teilhard de Chardin and the Piltdown Hoax (Teilhard Studies, No. 33, Spring 1996), a critique of S. J. Gould's implication of Teilhard in the famous hoax; including a bibliography of articles and books through 1995 (available from The American Teilhard Association, c/o Prof. John Grim, Department of Religion, Bucknell University, Lewisburg, PA, 17837).

12 Note the fact that this "triple grouping" as depicted in FIGURE 4, includes the terminal and juvenile "groups" of descendants of *all* radiations of the human layer up to *Homo sapiens*, all having taken the step of reflection. The human inflorescence shows all the phases through which the modern human must have passed in the course of phylogenesis.

13 At Le Moustier, type-site of the Neanderthal in the Dordogne, a succession of well-defined strata shows implements of the Aurignacian culture lying beneath the Solutrean, and the latter beneath the Magdelenian (in a juxtaposition of Middle and Upper Paleolithic cultural phases).

14 Cro-Magnon remains are the first human remains to be discovered from the upper Paleolithic or Aurignacian sites. In 1868 the apparently buried remains of five people belonging to the *Homo sapiens* complex were found in a rock shelter at Cro-Magnon in the Vézère valley (Dordogne).

15 The Aurignacian human is the upper Paleolithic human type of the Aurignacian cultural phase of the Cave Bear and Mammoth, characterized by worked bone and staghorn found in 1852 together with flint implements near Aurignac (Haute-Garonne) and at similar sites.

16 In MS B 1940, p. 212 Teilhard eliminated a reference he had originally made to Boule: "With Professor Boule, I see things in a different light."

17 The Age of the Reindeer is the cultural phase of the human at the upper Paleolithic, characterized by worked bone, flint tools, burial, and artistic endeavor.

18 MS B 1940, p. 214 and MS 1949, p. 105 have "naturellement" whereas Seuil, p. 224 has "actuellement."

19 *"Trois Frères"* refers to a sanctuary in a series of caverns and galleries in a hill through which the Volp river flows, found on the estate of Count Napoléon Henri Bégouën at Montesquieu-Avantès in the Ariège (Pyrénées). The site was named for the Count's three sons, Max, Louis, and Jacques Bégouën. In 1912, with François Camel, Max and Louis first discovered a chamber with clay models of bison and an alcove at the height of children which showed phallic symbols, and holes and heel prints on the clay floor. In 1916 they discovered a further series of galleries and the sanctuary, full of niches that led to a winding corridor covered with engravings of horses, bison, cattle, humans disguised as animals, creatures in human shapes, sexual symbols, and sorcerers. It was there the Dancing Sorcerer Teilhard refers to was found.

Teilhard met Max Bégouën for the first time on the Belgian front in 1915, when he served as a stretcher-bearer in the same regiment as Max and Jacques. Later that same year, in Artois, under fire and at great risk to his life, Teilhard dragged the wounded Jacques to safety. Teilhard visited "Trois Frères" in August 1928 with his mentor and colleague Abbé Henri Breuil. Max and his wife Simone's close friendship over many years provided fundamental support to Teilhard and his work. See Max Bégouën in "Reflexions sur le bonheur," inédits et témoignages," *Cahiers Pierre Teilhard de Chardin*, II (Paris: Éditions du Seuil, 1960), 15–38; and Alan Houghton Broderick, *Father of Prehistory: The Abbé Henri Breuil, His Life and Times* (Westport, Conn: The Greenwood Press, 1973), 115–26.

20 "Art is the zone around increasing human energy where nascent truths condense, are preformed, and come to life before they are formulated and definitively assimilated. . . . Art through its power of symbolic expression gives a first body, a first face, to the spiritual energy being born on Earth." But most important, "Art communicates with it and preserves its specifically human mark by personalizing it" (my translation). These words come from Teilhard's talk on "Understanding and Using Art Along the Lines of Human Energy," a talk given to artists in Paris on March 13, 1939 (*Oeuvres*, XI, 93–7). At the time of writing this passage on *Homo sapiens* at the Age of the Reindeer, Teilhard was in touch with the American sculptor Malvina Hoffman, whom he had first met at the Field Museum in Chicago in 1926, where she was preparing her journey around the world to sculpt "The Family of Man." He met Hoffman again in Peking and Paris; and in New York, in this spring of 1939, they visited the New York World's Fair together, where she had

sculpted a circular relief of dancers, displayed in a pool. Hoffman completed two bronze busts of Teilhard. They conversed at length about her art and his work. Teilhard's renewed contact with Hoffman in New York, just before his exile because of the war, increased his awareness of the single spirit inspiring both artist and scientist. The contact gave him strength and consolidated the direction and purpose of *Le phénomène humain* as he continued parts II–IV through the fall and winter of 1939 and the spring and early summer of 1940. The correspondence of Teilhard and Hoffman (along with photos of Teilhard) is in the J. Paul Getty Museum Library and Photo Archives at Malibu, California.

21 According to Teilhard every zoological phylum has a "scale" structure, like that of a pine cone or artichoke leaf, where a single element holds the structural law of the entire fruit. This is particularly true of the human phylum, with its structure of "overlapping scales." A "scale" is a *sub-phyletic* unit marked by individuality in form and habitat and by a weak ability to intermingle with other elements of the phylum. It possesses considerable power of mutation in its beginnings, and has an aptitude for prolonging itself at length in a residual form. Taken together, the Java and Peking humans form one "scale." The Peking human is a foliation of the true prehominids, and is disseminated along a perfectly defined coastal band that threads its way north to Peking from a center in Malacca. (See "Le groupe zoologique humain," *Oeuvres*, VIII, 98–104 and fig. 5.) The use of the structure of overlapping scales was Teilhard's suggestion for putting order into the discoveries of human paleontology while maintaining the fundamental unity of humankind, including the prehominids, by virtue of having taken the step of reflection.

22 "The chaos we are caught up in [in the modern age] is only a momentary simple phase of interference and adjustment between ancient and new currents that collide and break only to become more deeply harmonized in some kind of ground swell" (my translation). See *Oeuvres*, XI, 163–4.

23 For "endomorphosis," see Prologue, note 1.

24 See the final four paragraphs of section 3 for Teilhard's complete thought in this context. For the development of Teilhard's ideas on East and West, see "La route de l'Ouest: Vers une mystique nouvelle" (written in 1932), *Oeuvres*, XI, pp. 45–64; L'apport spirituel de l'Extrême-Orient: Quelques reflexions personnelles" (1947), *Oeuvres*, II pp. 147–60; Teilhard's correspondence with Ida Treat, *Letters to Two Friends by Teilhard de Chardin: 1926–1952* (Cleveland: Meridian Books, 1969), I; *Lettres intimes* and the introduction and notes by Henri de Lubac; and Ursula King, *Towards a New Mysticism: Teilhard de Chardin and Eastern Religions* (London: Collins, 1980), and *Spirit of Fire: The Life and Vision of Teilhard de Chardin* (Maryknoll, New York: Orbis Books, 1996).

25 This human image describing "old" China is reminiscent of Malvina Hoffman's bronze statue of "Elemental Man," or, as Teilhard described it, "Man emerging out of elemental forces" (see jacket). Photos of "Elemental Man" were used by Hoffman as illustrations for *Sculpture Inside and Out* (New York: W.W. Norton, 1939), a copy of which she sent to Teilhard on his return to Peking in August 1939. The bronze statue of Elemental Man

stands in New York state on the campus of Syracuse University, as Hoffman's tribute to the sculptor, Ivan Mestrovic.

26 An "anticyclone" is where a storm or winds move spirally outward from a center of high pressure that is the larger movement upon which the cyclones and anticyclones are borne.

Part III, Chapter III   The Modern Earth

1 The "unknown sea" refers to the "sea" of space–time, which is the subject of section 1 and all that follows.

2 Henri Breuil (1877–1961). Teilhard's life was interwoven with this French prehistorian, and an extensive correspondence between the two exists. Teilhard met Breuil when the latter was professor of paleontology at the Institut de paléontologie humaine (Paris). Breuil initiated Teilhard into the science of prehistory, just then at its beginnings, taking him on visits to the site at Altamira (Spain) in 1913, where he saw the famous bisons, at Niaux (Ariège) in 1921, and, with Dorothy Garrod, at Ipswich (England) in 1925. Boule's celebrated paintings captured the movement of the cave drawings, and Breuil himself could fashion stone implements. In 1927, the year after Breuil had been named professor at the Institut d'anthropologie at the Sorbonne, Teilhard and Breuil, again with Dorothy Garrod, visited the caves of Count Henri Bégouën (see ch. II, above, n. 19). In 1929 a chair at the College de France was created for Breuil. In 1947 Teilhard and Breuil had planned a voyage to South African sites, but this plan was interrupted by a heart attack Teilhard suffered on June 1, 1947. Upon Breuil's retirement, Teilhard was offered Breuil's chair at the College de France, but the appointment was opposed by Jesuit superiors. See Teilhard de Chardin, *Lettres à L'abbé Gaudefroy et à L'abbé Breuil* (Monaco: Éditions le Rocher, 1988) and Alan Houghton Broderick, *Father of Prehistory*.

3 In MS 1949, p. 113, par. 2 a break between paragraphs was omitted, and the omission was carried over into the Seuil text, p. 238. Compare to MS B 1940, p. 231, pars. 2–3.

4 "The center of the spheres was incorrectly placed," in contrast to the Omega Point. See Part IV, ch. II, section 3.

5 The following lines, omitted by Teilhard in revision, give his argument a position in the context of the thinkers of this time: "Yes, I know. In spite of great voices of those such as Eddington, Compton, E. Le Roy, even Einstein, and many others, the vast number (perhaps the majority) of biologists and physicists still resist the obvious. Contrary to all logic, they still behave as though their thought, like some extra-scientific epiphenomenon, could continue to float, impervious, on a duration whose universality is proved a little bit more by each of their own accomplishments. Their position is doomed. From now on no one can restrict the tide's spreading and rising any more than they can an intuition just unleashed by our intelligence. Once recognized in a single point of things. . . . " (MS B 1940, 238, my translation).

6 This quote, applied here to the human being, rephrases part of Teilhard's definition of *tâtonnement* as it applied to single cells or clusters of cells and to the

subject of "profusion." Groping, or trial and error, is one of the three ways life proceeds at all levels (see Part II, ch. II, 1, Corollary).

7 Teilhard addresses the human person using the familiar "tu" form of the personal pronoun, the intimate form of address one uses for oneself, for an intimate friend, or for family—a distinction that has almost disappeared in English. The dialogue form used here suggests the kind of debate found in Pascal's *Pensées*, which Teilhard so often had in mind throughout *Le phénomène humain* and which he brings to the fore below in subsection C "The Dilemma and the Option." Pascal, however, did not use the familiar form of address.

8 MS B 1940, p. 252 and MS 1949, p. 123 have "elles briseraient immédiatement le ressort," whereas Seuil, pp. 256–7 has "il en briserait immédiatement le ressort." This translation follows the earlier two texts.

9 Because of a mistyping in MS B 1940, p. 124, a confusion of reference arose and Teilhard's cross-reference to section 2 in Part IV on "Love-Energy" was omitted by MS 1949, p. 124, n. 1 and Seuil, p. 257, n. 1.

Part IV, Chapter I   **The Collective Way Out**

1 Teilhard's reference to FIGURE 4 here was omitted from MS 1949 and thus from Seuil. The omission was due to a confusion of numbers that resulted from Teilhard's having omitted three of the diagrams included in MS B 1940 (see Editor-Translator's Introduction, II.).

2 A small isolated mass of one type of tissue within a different type.

3 See "Sur la nature du phénomène social humain et sur ses relations cachées avec la gravité" (1948), *Oeuvres* VII, pp. 171–4. This essay more fully describes the process of collective unification, or "totalization," from gravitational compression, to biological organization or complexification, to psychic centration and emersion.

4 "The fundamental law of convergence is not only within ourselves, but above ourselves" (my translation). For Teilhard the superhuman is the stage when human individuals, organized by the control of a thinking mind, become elements subjected to a higher soul above. See *Oeuvres*, VI, 80–1.

5 Léon Brunschvicg (1869–1944), French philosopher of science.

6 In MS B 1940, p. 274 the original title of subsection C "Unanimity" was "Conspiration" (see below, ch. II, note 17). The title was revised after Teilhard's return from China in 1946.

Part IV, Chapter II   **Beyond the Collective: The Hyperpersonal**

1 As Teilhard explains in a letter to Ida Treat, March 13, 1927, repulsion, or the force with which particles or similar forces repel one another, has its psychospiritual dimension in the human being's antipathy toward the human being. What we really fear and hate in the human being is the *other*; and as soon as we find a way of bringing this "other" back into unity with us, this aversion ceases. See *Letters to Two Friends: 1926–1952* (New York and Cleveland: Meridian Books, 1968).

2 Neomatter. Teilhard emphasizes here the negative and mechanized results

obtained by the regressive aspects of that new or "secondary" matter deposited by the human races as they age or are exhausted. These include the "crust" of social wrappings, sterile conformity, and the hardening into collective and individual routine (see *Oeuvres*, III, 101).

3 In MS B 1940, p. 281 Teilhard attributes this phrase to Jules Romains (1885–1973), principal representative of the literary school of "Unanisme," proposing to give universal expression to the variety of feelings and impressions of broad human groups.

4 This passage refers back to Part I, ch. III, sec. 1 (a), to the contrast Teilhard made between the world of mineral and the world of organic compounds; between the crystal structure, in which molecules link together exteriorly, molecule to molecule, and polymerization, in which molecules manage to join in an ever larger and more complex molecule.

5 *Eppur si muove*! And yet, it turns. Words attributed to Galileo as he left the tribunal after renouncing his theory of gravity, and stepped upon the Earth (from interview with Pierre Noir, SJ, Colmar 1983). See Teilhard's impassioned identification with Galileo's words in 1920, Oeuvres, V, pp. 36–7; and Teilhard's statement in the spring of 1949, after he had traveled to Rome in a final, fruitless effort to receive permission for the publication of *Le phénomène humain*: "Four hundred years later we find ourselves in the same position as Galileo was, one turn higher on the spiral," at the "bifurcation" between geocentrism, with the "absolute" rotation of the Earth around the sun, and the more profound concept of a universe in motion, with the Earth's psychic enfolding on itself at the heart of a new "space of complexity" ("Une nouvelle question de Galilée: Oui ou non; Humanité se meut-elle biologiquement sur Elle-même?" *Oeuvres*, V, 331 ff.) See Teilhard above, on the human "rebound."

6 In MS B 1940, p. 282 the title of section 1, "Convergence of the Personal and the Omega Point," originally read "Convergence of the Spirit and the Omega Point. (This revision was not carried out in the table of contents—see Seuil.) The title of sec. 3 below, "Attributes of the Omega Point," originally read "Spirit and Entropy" (MS B 1940, 295). Teilhard's revisions shift the focus of the text from the wider context of the first law of thermodynamics to the category of the collective as Teilhard applies it to a "granular" grouping of thoughts influenced by the supremely autonomous focal point of unification, the "Omega Point."

7 Alpha and Omega, or "the beginning and the end," are terms found in the Book of Revelation applied to God and to Christ at the end of time. In Teilhard they refer to both the beginning and end of space–time and to the universal Christ. The Greek letter symbol Ω for "Omega" often appears in Teilhard's retreat notes, Jan. 12, 1940, ff. (library of Les Fontaines, Chantilly, France).

8 Here Teilhard adds a third movement, the collective converging movement of human personalization, to "the double movement in one" of individual personalization first described above in Part III, ch. I, sec. 2 (a).

9 Teilhard uses "Weltanschauung" in the sense of a "vision of the world" (see *Oeuvres*, VIII, 163).

10 The French word "esprit" is used to refer to both "mind" and "spirit," as well as sometimes to "soul." The tragic split into the two terms "mind" and "spirit" in English makes it ultimately impossible to convey in English the profound unity of Teilhard's thought. I have chosen the all-inclusive word "spirit" over "mind" here to lead forward to Teilhard's culminating statement at the end of this section: "There can be no spirit without synthesis."

11 Here Teilhard ends the long detour, begun at the end of Part III, ch. I, sec. 1, subsec. A (a), to arrive at personalization of the individual by the hominization of the entire group in its phases of expansion, inner awakening through the discovery of evolution, and transition to the modern dilemma.

12 With the terms "collector and conserver of consciousnesses," Teilhard refers here and in section 3 to the first law of thermodynamics which he introduced in Part I, ch. I, sec. 3 "The Evolution of Matter," but now it is interiorized to include thought and thus takes on a positive value in space–time of heightening energy.

13 Here, in the physicopsychical dimensions of love energy *exaltation* has the sense of intensifying and heightening activity.

14 See Part I, ch. II, sec. 1 "Existence."

15 Teilhard first wrote this paragraph as follows: "Humanity, the spirit of the Earth, the synthesis of the individual and peoples, the paradoxical reconciliation of the element and the whole, of unity and multitude—all these things, just as necessary to our thought as staggering for our imagination, can only be born from *a universal human love*—a love that is armed with the force we still only lend to violence" (MS B 1940, 293, my translation).

16 In MS B on p. 293, Teilhard attributes these thoughts on the limits of the heart's radius to a soldier in the novel *Clarté* by Henri Barbusse (Paris: Librarie Ernest Flammarion, 1919), ch. XII.

17 "Conspiration," from the Latin *conspirare*, to breathe together, agree, conspire, is a term Teilhard attributes to Edouard le Roy. The sole way out ahead is in the direction of a common passion. See below, ch. III, note 11 as well as "Hominisation" (1925), *Oeuvres*, III, pp. 88–9; Energie humaine" (1937), *Oeuvres*, VI, p. 173, pp. 178 ff., pp. 189–90; and "Singularités de l'espèce humaine" (1954), *Oeuvres*, II, pp. 349–56.

18 In MS B 1940, p. 295 the original title of section 3 "Les attributs du point Omega" (Seuil, 302) was "Esprit et Entropie" and refers back to the third of three major questions posed at the end of Part I, ch. II on spiritual energy. It also refers to the law of entropy and the arrow of time. (See Part I, ch. II, sec. 3.) Irreversibility is an attribute of the arrow of time. Teilhard's revision of the title shifts the focus from entropy and forward to the reversal of direction and convergence at the Omega Point in chapter III below.

19 H. G. Wells, *The Anatomy of Frustration: A Modern Synthesis* (New York: Macmillan Company, 1936).

20 This paragraph not only links the beginning of *Le phénomène humain* to the end, but completes the centered and planetary form of energetics that underlies the whole structure of the human phenomenon. What follows resolves the three questions on energy left open at the conclusion of Part I, ch. II. The paragraph is confusing, however, because incompletely revised. It still contains a

reference to the two omitted diagrams and to the much longer description of the interrelationship between tangential and radial energy that had been omitted from Teilhard's text in 1946 and replaced by the simpler description given in Part I, ch. II above. For the omitted diagrams and the text, see Editor-Translator's Appendix A.

21 Note p. 184, line 13, "hemisphere and pole," where "The Development of Energy in a Universe of Psychic Stuff" was originally inserted and explained.

22 "Emersion" refers to a passage to the transcendent, which, in contrast to the durational process of emergence, designates an instantaneous, "punctual" or perfective, critical threshold (*Nouveau lexique*).

Part IV, Chapter III The Ultimate Earth

1 William D. Matthew (1871–1930), a Canadian-born paleontologist of the American Museum of Natural History in New York, specializing in fossil fauna of China and Mongolia, who took part in Roy Chapman Andrews's Third American Expedition in 1926 (see Part III, ch. II, n. 4).

2 There is a contrast in the French between "la branche humaine" as the main axis of the tree of life and "un autre rameau pensant" as a lateral or secondary branching.

3 *L'Homme se trouve former la flêche de d'Arbre*; i.e., the human being points the direction of the tree of life. The French term "flêche" implies Teilhard's double sense of axis and arrow, which is lacking in English. See n. 18, p. 266.

4 Again Teilhard introduces life's powerful action of directed chance born of life's groping or trial and error (See Part II, ch. II, sec. 1 A, and n. 2). This paragraph reveals the profound contrast in terms of human consequences between the viewpoint expressed in Pascal's "wager" and Teilhard's "option" for a future founded on the "promise of a whole world" (Part III, ch. III, sec. 2 C).

5 Note in the following pages how the three "lines of attack," or phases, of this progression continue the forward and centering movement of the whole toward Omega and the Omega Point, and how the "lines" embody the personalizing movement of human consciousness and of the universe itself. Each phase, each subsection, is like a spiraling vortex that draws us to a point of focus (like the contracting circles of a cone). As we arrive at each center point or term, the point opens out to form, itself, the outer circle of the next phase. Humanity forms new eyes. The eyes focus on the human object (below us, above us, within us). Then, in a conjugated act of science and religion, humanity turns its eyes away from the slopes of the summit toward what is totality and future.

6 *Crescit eundo*. It grows by going.

7 *L'homme, cet inconnu*, the title of a work by Alexis Carrel (1873–1944), French surgeon and physiologist, specializing in tissue grafting.

8 For the full context of geoeconomics, geopolitics and geodemography, see Index, "Geobiology," and Brian Swimme and Thomas Berry, *The Universe Story: From the Primal Flaring Forth to the Ecozoic Era—A Celebration of the Unfolding of the Cosmos* (San Francisco: Harper San Francisco, 1992).

9 In the Seuil text, p. 317, "some higher state for humanity" is a revision of what in MS B 1940, p. 314 read, "some superhumanity" (my translation)—a term referring to the earlier theme of ch. I, sec. 1 B "Megasynthesis": that the way out is not only for a chosen race, but the result of collective pressure by the whole of humanity.

10 Teilhard's term is *s'excentrer*: "pour s'excentrer sur le *Centre transcendant de sa concentration grandissante*" (Seuil, 320). See "La centrologie: Essai d'une dialectique de l'union," *Oeuvres*, VII, pp. 103–34.

11 This paragraph describes the period of "conspiration" referred to at the end of "Love Energy," where unanimity reaches its highest point and tension.

12 "Discordant" has its geological meaning of strata lacking parallelism of bedding or structure, as well as its social meaning of being at variance.

Epilogue: The Christian Phenomenon

1 The basis of my translation is Teilhard's French: "Il n'y aura plus que Dieu, tout en tous" (Seuil, 327), a biblical reference to 1 Cor. 15:28.

Summary or Postface: The Essence of the Human Phenomenon

1 " . . . cette interprétation organiciste du fait social." The word "organiciste" refers to the explanation of life and living processes in terms of levels of living systems rather than in terms of the properties of their smallest components.

2 A note by Teilhard on evil included here in the carbon copy of the "Summary or Postface," typed in Rome in October 1948, was omitted from the stencilled version of *Le phénomène humain* in 1949 and hence from Seuil: "While evil (whatever its quantity in the world), still at the level of experience, would only appear to be a statistically inevitable sub-effect ("bad luck") of the trial and error of universal arrangement."

Appendix: Some Comments on the Place and Role of Evil in an Evolving World

1 Matt. 18:7 (The *New American Bible* translation [Nashville: Thomas Nelson Publishers, 1983]). Teilhard's words are in Latin, modifying the text: *Necessarium est ut scandala eveniant* (see *Oeuvres*, X, 227, n. 1).

2 In November 1947 Teilhard had written an article on original sin for theologians to clarify his views. Original sin "affects" and "infects" the whole of time and space—just as the resurrected Christ covers the whole world (as seen in John's Gospel, or in the letters of Paul). The Fall is not an isolated fact but a general condition affecting the whole of history. (See *Oeuvres*, X, 217–30.) It was an early note on this subject in 1922, written at the request of the Belgian Jesuit Louis Riedinger, that occasioned the termination of Teilhard's teaching at l'Institut Catholique and his being sent to work in China as a geologist (*Oeuvres*, X, 59–70).

Editor-Translator's Appendix A: The Sphere

1 Note in the equation that instead of the division sign used in MS B 1940, I have substituted the addition sign, "+," as found in MS Avant Carmaux, p. 37 and in keeping with the meaning and context of the equation.

INDEX

INDEX

The British Teilhard Association

is a non-sectarian society which helps people from all walks of life to work and meet together to study and build on Teilhard's deep spiritual and mystical vision of a dynamic universe in movement towards ultimate completion in a cosmic centre of convergence he calls the Omega Point.

The Association rejects exclusivity and stresses inclusivity. It encourages its members to deepen their understanding of Teilhard's ideas and to apply them to contemporary situations. With Teilhard, members look to the future, not the past. They share mutual concerns such as ecological sustainability, economic stewardship, ethical values, wholism rather than reductionism, the sacredness of all life forms . . .

Members are encouraged to "help themselves" by setting up local groups to focus on these and other issues inspired by Teilhard's profound conviction: "The future of the thinking earth is organically linked to the transformation of the forces of hate into forces of charity." And this, he believes, can only be brought about through love—"the most universal, the most tremendous and the most mystical of cosmic forces."

Please mail the Secretariat in Beaumaris for further details and membership application.

The British Teilhard Association
Plas Maelog
Beaumaris LL58 8BH, Wales, UK
     Tel: 01248 810402   Fax: 01248 810936
          E-mail: sion.cowell@btinternet.com

The American Teilhard Association (ATA)

explores Teilhard's thought in such contemporary areas of concern as issues of religion and science, social and ecological justice, and the relationships of Teilhard's thought to contemporary thinkers such as Thomas Merton, Barbara McClintock, and Thomas Berry.

Our international membership is $40 annually, and our regular US membership is $30 for which a member receives two Teilhard Studies, a booklet series on Teilhard's thought published by the ATA, and our newsletter, "Teilhard Perspective." For further details please write to:

The American Teilhard Association
c/o Bucknell University Religion Department
Lewisburg, Pennsylvania 17837
USA